ETHICS

in the Community of Promise

ETHICS

in the
Community of Promise
Faith, Formation, and Decision

James M. Childs, Jr.

ETHICS IN THE COMMUNITY OF PROMISE
Faith, Formation, and Decision

Cover image: Ballroom 1999, Diana Ong (b. 1940/Chinese-
American), Computer graphics © Diana Ong/SuperStock
Cover design: Brad Norr Design
Book design: Allan S. Johnson, of Phoenix Type, Inc.

Library of Congress Cataloging-in-Publication Data

Childs, James M., 1939–
    Ethics in the community of promise : faith, formation, and
decision / James M. Childs, Jr. — 2nd ed.
        p.   cm.
    Includes bibliographical references and index.
    ISBN-13: 978-0-8006-3797-2 (alk. paper)
    ISBN-10: 0-8006-3797-6
    1. Christian ethics.   I. Title.
    BJ1251.C48   2006
    241 — dc22   2006009372

The paper used in this publication meets the minimum
requirements of American National Standard for Information
Sciences—Permanence of Paper for Printed Library Materials,
ANSI Z329.48–1984.

Manufactured in the U.S.A.

CONTENTS

In Loving Memory of James M. Childs, Sr.
and Evelyn L. Childs;
and for
Cameron, Nicholas, Sophia, Alex, and Lilly

Preface to the Second Edition

The first thing to be noted about this second edition of *Faith, Formation, and Decision* is that it is now entitled *Ethics in the Community of Promise*, which was the subtitle of the first edition. *Faith, Formation, and Decision* now becomes the subtitle and provides the three-part structure of the book as in the first edition. The title change was prompted by the conviction that the new title more clearly conveys the nature of the book.

I have retained the basic approach of the first edition and much of the original text. The theological and methodological perspectives presented in the first edition continue to express the view of the Christian life and ethic that I want to convey. There have, however, been some changes in the text. Additional biblical references have been included at various points. The issues used to illustrate the matters that concern the Christian ethic in our time have been updated and new ones added or substituted to reflect changes in areas of concern, such as bioethics, public policy, and social thought. There have been recent developments in public expressions of religious convictions with the purpose of influencing public policy. This phenomenon finds its place in the discussion. Environmental concerns were missing in the first edition. They are addressed to some degree in this edition. The discussion of the Beatitudes has been expanded somewhat to include a brief discussion of the virtue of courage. A greater stress has been placed on the dialogue of the church as a community of moral deliberation. The theology of the cross, implicit in the first edition, is here made a bit more explicit. One can find some references to recent Trinitarian discourse and its relevance for the Christian ethic. The endnotes have also been expanded with inclusion of new references, some of which represent more recent resources that further support points supported in the first edition by earlier sources.

Discussion questions have been added to the end of each chapter in the hopes that this will be helpful in the use of the book for classes and study groups. In addition to the brief cases scattered throughout the text, I have added four longer cases with discussion questions in the appendices.

I am grateful to Trinity Lutheran Seminary and its board of directors for a generous sabbatical policy that has allowed me the time to work on this second edition. I am also grateful for the many students and others in various church venues with whom I have had the privilege, over more than a decade, of sharing and discussing the Christian life and ethic on the basis of the first edition. Their faith and their genuine quest for the truth of the Christian witness in a very conflicted and often confusing world have been a source of encouragement and inspiration. Thanks go to Fortress Press and Michael West for their willingness to publish a second edition. I have deeply appreciated my partnership with them, and I am grateful for their confidence in my work.

Most people find strength for life's tasks in the blessings of family, and I am no exception. I thank God for all of them. The first edition was dedicated to my father. Since that time, he has joined my mother in the church triumphant. The first dedication is in their memory. There has also been new life in the family. These are the wonderful grandchildren to whom this book is also dedicated. In family and in a wide variety of relationships with our neighbors, God gives us the blessing of one another in the promise of ultimate community in Christ and calls upon us to love as we have been loved. As we struggle to answer that call, we anticipate in faith, hope, and love that glorious future God has promised us in Christ. That's what this humble little book is all about.

Soli Deo Gloria

PART ONE
Faith

1

ETHICS AND THE CONGREGATION

Christianity means community through Jesus Christ and in Jesus Christ. No Christian community is more or less than this. . . . We belong to one another only through and in Jesus Christ.

What does this mean? It means, first, that a Christian needs others because of Christ.

—Dietrich Bonhoeffer, *Life Together*

It is an ancient scene. Small groups of people, families and neighbors together, are converging on the temple in Jerusalem. As they approach the walls that surround the temple courtyard, a cantor at the gate sings out:

> O LORD, who may abide in your tent?
> Who may dwell on your holy hill?

The gathering crowd of worshipers responds:

> Those who walk blamelessly, and do what is right,
> and speak the truth from their heart;
> who do not slander with their tongue,
> and do no evil to their friends,
> nor take up a reproach against their neighbors

The cantor returns the chant:

> in whose eyes the wicked are despised,
> but who honor those who fear the Lord;

At the temple gate now, the people finish the thought as the antiphonal song proceeds:

who stand by their oath even to their hurt;
who do not lend money at interest,
and do not take a bribe against the innocent.

As the people move through the gates, the cantor finishes the psalm:

Those who do these things shall never be moved. (Psalm 15)

It is a modern scene. Cars converge on the church parking lot. Families congregate in small groups with neighbors and friends. Greeters are there at the door to welcome them as they enter the church, offering a friendly word or a timely question of concern about a member of the family or a recent event of importance in their lives—a wedding, a birth, a graduation, or a new job. Soon after they have found their seats, the first hymn rings out:

Let justice flow like streams of sparkling water, pure,
Enabling growth refreshing life, abundant, cleansing, sure.

The choir responds by picking up the second stanza:

Let righteousness roll on as others' cares we heed,
An ever flowing stream of faith translated into deed.

All join in the concluding stanza:

So may God's plumb line, straight, define our measure true,
And justice, right, and peace pervade this world our whole life
    through.[1]

In the temple of Jerusalem, the worship is proceeding. There is recitation of the Scripture, a statement of the people's faith in God's dominion and God's deliverance and a description of their life as a chosen people:

Hear, O Israel: The LORD is our God, the LORD alone. You shall love the LORD your God with all your heart, and with all your soul, and with all your might. Keep these words that I am commanding you today in your heart. Recite them to your children and talk about them when you are at home and when you are away, when you lie down and when you rise. Bind them as a sign on your hand, fix them as an emblem on your forehead, and write them on the doorposts of your house and on your gates. When the LORD your God has brought you into the land that he swore to your ancestors, to Abraham, to Isaac, and to Jacob, to give you—a land with fine, large cities that you did not build, houses filled with all sorts of goods that you did not fill, hewn with cisterns that you did not hew, vineyards and olive groves that you did not plant—and when you have eaten your fill, take care that you do not forget the LORD, who brought you out of the land of Egypt, out of the house of slavery. (Deut. 6:4-12)

Over twenty centuries later, the gathered people of God echo their ancestors in the faith as they rise to say their creed:

> I believe in God, the Father almighty,
> creator of heaven and earth.
>
> I believe in Jesus Christ, his only Son, our Lord
> He was conceived by the power of the Holy Spirit
> and born of the Virgin Mary.
> He suffered under Pontius Pilate,
> was crucified, died, and was buried.
> He descended into hell.
> On the third day he rose again.
> He ascended into heaven,
> and is seated at the right hand of the Father.
> He will come again to judge the living and the dead.
>
> I believe in the Holy Spirit,
> the holy catholic Church
> the communion of saints,
> and forgiveness of sins,
> and resurrection of the body,
> and the life everlasting. Amen.

A common theme characterizes both these scenes, ancient and modern, despite their outward differences. In both cases the message is that community worship is the place of commitment to the good and right in the eyes of God and for the sake of the neighbor. It is a commitment couched in the recognition and assurance that the world belongs to God who in love has created it, redeemed it, and called it to new life and new possibilities. The great *Shema* (in Hebrew *shema* means "hear") of Deuteronomy 6 functioned as a creedal confession for the people of Israel in which the memory and promise of God's deliverance is woven together with a reminder that their lives are to be lives of joyful obedience in which the will of God permeates every facet of their existence as water suffuses every fiber of a sponge. The Apostles' Creed does not speak directly of the life of obedience, but it is no less powerful in its testimony to an all-powerful and all-gracious God. It places a frame of meaning and hope around the Christian life, giving impetus to our response of love.

Another way to say this is that, in the tradition of biblical faith, the life and worship of the congregation provide the occasion for the development of faith, formation, and decision. By *faith* I mean our understanding and trust in God and God's promises. By *formation* I mean the manner in which our outlook on life, our values, and our attitudes toward others and their needs are shaped by our understanding of God and God's promises. In short, formation is the development of character and the virtues that express it. By *decision* I mean the choices we make concerning right and wrong, in our own lives and as we address our Christian witness to the moral issues in the world around us. Faith, formation, and decision go together in Scripture, in song, in liturgy, in educational programs, and in the conversation of the faithful. There is a constant disclosure of who God is, what God cares about, and how God loves us and promises to be with us. God's gracious power is at work through this disclosure, enabling us to trust in the one we have come to know.

This trust and understanding take shape concretely in the sorts of people we are, individually and as a group. To know the love of God and trust in it is to become a people of love. To know the mercy of God is to become a people who are merciful. To know the creator God who cares for the earth and every-thing that is in it is to become a people who are good stewards of that creation. To know God in Jesus Christ as the one who gave himself up for all people is to be a people ready to receive and affirm the worth of all people, even our enemies. To know God in Jesus as the creator and redeemer of all life is to be a people who uphold the value of life. In these and many other ways we are formed out of faith by the grace of God; we become a people whose choices in life for the right and the good are a reenactment of God's action in our life. Or, to cite another way of saying it, "Our God is a performing God who has invited us to join in the performance that is God's life."[2]

Faith, formation, and decision go together whenever we think about ethics, Christian or otherwise. Ethics can never be understood simply in terms of a set of principles that tell us what is right and wrong. Unless those principles are a consistent expression of our basic outlook on life, our faith, and dispositions, they may not make much sense to us or they may not be very important to us.

Some years ago I accepted an invitation to speak to a group of business-people. They were a diverse group of many different backgrounds who were strangers to me. I was able to speak of principles of morality and say some-thing about how they applied to contemporary problems of business. It was not a bad speech, and I am sure that some of the listeners appreciated some of the things I had to say. However, I walked away without a clear sense that I had communicated effectively. I could not gauge whether the convictions I expressed were in the least bit persuasive. I realized afterward that the reason for these feelings of uncertainty was that I had no way of knowing whether my listeners and I shared a common basis for thinking about ethical questions. I did not know how many shared my faith; I did not know what sorts of people they were. In order to understand how people feel about ethical principles or how they might decide on certain issues, you must first know something about their faith and their outlook on life. What do they think is of ultimate importance and greater than themselves? What forces have shaped their character in what ways?[3] That same experience repeated itself in the years following, during which I regularly taught business ethics in an MBA program. Though I got to know my students, we were all aware of the variety of different, often unspoken, presuppositions people brought with them to the discussions. All realized tacitly that those different perspectives would condition individual reactions. In papers and presentations students would say what they felt was expected, but there was no guarantee in every case that it was what they truly believed.

There are a multitude of additional illustrations that help make this point. For example, not too many years ago it was common for family members and their pastors who kept vigil with a dying loved one to sometimes find themselves at odds with the doctors over whether or not to continue every possible effort to keep the patient alive. In faith the family and pastor may have felt that it was the fitting time to die; they knew the gospel promise; they knew that death is not the last word. But the doctors may have resisted. They may have felt that every step possible to keep the body alive is obligatory. The world of medicine is dedicated to forestalling death; death is defeat. For the family it was right to let death happen. For the doctors it was right to work their hardest to keep that patient alive. Both family and doctors cared very deeply about the dying one. They differed on what is right because they had different outlooks on life and death.

Nowadays such a conflict is less likely since medicine has more readily embraced practices of care for the dying and tempered its drive to keep persons alive at all costs. However, similar tensions have emerged in the wake of interest in physician-assisted suicide or other forms of assisted dying for the suffering terminally ill. Some people of faith may oppose it in the belief that only God can take life. Other people of faith may approve it as consistent with their belief in a compassionate God. Secular thinkers sometimes champion the practice as an expression of our personal rights. Doctors are frequently opposed to physician involvement on the grounds that their vocation is to preserve life, but some who share a concern for compassion and the relief of suffering would help persons die if it were legal.[4] We shall have further discussion of assisted dying in chapter 9. For the present the point is simply to observe that different outlooks on life and death are operating in this debate to produce very different responses to the ethical challenge.

Faith, formation, and decision go together in all our thinking about ethics just as they have always gone together in the gathered life of the people of

God. Without belaboring the matter, it seems clear that Christian ethics and congregational life need each other. The purpose of this book is to provide an understanding of formation and decision that is consistent with the faith we nurture and proclaim in the life and worship of the congregation. The reason for doing so is to undergird Christian people in their moral struggles as they seek, individually and corporately, to give a faithful witness to the gospel of Jesus Christ in the world of our time. To emphasize the congregation as the place where this can happen is important because that is the place where most Christians experience community in the body of Christ, the place where the resources for faith, formation, and decision are present in great abundance.

In a recent reflection on his journey as a theologian, Douglas John Hall raised the concern that both congregations and theologians have failed to make the serious work of theology a part of the churches' ongoing concern. The churches have failed to nurture and appreciate the theologians, and the theologians have too often restricted their work to the academy. In the end the churches are the biggest losers, for they will be deprived of needed theological depth and insight in a time when Christianity is struggling in a secular and pluralistic world.[5] I think the same concern for the life of the church can be raised in connection with that expression of theology we call Christian ethics.

It seems to me that there is more than one reason why pursuing the integration of faith and ethics is a worthwhile purpose. Our contemporary world is marked by a staggering array of ethical problems that appear to have sent our society into a moral tailspin of confusion and uncertainty: duplicity in government, shady dealings in the top echelons of the business world, exploitation and inequality in the domestic and global economic order, a morass of unsettled arguments about critical environmental issues, deep questioning over the morality of recent military initiatives, disturbing patterns in our sexual behavior and in the erosion of the institution of marriage, and the intrusion of medical science into heretofore sacred precincts of life. Surely Christians have a responsibility to speak with a clear voice to a world that seems to be cut adrift from its ethical moorings. There is so little trust in the institutions of our common life. There seems to be so little hope for change. The profound skepticism and confusion of the general public regarding moral concerns and the fact that these concerns deal with problems that threaten the very meaning and existence of life as we know it is a situation for strong Christian witness to provide direction and hope. However, even as the Christian community seeks to meet this challenge and opportunity, it must address what many consider a crisis of moral authority in both the church and society at large.

The Enlightenment, the dawn of the "age of reason" in the seventeenth century, marks the beginning of what we have come to call the modern era.

Faith in critical reason and the empirical method greatly weakened the traditional sources of moral authority that we depended on in the past. Scripture, belief in a natural moral law, the doctrine of the church, and tradition or custom once had a much stronger hold on the general public and many churchgoers than they now do. Value judgments and creeds once considered absolute became relative matters of personal preference. Authoritative teaching became harder and harder to defend in a modern world that considered the Bible and church doctrine to be developments of the past that no longer may be totally relevant in an ever-changing world. The spirit of secularization, so much a part of modernity, was one of celebrating freedom from the old authorities that once prescribed obedience and commanded our loyalty.

Now we have entered the era under the sway of what philosophers like to call "postmodernism." The modern era characterized by the Enlightenment's faith in the power of reason to lead us to truth in all matters including ethics eroded the influence of religious authority. However, the promise of a rational attainment of universal truth has never been realized as the successor to the previous authority of religious traditions.[6] Consequently, in this postmodern era there is no overarching faith, philosophy, or worldview that unites us. Instead, we live in a pluralistic world of many faiths and many different outlooks shaped by the influences of our particular social and cultural circumstances.[7]

Reactions to this postmodern state of pluralism are predictably diverse. This is true within Christian communities as well. At one end of the spectrum we find a rigid traditionalism that has condemned the lingering secular spirit and the postmodern celebration of diversity. They call for a return to the old values and as a focal point of that cause often choose a few select issues such as abortion, gay marriage, and prayer in public schools. At the other end of the spectrum, more liberal church leaders have maintained that the church must modify its teachings in light of new understandings and situations. This, they maintain, has always been the church's task throughout the ages. In the former case, an understandable desire to defend certain values can easily lead to a closed-minded absolutism and a truncated inventory of Christian concerns. In the latter case, accommodation to change can easily slide into relativism.

If there is a way to get our bearings in today's confusing circumstances, it is only in community. For only in community do we discover a shared vision of the meaning and hope of life that can provide a solid basis on which to address moral questions. The people of God gathered around the Word of God discover the ethical insights of their faith and the power of that faith to provide a moral compass by which to navigate among the competing and ambiguous choices of our contemporary world. Allen Verhey reminds us of Paul's description of the church at Rome as "full of goodness, filled with all knowledge, and able to instruct one another" (Rom. 15:14). It is a reminder that it is in the gathered communities of the faith, blessed by the Spirit with the same gifts as the church at Rome, that people find wisdom and direction. The work of Christian ethics exists to serve those communities.[8] I share that conviction. It is out of the community in which our moral vision is born of the faith and nurtured in the faith that we emerge as from a chrysalis ready for flight in a world that needs this faith-based witness.

We really do need each other. The lonely pursuit of the moral life is an exercise in despair; none of us has what it takes to understand all that needs understanding and do all that needs doing. It is part of the good news of our salvation in Jesus Christ that our salvation is not an individual happening but that the grace of God has created us anew in community, intimately linked to one another as the body of Christ. The pursuit of Christian virtue is not a solo performance. Instead, our pursuit of the Christian ethic is more like playing in an orchestra in which each of us has his or her own particular part to play in harmonious concert with others and each one of us shares in the ownership of the total sound that is produced. My gifts are your gifts and your gifts are mine. Not all of us are effective as advocates for justice, but the church is endowed with members who are and, as a part of the total community, we are all advocates for justice. Not all of us have the patient endurance to bear quietly the burdens of those who suffer, but the church is endowed with those who can, and all of us, as part of the community, are those who bear the burdens of others in love. Not all of us have the insight to reason through some of the complex moral dilemmas created by modern medicine, but the church is endowed with many who can, and all of us as a community share in that witness to what is responsible on behalf of life. And so it goes. This is Paul's image of the body of Christ after all (1 Cor. 12:12-31). It is indeed good news that we are saved as a community, as a people, and not merely as individuals. It invites us to value the gifts that all of us bring to our common tasks. It invites us to treasure the experience of those from different cultures and with different histories who can be our teachers, even as they are our brothers and sisters in Christ.

When I think about the church as a community and the manner in which we support and complement each other, I often recall a story I enjoyed reading to my children. In one of the Dr. Seuss selections called *Sneetches*, there is a little piece entitled "Too Many Daves."[9] The story tells of a woman named Mrs. McCave who had twenty-three sons and named them all "Dave." As a result, when Mrs. McCave calls out for Dave, all twenty-three of her children come running at once. The fun comes when Dr. Seuss goes on to mention all the silly, different names she might have chosen instead of naming them all

"Dave." But the point is, it seems to me, that when everyone has the same name there is chaos and not order. The same holds true for the life of the church. If all of us had the same gifts, the church could not function. However, since we are not the same and each of us brings a variety of different gifts that sustain and support each other in our common faith and calling, there is order rather than chaos. That is the case, at least, when we use all the resources that God has given us in each other. The apostle Paul opens his first letter to the Corinthians with the assurance that God has blessed them with every spiritual gift they require and is faithful in seeing them through the challenges of this life to the very end (1 Cor. 1:4-9). It remains an assurance for us today.

Nonetheless, the life of the church as we experience it in the congregation frequently can be rather narrowly focused and characterized by the avoidance of difficult issues that should be a matter of Christian reflection and growth. I still remember an occasion when I was asked to present a series of lectures to an adult class at a local congregation. The subject was social ethics, and the topics included such controversial matters as economic justice and making peace in a nuclear age. As the sessions progressed, I could sense a growing restlessness among some of the people in the group. Finally, one man spoke up and expressed the feelings of a good number of the class. "I don't know why we are talking about things like this in church," he said. "We have a happy, friendly congregation here. We are all united in our love for Jesus; we like to come to church and hear the Good News. If we start talking about issues like these, it will only divide us and spoil our peaceful congregation."

The idea expressed here appears to be that community is created by preserving the outward unity of the congregation through the reduction of its commitments and convictions to the lowest common denominator. Where this kind of view is operative, we not only avoid discussing certain important aspects of our calling as Christian witnesses in the world, but also we deny each other the gifts we can bring to the task through sharing in the congregational community. We are left to our own devices to struggle with the ethical issues of life. And, unless we make the connections for ourselves, we must carry on those struggles without the benefit of understanding how our faith and hope in Jesus Christ can provide the moral compass we require.[10] Such a view stands in stark contrast to our opening scene from ancient Israel where life with God and life itself came together as the people came together.

The problem of avoidance remains with us. During the past several years I have been serving as the director for the Evangelical Lutheran Church in America's studies on sexuality. The first phase of the study process was focused on homosexuality with reference to questions of blessing same-sex unions and admitting persons in such committed unions into the ordained and other ministries of the church body. In my travels across the country to explain the study process and encourage congregations to participate, I often met the objection or fear that such a discussion will cause strife within the congregation and even result in loss of members. Such fears are understandable and yet not helpful to the witness of the church.

The irony of the claim that we should avoid controversial, ethical discussions and stick to the gospel is that, whenever we gather around the gospel, its power and promise (if we are open to it) inevitably involve us in the enterprise of ethics. Moreover, many of the ELCA congregations that did do the study I just mentioned reported a very different kind of experience from internal strife. Over 80 percent of the thousands who participated and sent in their responses indicated that they now understood each other better and had learned something. Trusting in the Spirit's promised gifts, they engaged in responsible study and dialogue and emerged from the experience enriched.[11] Not only were they enriched, but they were being faithful to the church's vocation to be a community of moral deliberation, a subject to which we shall return in part 3.

This book begins and ends with the conviction that the concerns of Christian ethics are an integral part of our gospel faith and that the Holy Spirit will guide, strengthen, and sustain the Christian community in even its most challenging tasks of moral discernment.

Questions for Discussion

1. Look through your hymnal. What hymns and other parts of the service can you find that link the gospel and our call to Christian love and ethical concern?

2. What are some of the most urgent ethical issues in our day, which Christians need to address in their personal lives and public witness? Are there issues you believe the church should *not* get involved with? If so, why?

3. Are the pressing ethical issues of the day being addressed in your congregation? How is this happening? If some things are not being addressed can you think why? What can be done constructively to integrate ethical awareness and commitment into the life of your congregation?

2

GRACE, FAITH, AND THE GOOD

It is always necessary that the substance or person be good before there can be any good works, and that good works follow and proceed from the good person, as Christ also says, "A good tree cannot bear bad fruit, nor can a bad tree bear good fruit."

—Matthew 7:18

As faith makes one a believer and righteous, so faith does good works.
—Martin Luther, *Treatise on Christian Liberty*

Ethics is a way of life. Teachers of ethics will tell you that *ethics* is an academic discipline. It is the reasoned study of how we determine the good and the right. It involves careful reflection on such matters as virtue and systems of decision making. It involves a comparative discussion of different approaches to moral questions. In short, it has all the characteristics of a field of study like that of many other fields of study. Nonetheless, from the Christian standpoint, the first thing that must be said of ethics is that it is a way of life. The study of ethics is, then, a discipline that serves to assist us in that way.

Faith and Ethics: Living the Given Life

Ethics is an integral part of that way that we call faith. Faith is more than the act of believing something to be true. To have faith, as Christians understand it, is to trust completely in the promise of God and to freely direct our lives according to the hope that we have in that promise. That promise, of course, is what we call the gospel, the good news that, in Jesus Christ, God has overcome sin and death and offers to all humankind forgiveness and everlasting life. That promised life is the free gift of God that has the power to create in us the trust of faith. The trust of faith, free from fear, is free to express itself in a way of life that embraces the teachings and example of its Lord and Savior, Jesus Christ.

Faith as a way of life is the matrix for ethics when we understand Christian ethics to begin with Christlike love and concern for the neighbor. This was a great insight that Martin Luther had and that he expressed clearly in these memorable words:

> Behold, from faith thus flow forth love and joy in the Lord, and from love a joyful, willing, and free mind that serves one's neighbor willingly and takes no account of gratitude or ingratitude, or praise or blame, of gain or loss. . . . Hence, as our heavenly Father has in Christ freely come to our aid, we also ought to help freely our neighbor through our body and its works, and each one should become a Christ to the other that we may be Christ to one another and Christ may be the same in all, that is, that we may be truly Christians.[1]

Whenever I hear these words of Luther, I cannot help but remember an incident from my childhood. It was on a Sunday morning a long time ago in a church basement in Chicago during the opening service of our Sunday school. The superintendent had us all stand up by our little chairs to say an opening prayer. She told us, as we were about to pray, that if we closed our eyes really tight, we could see Jesus while we prayed. I squeezed my eyelids shut as hard as I could but to no avail. It is only recently that I have admitted openly that I could never see Jesus. I thought for sure that I was the only little boy in the whole Sunday school who could not. But I have also thought since that time that if she had told us to look around us at each other, then all of us would have seen Jesus. In faith Christ is alive in us and we are alive in Christ.

Another way to speak about these matters is to talk about Christian ethics in contrast to philosophical or secular ethics. The German theologian Helmut Thielicke has provided us with a helpful way of understanding this contrast. He explains that both Christian ethics and philosophical or secular ethics must deal with the same sorts of moral choices and follow similar patterns of reasoning in making their decisions. However, what distinguishes the two approaches is that they each have different starting points. Philosophical ethics begins with the *task*, the task of doing the right and achieving the good in each situation of decision. Christian ethics has the same task, but it does not start with the task; it starts with the *gift* of God in Jesus Christ. To begin with the gift is to recognize that it is the grace of God at work within us that motivates us to undertake the ethical task. For secular ethics, ethical decision and action is understood as the moral achievement of the person who has undertaken the task. For

Christian ethics, each decision and action is understood to be an expression of the grace of God at work in and through that person. Moreover, persons of faith approach the ethical task with confidence in that grace of God, trusting that God is with them to uphold them and sustain them throughout the moral struggle.[2]

Everything that we have been saying has pointed in the direction of a simple but critically important truth for the life of faith: the grace of God is the beginning of ethics for the people of God. This is the meaning of John's statement that we love because he first loved us (1 John 4:19). In ancient Israel and among the people of the New Testament concern for morality out of love for God and the neighbor has always been a response to God's saving activity and the people's faith in the promise of God which that activity proclaims. The idea of an ethic that we obey in order to earn divine favor for our salvation is strange to biblical faith.[3] Thus, when we consider the nurture of Christian ethics in the life of the congregation, two things follow. First of all, when Christian people gather to hear the gospel, in preaching, in the Scripture readings, through participation in the sacraments, and through Christian conversation, the foundations of ethics have already begun to be built. Second, when we speak explicitly of the good and the right to which Christian people are committed in response to the will of God, we see the divine commandments and precepts not as a burden, but as a joy, a statement of what God has made it possible for us to be in living out our lives as those redeemed by grace.

The second point deserves further emphasis. In the minds of many Christians, the commandments of God (especially the Ten Commandments), which provide the content of biblical ethics, function primarily to show us how we are sinners who have broken the law of God. They make clear what God expects and reveal how we have failed to meet those expectations. The commandments, then, are reduced to the role of accuser and judge. As a result, people may relate to the commands of God in a number of ways that are less than positive. Two are worthy of mention.

The first is simply to take refuge in God's forgiveness and to regard all further attempts to take God's teachings to heart as being futile and unnecessary. This is the sort of Christianity that prompted Dietrich Bonhoeffer's criticism of a discipleship based on "cheap grace." To operate with cheap grace is to rely on God's forgiveness as an excuse for not being involved in the struggles of living out God's will for us.[4]

It is an easy Christianity in which the grace of God's forgiveness frees us from any particular demands on our lives. There is very little agonizing over which choices and values might best fulfill our calling as God's people in the world. There is very little wrestling with conscience, for conscience is stilled by the forgiveness we confer upon ourselves in the name of God's mercy. In this outlook, grace provides the freedom to let everything remain pretty much unchanged. Thus, there is very little repentance, for repentance, in its true sense, always involves a passion for change.

At the opposite end of the spectrum there is a second kind of response. Our persistent sense of being accused and judged by divine law is sometimes met by pretentious claims of having satisfied that law or at least having demonstrated moral superiority. We have all met self-righteous religious people who disturb us with their prideful attitudes. Often such persons fasten on to a few high profile moral issues and make their stance on those matters the emblem of their rectitude. We rightly suspect that they have underestimated the true depth of God's expectations. If they really understood the will of God, they would not be so smug.

Jesus has little patience with moral arrogance. In Luke 18:10-13 he tells the parable of the Pharisee and the tax collector who went to the temple to pray. The Pharisee congratulated himself by thanking God that he was not like other people, "thieves, rogues, adulterers, or even like this tax collector." The tax collector by contrast confessed himself to be a sinner and prayed for God's mercy. It is he who went home justified, Jesus said. The text also tells us that Jesus "told this parable to some who trusted in themselves that they were righteous and regarded others with contempt" (v. 9). Jesus' encounter with the wealthy ruler recorded in the same chapter (vv. 18-30) provides a similar example. The man attempted to show himself worthy of salvation by his claim that he had kept God's commandments from his youth. Jesus' reply cut through to the heart of his self-deception. "You lack one thing," Jesus said. "Sell all that you have, distribute it to the poor and follow me." The ruler walked away sorrowfully, we are told, because he had great riches.

In our secular world, people who strive to satisfy the law and justify their lives most often do not even identify that law as God's law. They draw their ideas of the successful life from the standards of society; these societal standards function in the place of divine commandments. In our performance-oriented world, meeting these standards is their hope and the measure of a worthwhile life. Religion teachers are fond of using Willie Loman, the main character in Arthur Miller's *Death of a Salesman,* to illustrate this point. Willie was captivated by a god of success and riches. He longed to be a supersalesman, wealthy and well-liked. He could not fulfill the law of the god he had chosen to serve; he was a failure. His sales trailed off to nothing; his sons were a disappointment; his company let him go. Accused, judged, and condemned, his life ended tragically in suicide.

Much of the literature dealing with ethics in the world of business uncovers the fact that Willy Loman's tragic drama continues to be replayed with relatively slight changes in script. Far too many people are prone to linking self-worth to generally accepted indicators of success in the world of work. Identifying self-worth and job success means that for many, career failure equates with failure in life. The stronger this threat, the more blinded some become to the moral compromises they are willing to make in pursuit of success. Thus, people get caught in the irony of sacrificing their personal integrity in order to feel good about themselves.[5] The highly public corporate scandals of recent years are simply the most visible signs of this problem. Many more succumb daily to garden variety compromises in obedience to the law of success.

When we see the commands of God—either identified as such or cloaked in worldly guise—as judge and accuser whom we must satisfy to justify our existence, the end is disappointment and, ultimately, no more than death.

Dietrich Bonhoeffer is worth quoting at this juncture: "The commandment of God is permission to live before God as a human being. The commandment of God is *permission*. It is distinguished from all human laws in that it *commands freedom.* . . . This is the lofty aim of God's commandment."[6]

Persons of faith who know the grace of God in Jesus Christ are free from the condemnation of the law, free to see the commands of God in a healthy and helpful way as God's gift for our lives as God's people. Their self-worth is assured by God's acceptance and affirmation in Christ Jesus. They have no need to win God's favor or the favor of the secular gods. With specific reference to the Ten Commandments, Jan Milic Lochman reminds us that the two tables of the Decalogue were kept in the Ark of the Covenant. Since the Ark symbolized the saving love of God for Israel, this arrangement provided a visible sign that the commandments were not the way to salvation but the way of those who had received salvation. Consequently, Lochman calls the Ten Commandments "sign-posts of freedom" in the Christian life, a practical guide to a life lived in the joy of freedom from condemnation.[7]

God's Promise and Our Good

Thus far we have spoken, for the most part, about the faith *with* which we believe, the trust we have in the gospel promise, which includes love for the neighbor. We need also to speak of the gospel promise as the faith in which we believe. In so doing, we will be led to a vision of the *good*, the goal of our moral striving. In this vision of the good we will find the Christian ethic's answer to a primary question all ethical systems must address, "What is the good?"

At this juncture, I want to emphasize a word we have used but not stressed—the word *promise*. In the opening pages of this chapter we have referred occasionally to the gospel promise of God's salvation that gives birth to faith. Promise in this sense is much like the promises people make to each other when they enter into covenants. So, for example, spouses promise their undying love and faithfulness upon entering into the marriage covenant. Indeed, the theme of marital fidelity is an image the Bible frequently employs to describe the steadfast love of God for the world. Each time we gather in worship to celebrate the Lord's Supper, the opening lines of the ancient Eucharistic prayer recall for us God's faithfulness:

> Holy God, mighty Lord, gracious Father:
> > Endless is your mercy and eternal your reign.
> You have filled all creation with light and life;
> > heaven and earth are full of your glory.
> Through Abraham you promised to bless all nations.
> > You rescued Israel, your chosen people.
> Through the prophets you renewed your promise;
> > and, at this end of all the ages, you sent your Son,
> > who in words and deeds proclaimed your kingdom
> > and was obedient to your will, even to giving his life.[8]

The prayer puts us in mind of the fact that God is and always has been "Emmanuel," which means "God with us," relentlessly loving us even when we have turned away. This truth is spelled out further as we confess our faith in the Nicene Creed. In reciting the creed, we voice the manifold ways in which our triune God, Father, Son, and Holy Spirit, has been and continues to be with us.

But there is still another sense in which we speak of the promise of God. God's promise is also expressed in providing a future for the whole of humanity in the ultimate realization of divine dominion, which the Bible speaks of as "the kingdom of God," for which we will employ the more inclusive terms *dominion* and *reign of* God. In the Old Testament, "it is the kingdom of God toward which all history moves. There justice shall reign [Isaiah 11:3-5]; there peace will be unbroken [Isaiah 2:2-4 and Micah 4:1-3]. There Israel shall find at last her destiny to be a blessing to the entire world [Isaiah 2:3; Micah 4:2; Genesis 12:3]. God is the real ruler of that kingdom. . . . It is God's kingdom and it will endure forever."[9]

The promise of the final, future reign of God, which weaves its way through the Old Testament, is echoed during the period between the testaments by various writers who kept alive the hope of their ancestors. In a book called

The Assumption of Moses, we read this eloquent testimony concerning God's promise for the future of all creation.

> Then God's kingdom shall appear throughout all
> God's creation
> And then Satan shall be no more
> and sorrow shall depart with him.[10]

Against the backdrop of this long tradition of expectation for the reign of God, Jesus came preaching the dominion of God. He identified his person and his work with the consummation of centuries of hope and longing for God's dominion. Biblical theologian N. T. Wright has provided a very helpful account of Jesus' self-understanding in relation to the coming of God's reign. Jesus, he contends, believed that God intended to work through Israel to bring about that reign and that its realization would be for all people, not simply the liberation and restoration of Israel, which was the prevailing hope. Moreover, he believed that he was the Messiah who would inaugurate God's dominion in a most unexpected manner: crucifixion and resurrection. As Wolfhart Pannenberg had shown earlier, it is the resurrection that established Jesus as the Messiah and gave birth to the conviction that the reign of God had dawned. The arrival of this new age and new covenant in the resurrection of Jesus was the prolepsis of the general resurrection of the dead and the arrival of that future in which God would be all in all. The universality of that vision provides the foundation for the mission to the gentiles.[11]

Having thus identified Jesus' person and work with the hopes for God's future dominion, where does it lead us in our further understanding of the Christian ethic?

When the disciples of John the Baptist came to Jesus to inquire on John's behalf whether Jesus was the expected Messiah who would bring in the reign of God, Matthew tells us (11:4-5) that Jesus answered with this statement, "Go and tell John what you hear and see: the blind receive their sight, the lame walk, the lepers are cleansed, the deaf hear, the dead are raised, and the poor have good news brought to them." Jesus' statement is a quotation from the prophet Isaiah concerning the signs that would signal the entrance of God's final dominion. This was the way in which Jesus invited people to understand the meaning of his ministry. He sets that forth also in what might be called the inaugural address of his earthly ministry in Luke 4:

> He unrolled the scroll and found the place where it was written:
>
> > The Spirit of the Lord is upon me,
> >   because he has anointed me
> >   to bring good news to the poor.

> He has sent me to proclaim release to the captives
>   and recovery of sight to the blind,
>   to let the oppressed go free,
>   to proclaim the year of the Lord's favor.

> And he rolled up the scroll, gave it back to the attendant, and sat down. The eyes of all in the synagogue were fixed on him. Then he began to say to them, "Today this scripture has been fulfilled in your hearing." (Luke 4:17-21)

Jesus healed the sick, accepted and gave comfort to the poor, and, finally, defeated death itself. In all of this Jesus made it crystal clear, for those who were willing to hear and see, that the reign of God had dawned, the future dominion of God had been revealed.

In reviewing Jesus' earthly ministry and his victory over sin and death in the resurrection, we get an idea of what the promised future of God holds in store for us. It is a dominion from which none is excluded. "The power of God's *basileia* [kingdom] is realized in Jesus' table community with poor, the sinners, the tax collectors, and prostitutes—with all those who 'do not belong' to the 'holy people,' who are somehow deficient in the eyes of the righteous."[12] As Saint Paul has put it, "God proves his love for us in that while we still were sinners Christ died for us" (Rom. 5:8).

God's dominion is a hope for wholeness, in body and in spirit, individually and in community. "The *basileia* [kingdom] vision of Jesus makes people whole, healthy, cleansed and strong. It restores people's humanity in life. The salvation of the *basileia* is not confined to the soul, but spells wholeness for the total person in her/his social relations."[13]

Indeed the whole creation is the object of God's redeeming activity. At the very beginning of John's Gospel the evangelist tells us that the Word who was made flesh and dwelt among us was in the beginning with God and "all things came into being through him." John wants us to make the connection between the creating and redeeming activity of God; in Jesus God follows through on the hope of the creation. The scope of divine redemption is as wide as the universe of God's making (John 1:3). Thus, Saint Paul speaks of the salvation of the whole creation as part and parcel of our hope for salvation. "The creation itself will be set free from its bondage to decay and will obtain the freedom of the glory of the children of God," he says (Rom. 8:21).

Christians have often thought of salvation in very individual and spiritual terms. It is the hope of heaven, as the resting place of the soul, for those persons who are saved. But our brief review of the biblical understanding of God's promise for the final reign is much grander and more glorious. Ours is a hope for the redemption of the whole person and the whole world. The arrival of God's future dominion will bring about the fulfillment of history and the perfection of all that is. Joseph Sittler captured this promise in his discussion of Col. 1:15-20 in which the writer invites us repeatedly to see "all things" (*ta panta*) in and through Christ:

> God's restorative action in Christ is no smaller than the six-times repeated *ta panta*. Redemption is the name for this will, this action, and this concrete Man who is God with us and God for us—and all things are permeable to his cosmic redemption because all things subsist in him. He comes to all things not as a stranger, for he is the first born of all creation, and in him all things were created. He is not only the matrix and *prius* of all things; he is the intention, the fullness, and the integrity of all things: for all things were created through him and for him. . . . A doctrine of redemption is meaningful only when it swings within the larger orbit of a doctrine of creation.[14]

The scope of God's promise is nothing less than the redemption of "all things" (*ta panta*). This is the good news that is spoken of by the prophets and revealed in Jesus Christ. This is the faith in which we believe.

Jürgen Moltmann sees the fullness of God's coming future as the realization of the new creation (Rev. 21:5), the transformation of all things, not their annihilation. Like Sittler before him, Moltmann sees this cosmic hope as the grounds for Christian commitment to ecological responsibility as an integral part of faith and ethics.[15]

Our vision of God's everlasting dominion provides us with a vision of the good toward which we strive through love in faith and hope. Jesus' victory over sin and death forges an everlasting bond of unity between God and the world and everlasting community among people with each other and with God and the whole new creation. The ultimate good of human existence is to participate in this everlasting community.

This theological answer to the ethical question, "What is the Good?" can be expressed in more precise terms by listing the values it represents. Those values are: life, wholeness, peace, equality among all (justice), community and unity (reconciliation), joy, and freedom from all bondage to sin and evil (personal, social, and political).[16] The goal of the Christian ethic is to actively pursue these values, as much as possible, for our neighbors, our society, our world, the good earth, and ourselves.

Thus, when the people of God gather in congregation to rehearse in manifold ways the promises of the gospel of God's dominion, not only is faith awakened, the engine that drives our way of life in the Christian ethic, but we have a clear revelation of the good to direct our decision and our action. As we shall see in parts 2 and 3, the virtues that characterize the Christian life and the principles that guide our decisions about right and wrong will be very closely tied to this vision of the good and the values that define it.

Questions for Discussion

1. When people speak of Christian ethics, do you think they are thinking mainly of rules to be obeyed or of loving service to the neighbor out of joy in being loved by God, as Luther speaks of the Christian life? What resources do we have in the life of the church and the worship life of the congregation to help us promote an ethic that stems from joy in the Lord?

2. In what ways, if any, has this chapter changed your understanding of what is meant by "the kingdom of God" or the reign of God?

3. Some things are "good" because they are useful, such as a "good" automobile. But some things are *intrinsically* good, to be desired for their own sake. Name things that you think are intrinsically good. How do your selections fit with the values or "goods" of God's reign listed toward the end of this chapter?

3

HOPE AND WITNESS

Ethics as Anticipation

Blessed be the God and Father of our Lord Jesus Christ! By God's great mercy God has given us a new birth into a living hope through the resurrection of Jesus Christ from the dead.

—1 Peter 1:3

Always be ready to make your defense to anyone who demands from you an accounting for the hope that is in you.

—1 Peter 3:15

In Stephen King's novel *The Stand,* we are introduced to a winsome and wise character named Peter Goldsmith. Peter chooses these words in his effort to help his daughter Frannie better understand her mother.

> Carla was different in those days. She didn't change until your brother Freddy died. Until then, she was young. She stopped growing after Freddy died. She slapped three coats of lacquer and one of quick-dry cement on her way of looking at things and called it good. Now she's like a guard in a museum of ideas, and if she sees anyone tampering with the exhibits, she gives them a lot of look-out-below. But she wasn't always like that.[1]

Here we have a vivid portrait of a person for whom hope has ceased to exist, one for whom the future holds no promise. All that remains are the remnants of past values and a few comforting memories that need to be jealously guarded. It is not a picture of someone who is very old or dying, which might make it understandable. It is a picture of one who has lost hope and no longer anticipates anything new.

By contrast, we can easily imagine, let us say, a couple—not necessarily a young couple—who are engaged and planning to marry. For them the future holds great promise of new and wonderful adventures in their life together.

Their promising future exerts a tremendous power over them. Practically everything they do—day in and day out—is under the sway of this coming future.
Their plans and their very outlook on life are all under the influence of the
hope they have in each other for fulfillment and happiness. Theirs is a life of
anticipation.

We have spoken of faith, and we have connected it with love. It is time
now to speak of *hope* and, along with it, *anticipation*. Our discussion of God's
promise for the future at the end of chapter 2 has prepared the way for us. For
we have learned that the Bible is not a museum of ideas but a future-oriented
book, promising a new heaven and a new earth in the fullness of God's reign.
And the people of God are not a people who jealously guard the past. Rather,
they are like a couple in love, rushing ahead in anticipation to meet the future.
We are a people of hope. We are a people of anticipation called to engender
hope in sharing and acting out God's promise in Christ in and for a world that
often seems short on hope.

The renowned theologian of hope, Jürgen Moltmann, has recently offered
his lament that the century just past gave us little in which to hope. It provided
no new ideas or visions that could lend meaning to history. Instead, "In that
century progress left in its wake ruins and victims, and no historical future that
can make this suffering good. . . . If the achievements of science and technol-
ogy can be employed for the annihilation of humanity . . . it becomes difficult
to enthuse over the Internet or genetic engineering. Every accumulation of
power also accumulates the danger of its misuse."[2]

However, this kind of necessary realism does not cancel out hope. Hope is
resilient in the human spirit as Moltmann himself has surely taught us. "With
us there is a saying, '*La esperanza muere ultima.*' Hope dies last. You can't
lose hope. If you lose hope, you lose everything." These are the words of Jesse
de la Cruz, a retired migrant farm worker whose testimony gave Studs Terkel
the title of his latest book of interviews, *Hope Dies Last: Keeping Faith in
Troubled Times.*[3] Terkel's interviewees come from different eras in our recent
history, but they share a common characteristic of a tenacious hope for bad
times to get better through the efforts of ordinary folks who care.

Hope arises out of the contrast between what is and what ought to be. The
promise of the future energizes life in the present. Thus, the gospel promise of God's future revealed in the victory of the Christ speaks to the realism
of Moltmann's judgment on the past century and the hope against hope of
Terkel's witnesses. The key is in whom we place our hope. The focus of Christian hope is neither in the cumulative progress of human invention nor in the
admirable spirits of *Hope Dies Last.* Christian hope is in the Easter revelation
of God's will for the world.

Ethics as Witness in Anticipation

The vision of the good that we have in the promise of God's future is both a goal and a gift. We affirm it as our goal because it is God's promised gift. The values we have identified as a summary of that good—life, wholeness, peace, equality among all (justice), community and unity (reconciliation), joy, and freedom from all bondage to sin and evil (personal, social, and political)—are values we pursue in this life because we have hope that God's promise is true. Indeed, our hope goes forward in the certainty of Christ's resurrection through which the dominion of God is revealed and understood.

However, for much of Christian piety the promise of God's reign has been looked at as otherworldly in character. We touched on this briefly in the last chapter. Heaven is contrasted with earth; eternity stands over against history. This world is but a place of sin, decay, and death. History bears witness to the perversity of the human heart, and the institutions of society reflect the fallen state of humankind. Time-honored hymns give voice to this perspective:

> I'm but a stranger here, heaven is my home;
> Earth is a desert drear, heaven is my home;
> Danger and sorrow stand round me on every hand;
> Heaven is my fatherland, heaven is my home.[4]

Or, again,

> A pilgrim and a stranger, I journey here below;
> Far distant is my country, the home to which I go.
> Here I must toil and travail, oft weary and opprest;
> But there my God shall lead me to everlasting rest.[5]

Of course, even in this dismal account of historical existence, God is still interested in the course of history and human events. Divine providence has provided order and authority in this world in order to keep it from unraveling altogether. As youngsters in catechism class most of us probably learned that the Fourth Commandment imperative to honor our parents should be extended to include respect for law, order, and persons in authority in general. Perhaps this instruction in good citizenship was punctuated by passages from Romans 13 or 2 Peter 2 counseling obedience to government as established by God to punish the wicked and reward the good. However, in all likelihood, our teachers did not present these concerns for the institutions of history and society as central to the agenda of the church in the world. In the final analysis, the church's primary task is to proclaim the gospel that unbelievers may come to faith in Christ and enter into the hope of heaven.

In this view, Christians should certainly be concerned for peace, justice, and the common good as their God-given duty. However, the approach to this concern has often been rather conservative in nature, preferring stability to change and progress and accepting the unresolved problems of the world as the inevitable result of human sin in a world that is destined by God for destruction. In fact, too much emphasis on social concerns can make us forget that Jesus said that his dominion is not of this world. This is an attitude much like that of Carla in Stephen King's novel—a guarded attitude, one that has little hope for this world and expects little that is new.[6] In this perspective faith tends to be a purely private matter divorced from social and political concerns. One cannot help but conclude that this outlook gives aid and comfort to the sort of hard core secularism that wants to keep religion in the ghetto of personal spirituality.

However, when we review the biblical account of the gospel promise of God's reign, as we have done, we are, as one author has put it, "converted to the world."[7] That is, when we understand that the promise of our salvation is couched in the promise for the fulfillment of history and the entire created world, we begin to see that concern for this world is not misplaced. Striving for peace, justice, and the common good is not secondary to our purpose as a Christian community; it is an important part of our witness to the full scope of the gospel promise of God's reign through Jesus Christ.

Let us spell it out more fully. When Christians stand for the value of all life by standing against the wanton use of abortion or by standing for the acceptance, rights, and opportunities of the disabled, they anticipate the fullness of life that is part of the gospel promise of the reign of God. When Christians become advocates for a public policy that can help to provide a greater measure of health care for all people or when they become an influence for a sexual ethic that celebrates the joy of bodily life and respects it as an integral part of the self, they are acting in anticipation of the value of wholeness that is part of the gospel promise for the reign of God. When Christians become active agents of reconciliation at every level of life, from nuclear family to international family, they anticipate the promise of peace that is part of their hope for the dominion of God. When Christians oppose racism, sexism, and other isms that exclude and denigrate people for being what they are, they anticipate the value of equality that is part of our hope for the future reign of God. When Christians actively care for the earth and love the creation as God does, they anticipate the wholeness, life, and peace of the new creation when the wolf will lie down with the lamb and hurt and destruction will end forever (Isa. 11:6-9). When Christians reach out to people in their addictions and in their inner turmoil or when they actively address all forms of oppression, they anticipate the freedom from bondage that is God's future for us. When Christians do these and many more things that we could name, they sow the seeds of joy in anticipation of the new heaven and new earth of God's coming reign when every tear will be wiped away and death, pain, and sorrow will be no more (Rev. 21:1-4).

When Christians do these and many more things that we could name, they act in expectation of something new. They believe that the power of God's coming reign can exert itself now, bringing about that which is new in anticipation of the new heaven and the new earth, even as they know that, in Christ, they are a new creation (2 Cor. 5:17). In acts of anticipation the Christian community gives an account of the hope that is within it. The concerns of ethics belong to the witnessing life of the church; they are part and parcel of the gospel mission of the church in the world. Seeking peace and justice is not a substitute for proclaiming the good news, but it is not separate from evangelism either. This point is of critical importance for properly understanding ethics in the life of the church. If we fail to make the connection between ethics and the witness of the church, ethics will remain a second-class citizen and the church will fail to speak the whole truth concerning the promises of God. As Dietrich Bonhoeffer observed, the *penultimate,* our finite and imperfect efforts to embrace the good in the present, prepares the way for the *ultimate,* the fullness of the good that is ours in Christ.[8]

As I hope will be clear throughout, the position I am commending—now as in the past—is that Christian ethics and the gospel witness of the church are interwoven. This view stands in contrast to more than just the otherworldly tendencies mentioned above. It also stands in contrast to the heritage of the liberal Protestantism of the recent past and what some might call the emerging theocratic impulses of the present.

The Heritage of Protestant Liberalism

During the nineteenth century and in the early part of the twentieth, much of the Western world was swept up by a wave of optimism. Scientists, philosophers, industrialists, politicians, historians, and theologians contributed to the newfound understanding that the world is historical in nature, a place of constant change, development, and possibility. For the first time in human history, the idea of progress became an important notion: things did not have to stay the way they were; they could get better. Charles Darwin's account of evolution seemed to provide a scientific basis in nature for the hope of progress. Revolutionary movements on behalf of socialism sought to improve the quality of life by correcting the abuses of laissez-faire capitalism. A new spirit of humanism spurred efforts to reform social institutions such as prisons and schools in order to make them more humane and progressive in outlook.

Not surprisingly, Christianity produced some theological developments reflecting the general spirit of progressivism. Starting in Europe and spreading to the United States, so-called liberal theology turned its attention more and more to ethics and social concerns. Christianity was recast with a predominating emphasis on Christ as the moral teacher, enabling his people to provide moral leadership in the transformation of society. The ethical vision of Jesus could provide the blueprint for realizing the dominion of God on earth. One writer of this era described God's reign as "the commonwealth of love" and "the commonwealth of labor," brought on by "the progressive reign of love in human affairs," which "tends toward the progressive unity of mankind."[9] Christians in concert with other people of goodwill could achieve this hope through moral progress.

All this optimism proved to be premature, however. Events of the first half of the twentieth century brought it down like a house of cards. Utopian dreams were shattered by the long and bitter conflict we call World War I. Renewed expectations had a short life span after the war because, scarcely more than a decade later, the Great Depression caught up with our prosperity. If there were any liberal progressivists left after that, they had only another decade to wait for World War II, the horrors of the Holocaust, and the dawn of the nuclear age to complete their disillusionment.

Although the idea of progress and development has become a permanent feature of modern thought, even after these disastrous events, liberal tendencies in mainstream Protestant Christianity in particular and the human consciousness in general has given way to a more chastened view of things. Christian theology has recovered its keen sense of human sin and turned its hopes once more toward God's promise and not our own capacity to transform the world for the good. The reign of God is God's reign, and God will bring it to pass, not we.[10] In the account of Christian faith, hope, and ethics being offered in this book, this last conviction points to hope in God's promise for the coming future when all things will be made new and God will be all in all. However, there are and have been other ways of thinking about God's sovereignty.

Theocratic Impulses?

In his 1937 book, *The Kingdom of God in America*, H. Richard Niebuhr characterized the theocratic aims of the early Protestant colonists in America. Unlike the liberal tradition that came later, the Puritans and assorted other Protestant groups had no utopian notions of an ideal future toward which Christians would work. Theirs was a keen sense of the present sovereignty of God and a desire to live in a society where obedience to God's laws prevailed. Such a state of affairs was not dependent on human effort; a Calvinistic realism regarding human sinfulness bore none of the humanistic optimism of later liberal theology. God's rule was simply a fact to be acknowledged and honored in human affairs. The basis for all organization of life under God's sovereignty was God's self-revelation in Scripture. Indeed, in theocracy judicial and civil authority was strictly limited by divine rule as expressed in the revealed word of God. Moreover, the church too was subject to the same limitation of its power. The theocratic idea of limitation by divine rule did not mean that the church exerted power over the state, however. The separation of church and state was a hallmark of their commitment to the Reformation's protest against the church's usurping of secular power.[11] Ultimately, theocracy could not survive with the separation of church and state in a democratic capitalist society gradually moving toward diversity and secularization.

Nonetheless, despite the dissipation of that early Protestant experiment, theocratic impulses have consistently reasserted themselves. A prime example in more recent times is the famous Scopes trial. The "fundamentalist" movement in Christianity believed evolution to be a theory that denied the authority of an inerrant Bible and its account of creation. They sought to have states pass laws that would prohibit its teaching in their schools. They succeeded in Tennessee, and in 1925 a teacher, John Thomas Scopes, was brought to trial for violating that law.

The debate over the teaching of evolution in public schools has resurfaced in our time. In its present form the challenge from Christian conservatives is not to prohibit teaching evolution but to mandate the teaching of an alternative to evolution that makes room for divine initiative. Theologian Langdon Gilkey has lifted up this controversy as Exhibit A of the "religious right" or Christian fundamentalism's theocratic designs. He characterizes their brand of religion in politics in the following way:

> Most important in the union of fundamentalist Christianity and politics
> is the claim of fundamentalism to *absolute* truth, to possessing *the* gos-
> pel, the only true Christianity, or as one fundamentalist Christian put
> it, "God's religion." This means that to them, their religious and moral
> agenda represents an absolute moral obligation for everyone, a universal
> requirement.... Their views of social matters become "Christian" views
> of such issues, and no alternative views are tolerated: "dissenters cannot
> really be Christian."[12]

Other contemporary interpreters of the activities of the Christian right echo of theocratic impulses: efforts to pass an amendment to the Constitution defining marriage as between a man and a woman to the exclusion of gay marriage, a militant push for the reversal of the *Roe v. Wade* abortion ruling, vigorous political activity on behalf of elected officials and judges favorable to their moral agenda, support for school prayer, opposition to stem-cell research, and federal financial support for faith-based organizations that make evangelization an integral part of their service to clients.

On April 24, 2005, Christian conservatives held a broadcast rally from a church in Louisville, Kentucky, called "Justice Sunday." The event expressed opposition to a threatened Democratic filibuster in the Senate designed to hold up confirmation of some of President Bush's judicial nominees thought to be faithful to the values held by Christian conservatives. The presence of Senator Bill Frist, the Republican majority leader, as a speaker at this event reinforced existing concerns about the religious right taking over the Republican Party and the resultant legislation of a particular brand of Christian morality. Dr. Bob Edgar, general secretary of the National Council of Churches, offered one of the many critical responses to the event: "Taking a segment of Christianity and melding it with conservative Republican ideology and saying 'We're morally right, and everybody else is anti-Christian, anti faith'—I just think it's an outrage."[13]

Of course, one might regard the sorts of responses given by Gilkey and Edgar as simply expressions of a liberal bias. However, it is important to note that conservative evangelicals have also raised their voices in critical concern over an inappropriate mix of religion and politics.[14]

Encouraging the faithful to vote their conscience when important values are at stake is surely not a theocratic initiative. Faith-based involvement in politics manifests a theocratic inclination when it marries a dogmatic, exclusionary absolutism to the very machinery of political power. This is an orientation characteristic of a "theology of glory," which Douglas John Hall has contrasted with Luther's theology of the cross. The theology of the cross tells us the truth about ourselves and the realities of our fallen world. It entails a theology of humility, open to its own limitations and gratefully dependent upon the grace of God. By contrast,

> The *theologia gloriae* confuses and distorts because it presents divine revelation in a straightforward, undialectical, and authoritarian manner that silences argument, silences doubt—silences therefore, real humanity. It overwhelms the human with its brilliance, its incontestability, its certitude. Yet just in this it confuses and distorts, because God's object in the divine self-manifestation is precisely not to overwhelm but to befriend.[15]

Hall's words prompt a memory of Bonhoeffer's provocative statement in his famous book *Discipleship:* "The Word is weaker than the idea. Likewise, the witnesses to the Word are weaker than the propagandists of an idea."[16] The Word does not seek to overpower and control but offers itself in mercy and love ready to suffer the rejection of the cynical and mean spirited. Doctrinal absolutism advanced by political power verges on ideology.

Anticipation and the "Not Yet"

It is important to have taken this glimpse at recent history and present phenomena in order to make the point that the ethics of anticipation, which I am setting forth here, is neither a new form of the old liberalism nor a theocratic venture. The former was bathed in humanistic optimism, and the latter is marked by an overbearing certitude. Both in their own way place far too much weight on human knowing. Our focus in this account of ethics is on our faith and hope in God, not on our own activity. As I have written elsewhere, we proceed by "assurance," not certitude. The assurance is that of God's presence and blessing in the midst of ambiguous realities.[17]

The very word *anticipation* gives us a clue to a right understanding of the matter. To anticipate is to have and yet not have. The final reign of God and all that it promises has been revealed in the Christ, and its power is already at work in us now. However, the future of God has not yet appeared in its fullness. Sin is the lingering reality that continually confronts us and will continue to be with us until that future arrives. The very values of which we speak as the focus of our love and our hope rise up to judge us. The promise of life reminds us that we are surrounded by death. The promise of wholeness exposes our brokenness. The hope of peace underscores the violence of our world. The value of equality reveals to us how prejudice is so deeply rooted in the human spirit. Our expectation of community and unity in the reign of God forces us to recognize ever more clearly the divisions among us and how these divisions are deepened and perpetuated by various forms of injustice. The hope of freedom sharpens our awareness of oppression.

Thus, while we are formed in hope for the ultimate dominion of God and its promises, life remains cruciform. What I mean is that we continue to struggle with the reality of sin within ourselves and around us in the world. We continue to stand at the foot of the cross viewing the marks of human evil in the broken body of the crucified. This is apparent in the fact that even our best efforts are imperfect and incomplete. It is evident in the frustrations and setbacks that constantly occur in working for a better world. Persons who choose to become deeply involved in working for social change need the endurance of a long-distance runner. Partial success is often elusive, and complete success is virtually unheard of. The constant conflict of competing interests makes it extremely difficult to resolve the most basic problems of society. Anyone who reads the paper or watches the news knows this. Persons with good motives make bad decisions. And persons with bad motives get in the way of good decisions. We will get more deeply into the struggles and uncertainties of ethical decision later in this book. For now it is enough to make the point that we live in the "not yet." The reign of God has been revealed and established in the Christ, but it is "not yet" consummated in its fullness.

It is not only the large-scale and complex issues of social and global concerns which confront us with conflict and frustration; the more commonplace problems of personal decision can also be troubling. Most of the time our ethical decisions are simple and straightforward. For example, we normally tell the truth and keep our promises. Sometimes when we wrestle with whether or not to do that it is simply because we are tempted to lie or break a promise for the purpose of selfish gain. However, often moral decisions are not so straightforward, and struggles with them are not just struggles with the temptation to selfishness. What about telling the truth when it causes needless harm to an innocent party? Which obligations do you fulfill when circumstances beyond your control make it impossible to fulfill them all? Do you agree to the treatment of a dying loved one out of respect for life? Or do you consent to the withdrawal of further treatment so that suffering can end and the peace of death can come? How do you sort out conflicts between the needs of a spouse and the needs of children when all are not agreed? All of us can add further examples to the list without much difficulty.

When facing conflicts like these, we discover conflicting motives within ourselves. Why do I *really* want to resolve a moral dilemma one way rather than another? Is it because I am convinced it is the most responsible choice? Or, is it because it is the choice I want to make for selfish and unspoken reasons, while my spoken reasons are mere rationalizations? Sound familiar? We are "not yet" persons as well as people who live in a "not yet" world. Yet we are still a people surrounded by promise. "In other words, the bearing or stance appropriate to the church is not that of a community that has arrived but of one that is underway *(communio viatorum)*—that is, a community of hope. And that is precisely how the earliest church regarded itself."[18]

The People of Anticipation

In the New Testament, the church is understood to be the community of the end times.[19] The people of God have seen the dawn of the coming kingdom in the dawn of Easter morning. We are a people straining ahead for the future, restive with the "not yet" and impatient with ourselves, but filled with hope. We understand our hope because we understand the roots of despair. The story of Toby, related by one of his friends in Christ, comes to mind.

What impressed me most about him was his mental attitude, a combination of calmness and serenity. Toby had been severely disabled from birth. He was now middle-aged. We used to meet two or three times a week. How often we heard him say, "So what?" When the local football team was relegated, he cocked his head to one side, smiled, and said, "So what?" That I did not find hard to understand. But I was amazed when his wheelchair had a flat tire and Toby just cocked his head, smiled, and said, "So what?" When something like that happens to me, I usually begin to shout. When the doctor told him he had only weeks left to live and Toby again said, "So what?" even his mother could no longer understand him. "Aren't you carrying this too far, son?" she said. But Toby said simply: "Listen, Mum! Is Easter only about eggs or also about me?"

I thought that an absolutely wonderful remark, though it made Toby seem somewhat strange to me. But not later on when his mother told me that her son, who had died on an Easter Sunday, had very seldom talked of his disability. Only once. They were having tea together, and the boy—well he was actually grown up—knocked over a cup and began to cry. A middle-aged man began to cry over a broken cup! He sobbed to himself, "I'm just an old cripple." Now when I think of Toby, he no longer seems strange to me. That business about Easter and the business of the cup—they go together. Toby had ideals, very high ideals. But he was human enough to know that our ideals cannot always be reached.[20]

Even though our lives may lack the suffering and challenge that Toby faced, Toby can be for us a representative of the church in the world. As a people of anticipation, we live in the tension of cross and resurrection, the tension of broken tea cups and Easter morning.

Nowhere is this more evident than in the sacramental life of the congregation. In baptism we die to sin and are buried with Christ only to rise from those waters to newness of life. Although it is a one-time ceremony, it is for all of life. We are taught that it is a daily dying and rising because sin persists and God's covenant with us in baptism needs to be continually recalled in our hearts and minds. In some congregations this truth is symbolized by placing the baptismal font in a prominent location, always filled with water, always in view, as a way of saying that the pulse of life has the constant rhythm of repentance and hope.

It is all there in the drama of the Lord's Supper as well. The Lord's Supper is a memorial of our betrayal and Christ's death for human sin, but, at the same time, it is a foretaste of the heavenly banquet. In the midst of a world and a church divided by fear and hostility, it is the meal of unity and harmony with God and each other. In the bread and wine, Christ is present to offer forgiveness and life, but he is present also to send us out to proclaim that he is still coming.

At the Smithsonian Institute in Washington, D.C., one of the most popular exhibits is the Hope Diamond. People expect a great deal when they go to see this largest and most famous of diamonds. Sometimes they feel a sense of disappointment. It is big; it is impressive for its magnitude. But it lacks the luster and sparkle of smaller cut diamonds that we are used to seeing. For many in the world, looking at the church has the same effect. They expect a great deal and, perhaps, they may see it as impressive for its size and the magnitude of its name and influence. Yet it seems to lack luster. It fails in so many ways to be the shining example. There is much to repent in this judgment, a judgment we sometimes apply with even greater severity to ourselves. However, without excusing ourselves, the message of the gospel, spoken through faith, hope, and the struggle for the good, is the witness of the church, not our moral perfection. We become discouraged with ourselves and with how little good we seem to do in a discouraging world. But we should not despise even our humblest efforts. If Jesus could see giving a cup of water to a thirsty person as a sign of the kingdom, we dare not devalue the simple good we do and the efforts we are led to make. For these actions are signs of God at work through us to provide the world with anticipations of the promised future.

Questions for Discussion

1. To what extent do you think an optimistic belief in moral progress toward greater justice and the common good remains a part of our culture? Compare and contrast what you understand the Christian vision of reality to be.

2. Do you agree with the analysis of theocratic impulses showing themselves in our present religious and political situation? What do you consider the pros and cons of addressing matters of public policy with faith-based ethical convictions?

3. In what ways do Christian people concretely experience living in the tension of the "already–not yet"?

PART TWO
Formation

4

FORMED BY LOVE

I give you a new commandment, that you love one another. Just as I have loved you, you also should love one another.

—John 13:34

In Genesis 2 the narrative of creation portrays God shaping or forming the first human being from the dust of the earth. The verb for *forming* here is that used of a potter working the clay to make it into something. What was once nothing, a shapeless lump, is now, under the skillful hands of the potter, a useful vessel or perhaps even a thing of beauty. There is an analogy to this image of the potter at work in what we have been saying throughout the first part of this book. We have been shaped in faith, hope, and anticipation by the gracious hand of God. We have been formed by love, the love of God in Jesus Christ. Now it is time to describe in greater detail the specific contours of our formation as these display an ethical dimension.

There are two noteworthy places in which the apostle Paul uses *formation language* in speaking of the Christian life and ethic. In Rom. 12:2 he says, "Do not be conformed to this world, but be transformed by the renewing of your minds, so that you may discern what is the will of God—what is good and acceptable and perfect." Later, writing to the Philippians, Paul calls upon them to have the mind of Christ who, "though he was in the form of God, did not regard equality with God as something to be exploited, but emptied himself, taking the form of a slave" (2:5-7).

In both statements the form or shape of the Christian life is that of Christ himself. He provides the contours and the details. In the first passage it is implicit; in the second it is explicit.[1] In both statements Paul speaks of our formation in Christ as involving the mind. In both cases Paul's reference to *mind* is a reference to our understanding of life and the world and to the attitudes we have toward life and the world.[2] This is what we mean in ethics by the term *character,* our outlook on the world and the moral disposition it produces.[3]

Christian character, according to Paul, then, is to be formed in our understanding and attitudes by Christ, according to Christ, and in Christ. Or, we might say it is to be formed in love, the love Christ portrays in his person and teaching.[4]

Agape Love

That love Jesus teaches and embodied in his life and work is the love signified in the New Testament by the Greek word *agape.* Volumes and volumes have been written on this subject. We shall look at it here in terms of its outlook, disposition, and objective.[5] In *outlook* agape love is *universal* or *all-inclusive.* A great deal of evidence could be gathered from the New Testament to demonstrate the universal outlook of agape love that excludes no one from its concern and includes all in its outreach. However, the critical passage for making this point appears to be Matt. 5:43-44, where Jesus commands his followers to love their enemies and bless those who persecute them. There is nothing about the other person that can disqualify that person from being the object of the Christian's love. If even the enemy who would do us harm is not excluded, what other quality could a person possess that could conceivably exclude him or her from our loving concern? This is a difficult idea to understand and even more difficult to live out. Our natural inclination is to strike out against or at least avoid those who are hostile toward us. Those feelings are constantly reinforced in daily life by the attitudes and practices that prevail in the workplace, in politics, and in the various communities we are involved with. In addition, much of the violence that thrills the public on television and in motion pictures is built around the theme of vengeance.

Nonetheless, though it may be difficult to fully embrace the universal outlook of agape love, it is the teaching and the pattern that Jesus presents for us. It reflects the attitude of God. As Matt. 5:45 goes on to say, "He makes his sun rise on the evil and on the good, and sends rain on the righteous and on the unrighteous." It is echoed by Jesus' prayer from the cross that God forgive his enemies who were crucifying him. The love of God, especially as it is reflected in Christ, is universal. The implications of this all-inclusive character of agape love for Christian ethics will be spelled out in a variety of ways in the pages to come. But for now, it is obvious, for example, that the *agape* outlook cannot tolerate racism or sexism or any other *ism* that discriminates against people simply because of something they are. It is equally clear that agape love is not only something we extend to those who we think are lovable or somehow worthy.

When we understand this all-inclusive character of *agape*, we begin to understand that the disposition of love to regard all equally as the objects of our concern and care is another way of saying that each and every one of our neighbors is to be treated as an end in herself/himself. That is, our care for the neighbor is not conditioned by our perception of what the neighbor is worth to us or society. It is conditioned simply by the neighbor's needs and his or her innate dignity as one created in the image of God for whom Christ died.[6] This aspect of agape love in particular speaks powerfully to Christian attitudes regarding justice in our world, as we shall see later in chapter 10.

Closely associated with the all-inclusive outlook of agape love is its *disposition,* which can be described as *self-giving.* If the universality of *agape* is sometimes hard to appreciate or embrace, self-giving love is difficult to understand as well. We know that Jesus is our example in this matter; that he is the one "who emptied himself" and gave himself up to death for our sake (Phil. 2:4ff.). We know that in so doing he loved a human family that was sinful and undeserving. We are taught by his sacrifice about a divine love that, in contrast to most human loves, seeks nothing in return and does not even require the satisfaction that the beloved be lovable! We know that Christians throughout the centuries have been eloquent in their descriptions of how this self-giving love takes shape in the lives of believers in contrast to the self-centered and self-seeking impulses of sinful humanity.

No one has been more forceful in describing the radical character of *agape's* self-giving dimension than the devout Christian and former secretary general of the United Nations, Dag Hammarskjöld: "Your life is without a foundation, if, in any matter, you choose on your own behalf."[7] But is such a demand for self-giving love too radical? Will it not destroy the self? Is that really what God desires?

We expect critics of the Christian faith to attack the idea of a love so drastic that it virtually gives up all concern for self-fulfillment. After all, they do not appreciate Christianity to begin with. However, sincere Christians who have critically questioned whether we have properly understood the self-giving character of *agape* are not so easily dismissed. Some believe that the idea of agape love as self-giving love is easily distorted and misunderstood.

Dorothee Soelle, in her book *Beyond Mere Obedience,* struggles with one form of this distortion. The illustration she employs is a story written by Bertold Brecht about a middle-class woman who lived her whole life in self-giving devotion to her family and their needs, taking no pleasure for herself. Suddenly, at age seventy, with the death of her husband, she completely reversed her lifestyle and, during the remaining two years of her life, refused further service to her children and concentrated solely on pursuing her own interests in her own sometimes eccentric way. Soelle characterizes this woman's prior life as one of sacrifice and obedience to the role expected of her as a woman. In that life she was literally selfless. In her emancipated life, she expressed spontaneity and subjectivity. She became a self. However, Soelle observes that finally neither the old way nor the new way is really possible or healthy; the former was self-destructive and the latter was irresponsible.[8]

In the story, the distortion of the ideal of self-giving love that most concerns Soelle is the manner in which the woman's virtue of self-giving is exploited by her family and turned into a self-destructive kind of self-denial. Her story illustrates a society that manipulates women into accepting an oppressive set of expectations for their role in life by fostering the virtue and duty of self-sacrifice. In these observations, Soelle is very representative of many feminist theologians and other spokespersons for oppressed people who are suspicious of the Christian ideal of self-giving love. If that ideal is used to give moral and religious justification for unjust circumstances, to "keep people in their place" by appealing to a version of self-giving love that is always passive and patient in suffering, then the ideal is perverted and suspect. Speaking specifically from the feminist perspective, Lisa Sowle Cahill observes that, "Ideally, all Christians should experience a sacrificial and self-transcending love. At the same time, the cult of maternal and wifely sacrifice encourages in women the sin of self-negation rather than that of will-to-power."[9]

Self-giving love requires a self to give. Sacrificial love for the neighbor is meaningless unless we possess and care for the self that we offer. In creation and redemption God has given us life, ourselves. We are called upon to cherish and care for this precious gift, not to neglect our well-being and consider ourselves of no account. Out of the freedom and confidence of knowing our worth as children of God, we are able to give in love. We shall have to deal more with this difficult idea when we talk about the virtue of poverty of spirit in the next chapter.

At the same time that we need to protect the healthy pursuit of self-realization from distorted notions of *agape*'s self-sacrifice, we also need to keep in mind that Brecht's story points to perverse forms of self-realization as well. We are all aware of and dislike various forms of selfishness in ourselves and others. We know instinctively that this is alien to agape love and love in general. In our time, however, the cultural conditions seem unusually cooperative. In another book, I wrote of how two deeply rooted impulses of our cultural heritage have combined to enable individual and corporate greed and self-aggrandizement to flourish at the expense of the communal good. The cherished idea of individual freedom together with the belief in the limitlessness of wealth and opportunity combine to instill the further conviction that the freedom of individuals or specific groups to gain all the wealth and influence they can need not be restricted. There is always more, the argument goes. Therefore, the accumulation of some does not deprive others of the same opportunities. These assumptions live on. Thus, greed is not really challenged, even if not admired, and the success of the greedy may even be an inspiration or fascination to those less fortunate. Meanwhile the proposal that the needs of my neighbor ought to set some limits to my freedom for self-centered pursuits frequently takes second place, if recognized at all.[10] The political and economic orientations of the present seem to support this state of affairs to a remarkable degree.

The objective of God's love for us in Jesus Christ is to bring about unity and community within the self and among selves with God and each other. So also, for the Christian community the *objective* of agape love is found in these values of unity and community.

Human beings have often been confused about their own nature. Some have held the firm conviction that it is the soul or spirit that is really the essence of what we are. The body is unimportant and may even be the source of most of our problems. Others have held with equal certainty that the complex mechanism that we call our bodies is all that we are; there is no such thing as a spirit or a soul. As mysterious as the human emotions may be and as marvelous as the human mind may be, they are all capable of explanation in terms of the combination of molecules that has joined together through evolution to produce the human species. Some, especially in our American society, have made an ideal out of "rugged individualism." The completely independent and self-reliant person has often been our hero, the sort of person we would like to be. Actually, most of us know and experience the fact that people are spiritual and not just bodily and that our psychological life deeply affects our physical well-being and vice versa. We also know and experience the need for community and the support of human companionship; the ideal of total independence and radical individualism is a myth and, with few exceptions, those who seek to follow it discover only loneliness and desperation.

From the biblical perspective, human beings are a spiritual and physical unity created for intimate community with God and with each other. That is our true being as God intends it. Sin, therefore, is understood as a disruption and distortion of that pattern in which we find ourselves profoundly alienated from our true being: divided within ourselves and divided from God and from each other.[11]

Examples of how we are divided within ourselves and from each other, as well as from God, are numerous indeed. The intensity of these conflicts is perhaps nowhere more apparent than in our struggles to deal with our sexuality.

Various fears of the spiritual, physical, and relational dimensions of our nature come together in sexuality. Our passions both frighten and delight us. Our thoughts and our actions often conflict. We seek to give as well as receive, to love as well as be loved, to respect as well as to be gratified. We long for a perfect blending of a harmonious unity and community of body and spirit in relation to the other, surrounded by mutual commitments of caring and sharing that are woven into the intensity of the sexual union. But we often settle for a great deal less. Perhaps some of us give up on the ideal altogether. The sheer volume of literature dealing with human sexuality is a symptom of how deep and broad the problem is. However, our struggles for integrity and community in the expression of our sexuality constitute but one powerful example of the brokenness of the human situation. In Romans 7 the apostle Paul struggles with the problem of conflict within the self. His is the outcry of a troubled conscience. "For I do not do what I want, but I do the very thing I hate" (v. 15).

The self is divided within the self; sin is at war with love for God and God's will. In other words, Paul experienced the same sort of internal conflicts that we do. So intense was the war that raged within him that Paul cried out, "Wretched man that I am! Who will rescue me from this body of death?" The answer came immediately, "Thanks be to God through Jesus Christ our Lord!" (vv. 24-25).

For Paul, the forgiveness and the grace of God in Jesus Christ brought healing, wholeness, and peace to the self-destructive forces within the human spirit. And certainly this is the testimony of the whole life and work of Jesus. He healed the sick in body, but he also forgave their sins and restored them to the community. Wholeness, health, reconciliation, and life are among the many things in the New Testament witness that point to the fact that the objective of God's love is unity and community in every dimension of human existence. "The disunion of human beings from God, from other human beings, from the world and from themselves is ended. . . . Love thus denotes what God does to human beings to overcome the disunion in which they lived. This deed is called Christ, it is called reconciliation."[12]

As the agape love of Jesus Christ has brought us wholeness in life and life in community with God and each other, our agape love has the same objective. Love seeks an ethic in which our sexual union with another is the joyful expression of mutual love and respect and in which neither is merely the object of the other's gratification. Love seeks an ethic in which physicians and health-care workers treat patients as whole persons and not merely as cases. Love seeks an ethic in which society is based on equality and co-humanity and not on the divisions of race and class. Love seeks an ethic in which the quality of life that we strive to guarantee for each other is not measured simply in material terms but in terms of health and the richness of our relationships together in community. Unity and community are the objects of *agape*. In Paul's well-known "love chapter," 1 Corinthians 13, he tells us of the traits that love displays:

> Love is patient; love is kind; love is not envious or boastful or arrogant or rude. It does not insist on its own way; it is not irritable or resentful; it does not rejoice in wrongdoing, but rejoices in the truth. It bears all things, believes all things, hopes all things, endures all things. (vv. 4-6)

These are the attitudes and practices that build relationships and strengthen community and unity. Later we will observe more deliberately the relation between the character and direction of love and Christian commitment to justice. For now we can foreshadow that discussion a bit by pointing out that the Greek for what is translated "wrongdoing" in verse 6 can also be rendered "injustice" and the Greek for "truth" in the same verse is closely associated with the idea of justice—some would say a synonym for it.

In many congregations the sharing of the *peace* has become a regular part of Sunday worship. This is a marvelous opportunity to further understand and ritually express *agape's* objective of community and unity. There are at least several aspects to *peace* in the Old and New Testaments. First of all, peace is a wish for the health and wholeness of the individual. This is especially true of the Old Testament word for peace, *shalom*. But the New Testament also speaks of individual wholeness in terms of peace of mind in contrast to inner turmoil, anxiety, and fear (see John 14:27). Second, peace refers to peace with God. Paul tells us that "since we are justified by faith, we have peace with God through our Lord Jesus Christ" (Rom. 5:1). Finally, the peace of right relationship with God is that peace we seek by grace to duplicate in harmonious relationships with others.[13]

In sharing the peace with each other, we wish each other wholeness in body and spirit, harmony in relationship with God, and peace and love in our relationships with others. When we say, "Peace be with you," we act out in the worship setting what is to be the pattern and objective of the Christian life of agape love as it works for unity and community for the neighbor.

Character and Virtue

I have tried to say something about the character of love in which we are formed out of faith and by grace. Yet more needs to be said about the contours and details of Christlike character. Traditionally, character is further explained by talking about the virtues or traits that make it up. This is the next item on our agenda.

When I was ten years old, growing up in a town called Teaneck, New Jersey, there was a little street near my home named Catalpa Avenue. In those days Catalpa Avenue was not paved but simply covered with gravel. Since it connected my block to the blocks where most of my friends lived, I often rode my bike down Catalpa Avenue. On one particular morning when I set out, the town road crew had just laid down a fresh coating of new gravel. It was somewhat loose and not tamped down by traffic. When my bike tires hit this loose gravel, my bike went out from under me immediately and I fell onto the gravel, my bike falling on top of me. In the fall, the gravel dug its way into my arm, and I found myself hurt and bleeding. As I lay there on Catalpa Avenue crying and frightened, a woman who had witnessed my accident came walking by on the other side of the street. She called out to me, "Just pray, young man, just pray!" And, then, she kept right on walking by. I shall come to the point of this story in just a little bit.

When we speak of character and the virtues it displays, we are talking about the ethics of *being*. The ethics of being refers to what we are in our moral disposition, the sorts of people we are, morally speaking. In ethics discussions, the ethics of being are frequently distinguished from the ethics of doing. The ethics of doing refers to the directions we have for what we ought to do.

Protestant ethics has only recently recovered its interest in character, the ethics of being, as a topic of concern. Stanley Hauerwas has helped us to see that the Christian community is a community of character, the place where our moral vision and disposition are formed by the story of Jesus Christ that we share in our life together. This common story and its effect on us precedes and underlies any reasoned analysis of ethical decision making and action.[14]

The manner in which we are shaped in character and virtue by our faith-story has also been described by saying that Christians have a fellowship ethic, a *koinonia* ethic that helps form the consciousness of all members through shared worship, Sunday school teachers, friendships in the congregation, and the examples of pastors and other leaders.[15] Memories and stories of my late beloved father will continue to exert their positive influence on his grandchildren and great-grandchildren because his life was a story of reconciling love that kept our family together in many times of stress.

Finally, others have lifted up the importance of discussing the ethics of being by offering their opinion that the primary role of the Bible in Christian ethics is to shape what we are rather than to tell us what we are to do. That is, the examples, stories, images, and teachings of the Bible instill character and virtue in the believing community more than providing systematic instructions for directing us on what to do when faced with certain ethical decisions.[16] "Each gospel is a 'remembrance,' a literary commemoration of the crucified and risen Lord, forming character and shaping conduct into something worthy of the gospel."[17]

It is important not to make too strong a distinction between being and doing. Christian character and its virtues are not simply spiritual traits we possess; they have a "thirst for action," an inherent impulse to live themselves out in life with the neighbor.[18] This is the point of the story of my bicycle accident. I'm sure that the unknown woman's spirituality was genuine and sincere in urging me to pray, but the thirst for action was somehow missing—she simply passed by on the other side.

When, through Bible study and other means of sharing our story, we nurture the development of character and virtue in the life of the community, we are not dealing with harmless personal piety detached from the world. We are fueling the fires of moral passion; we are creating a thirst for action; we are already in the process of *engaging* the *real world*.

That unavoidable connection between virtue and its practice becomes apparent when we begin to study some of the biblical images of virtue in the chapters that follow. There is a wealth of material in the Bible that might inform our discussion of virtue in the community of the faithful. I have chosen to focus on a number of the terse but pregnant statements that we find in the first twelve verses of Matthew 5, those words commonly known as the Beatitudes. I suspect that most people reflecting on these statements find them rather intimidating. In fact, for centuries Christians have found the entire Sermon on the Mount, which begins with these Beatitudes, difficult to deal with. They see in these teachings a pattern of saintliness that appears quite beyond the reach of an ordinary person. The history of Christian reflection on the Beatitudes and the Sermon on the Mount has often been marked by various efforts to modify what seem to be its extreme demands.

The impression that we are dealing here with an impossible ideal is likely to be reinforced by the observation that the Beatitudes or other portions of the Sermon on the Mount have often been among the appointed readings for All Saints Day. Historically, All Saints Day was a festival to remember the heroes and the heroines of the faith, people whose faith and devotion seem to have been far beyond anything we aspire to or hope to accomplish as Christians. The Sermon on the Mount may have been their pattern for life, but can it possibly be ours?

However, since the time of the Reformation, the term *saint* has taken on new meaning. Now the whole church is referred to as the communion of saints. Each member of the church is a saint. The emphasis has shifted from focusing on the heroic faith of a fabled few to the fact that, through the grace of God in Jesus Christ, all believers are made holy and accounted as saints. We no longer venerate the heroes and heroines of Christianity. We give thanks to God for their inspiring example. But we also praise God that we too have received the same grace of the forgiveness of sins and a new life empowered for new possibilities.

We thus understand that the Sermon on the Mount and the Beatitudes are part of Jesus' proclamation of the reign of God. As such, they represent a statement of new possibilities initiated by Jesus in inaugurating that reign through his victory over sin and death.[19] Consequently, the Beatitudes are not virtues we must attain to be truly God's people but virtues that God makes possible for the children of the future promise. One biblical scholar has captured this nicely by making the point that the word *blessed* at the beginning of each Beatitude might better be translated as *congratulations*. Congratulations, you can be poor in spirit. Congratulations, you can be merciful, a peacemaker, and so on. That is the sense of it.[20] The idea is to stress that God confers new capabilities upon us as we are formed in love. Furthermore, as we reflect on the virtues signaled by the Beatitudes in the following chapters, it is important to note that their spirit is present in the virtues commended elsewhere in the New Testament in passages such as Col. 3:12-17; Phil. 2:2-3; Eph. 4:2-3, 32; and Gal. 5:22-23.[21] Here too the virtues listed are part and parcel of the new life in Christ that is ours by grace.

We began this chapter with the image of the potter shaping the clay. In concluding, I would like to come back to the image of pottery but with a different twist, for we may be likened to pottery in more ways than one. The love in which we are formed is the grace of God at work in us to bear witness to God's love in the gospel of Jesus Christ. This gospel is our treasure and the treasure for all people from God. "But," says Paul, "we have this treasure in clay jars, so that it may be made clear that this extraordinary power belongs to God and does not come from us" (2 Cor. 4:7). We are a "not-yet" people: humble, common, fragile, and imperfect, like earthenware pottery. Yet God has chosen to deliver the treasure of the gospel through the likes of us. God is shaping from the clay of our humanity a people equipped to help little children who have fallen from their bikes—to comfort them, to stop the bleeding, to help them find their way home, and to tell them to whom they can pray in time of trouble.

Questions for Discussion

1. Review the discussion of agape love. How would you explain it to someone who asks what all this talk about Christian love means?

2. What are some of the stories of Jesus that you can remember from reading the Bible that illustrate the kind of love we are called to live?

3. Who are people in your experience whose life stories display the character of Christian love in some specific way or ways?

5 POVERTY OF SPIRIT

Blessed are the poor in spirit, for theirs is the kingdom of heaven.

—Matthew 5:3

"The poor" worship at a throne as lowly as a manger, as self-forgetting as a cross. They do not need to search for heaven; it has already found them, and through them heaven invades our proud society to save us from an ever distant hell.

—George A. Buttrick, *The Beatitudes*

On the surface, poverty of spirit, like meekness that is mentioned later in the Beatitudes, does not seem to be a particularly attractive characteristic to cultivate. To be poor in spirit or to be meek does not suggest the kind of strength of personality that we find appealing. Rather, these words suggest a person who is mild-mannered, self-effacing, and even timid. In modern slang we might say such a person is a "wimp." And yet poverty of spirit is the cornerstone of all the other beatitudes. It is a quality that emanates from a profound faith in the gospel. It is possible only for those who have found true freedom in the gospel. Poverty of spirit is the virtue whose presence makes courage and strength of character possible.

Of Poverty and of the Spirit

Determining the basic meaning of this beatitude is itself a bit tricky. First of all, the beatitude echoes the Bible's concern for the welfare of the poor and the promise that their situation will be reversed in the fullness of God's future kingdom. The Old Testament passage that lies behind this thrust of the beatitude is Isa. 61:1. There, the prophet speaks of the Messiah who will come to bring good news to the poor. This is the passage that Jesus applied to his own person and work in Luke 4, indicating thereby that he was the fulfillment of that prophecy. The message of Isaiah and of Jesus in the Beatitudes is clear: God cares about the suffering of the poor and promises them deliverance.[1]

The poor referred to in the Bible are not simply those who are economically poor. All who are oppressed, powerless, and at the margins of society may be considered among the poor. The outcasts of that time and our time, the disabled, and the victims of injustice can all be numbered among the poor. As God is committed to the ultimate wholeness of all the downtrodden in the fullness of the kingdom, so the church, as a community of anticipation, is committed to fulfilling the needs and hopes of the poor as a witness to God's promise. Thus, this beatitude signals a mind-set and disposition consistent with that commitment, a mind-set of solidarity with the poor. However, there is more to it than that.

The words "in spirit" broaden the meaning of the beatitude beyond the focus on meeting the needs of the afflicted and being one with them in their needs. It suggests that there is a spiritual quality among the faithful who are poor that represents an ideal to be cultivated by all the people of God. Powerless as they were, the poor stood empty-handed before God in total trust and reliance upon the divine promises. Theirs was a faith without pretense. Out of their experience with oppression there emerged a keen insight into the true wonder of God's promise of salvation. Those with power, accomplishment, and the respect of their peers might be tempted to pride and fail to appreciate their deep need for God's mercy. This was not the case with the poor.[2] This spirituality of the poor leads us to an important insight concerning the full meaning of poverty of spirit.

The poverty that Jesus addressed was a harsh reality, not an ideal. That is the case today. Christian spirituality does not seek to cultivate poverty for its own sake. Indeed, the fact that Jesus promised that poverty would be overcome in the dominion of God indicates that the people of God should combat it, not cultivate it.[3] Consistent with that insight, James H. Evans has pointed out that the conviction that God is on the side of the oppressed poor sustained the faith of African American Christians in the days of slavery and beyond. Evans hastens to add that this divine compassion for the oppressed was not a consequence of their moral superiority; it was a matter of God's mercy.[4] Poverty is not an ideal, and Evans's point reminds us that we should also not idealize the poor and oppressed as inherently gifted with special holiness. However, what we can say is that the particular experience of the oppressed and the trust in God's promise that this experience has engendered for many means that solidarity with the poor involves more than just commitment to their needs and the redress of social ills. More important, it means a readiness to learn from them and to accept the mantle of their experience as a blessing. This reverses the customary role in which even the most compassionate of the privileged are often tempted to a demeaning paternalism in their attitudes of concern and in their charity toward the poor. Rather, the implication of this beatitude is that the poor should become our teachers. The impact of the promise upon their lives and the formation of their character can teach us much about the virtue of poverty of spirit.

The noted Latin American theologian Gustavo Gutiérrez has traced the biblical lineage of poverty of spirit. He defines it as being "totally at the disposition of the Lord." Poverty of spirit has the same meaning as the gospel theme of spiritual childhood, Gutiérrez contends. "God's communication with us is a gift of love; to receive this gift it is necessary to be poor, a spiritual child. This poverty has no direct relationship to wealth; in the first instance it is not a question of indifference to the goods of this world. It goes deeper than that; it means to have no other sustenance than the will of God. This is the attitude of Christ. Indeed, it is to him that all the Beatitudes fundamentally refer."[5]

I would like to close this section with a quotation from the widely read pastoral theologian, Henri J. M. Nouwen. His comment both serves as a summary of our present discussion and offers a bridge to the next section as we begin to look further at poverty of spirit and how it relates to several ethically significant issues of our time.

> I am increasingly convinced that one of the greatest missionary tasks is to receive the fruits of the lives of the poor, the oppressed, and the suffering as gifts offered for the salvation of the rich. We who live in the illusion of control and self-sufficiency must learn true joy, peace, forgiveness, and love from our poor brothers and sisters. As long as we only want to give, we remain in the house of fear—so much giving can be a way of staying in control.[6]

An Inclusive Church for a Just Society

In Christian tradition, three of the characteristics assigned to the church are that it is *one, holy,* and *catholic.* The oneness or unity of the church is the gift of God's grace in Jesus Christ. This is the overarching truth, despite the fact that the church has divided itself historically into a variety of denominations. The apostle Paul put the matter this way, "There is no longer Jew or Greek, there is no longer slave or free, there is no longer male and female; for all of you are one in Christ Jesus" (Gal. 3:28). Paul's declaration points also in the direction of at least one aspect of the church as catholic. To be catholic is to be universal or all-inclusive. The church as catholic includes all people everywhere throughout all times and all places. Both the church's oneness and its catholicity are part of its witness to the world. Oneness with God and each other that is inclusive of all people is the promise and hope of the dominion of God. As the church strives to express its unity and catholicity in all that it is and does, it anticipates the promise of God's future for the unity of all humankind in the bonds of life and love.

In the doctrine of the Trinity we understand the unity of the three persons in the one divine life to be a dynamic relational unity in which the Father, Son, and Spirit remain distinct while yet participating in the very life of each other in the most intimate and real way imaginable. It is a unity in difference solidified in the bond of mutual love. Various theologians have seen in this Trinitarian reality a pattern for the Christian church's commitment to the unity and inclusivity that is true to its catholicity. Jesus, the crucified Christ is the one visible image of the invisible God, and, as such, Jürgen Moltmann maintains, reveals the glory of the Trinity in the community of his body and the fellowship with the poor to whom he reached out. He goes on, then, to maintain that we need to think of our destiny for fulfillment in the image of God not simply in individual terms but also in social terms that reflect the divine life. Thus, the doctrine of the Trinity enables us to harmonize the personal and the social realities of our existence without sacrificing one to the other.[7] This is an important theological insight for the church's witness to a society where the rights of the individual have often trumped concern for the common good.

This aspect of witness points us in the direction of the church as holy. As a characteristic of the church, holy does not mean perfection. The people of God, the church in history, struggle with the problem of human sin and frailty as we all know. The institutional expressions of the church are far from perfect or free of corruption and evil designs. However, notwithstanding the church's many failings, it is holy in the sense of "set apart" by God to be witness to the promises of God. As such, it is consistent with its nature to strive for a strong witness to unity and catholicity in its own life so that, ethically speaking, it can be a powerful influence for a society marked by greater and greater equality, a truly just society.[8]

In this way the church's efforts to achieve true unity and to be all-inclusive in its own community serve as an example in its efforts to anticipate God's promises by striving for a society in which the oppression of racism, classism, and sexism is overcome. This kind of orientation is certainly consistent with that aspect of the beatitude concerning poverty of spirit that refers to concern for and solidarity with those who suffer oppression, those who are poor in that sense. However, poverty of spirit is an important virtue in the church's efforts for unity and catholicity in another way as well.

It is no secret that the church has often been guilty of prejudice and oppression just as much as society at large. In various ways churches and congregations have discriminated against persons of color, women, the poorer classes, and others who have not experienced genuine equality in our society. However, genuine equality within the church for all people will require more than simply efforts to insure a better representation of all people in the life and work of the church. What is needed is openness to what people who have suffered oppression can teach the rest of us concerning the meaning of the gospel promise. Theologians in Latin America representing the poor of those oppressed peoples, black theologians, and feminist theologians representing a variety of women's concerns have in recent years been trying to teach the church new insights concerning the church's message and mission from the perspective of those who have experienced long years of unrelieved oppression. However, they have not always been well received in what they have to say. Joseph Allen, a professor of Christian ethics, describes the situation this way: "Liberation theologians have stressed the Bible's concern for the oppressed and its demand for repentance and change on the part of oppressors. This stress is often received, understandably enough, in an unappreciative way by Christians whose circumstances are comfortable and who resist the idea that they share in the responsibility for the plight of masses of deprived people."[9]

In a similar way, James Cone, the well-known African American theologian, has observed that no white American theologian has taken racism and the black experience as a point of departure for his or her theology, despite the centrality of this issue in the history of American culture.[10] For Cone and others, it seems as though the majority of white teachers in the church have ignored the experience of African American people in talking about the significance of the gospel and its ethical implications for change in society. Moreover, as Cone concluded in an earlier work, "Unfortunately not only white seminary professors but some blacks as well have convinced themselves that only the white experience provides the appropriate context for questions and answers concerning things divine. They do not recognize the narrowness of their experience and the particularity of their theological expressions."[11]

Cone's critique of white and black seminary professors points to a cultural myopia that still remains true as a widespread characteristic of our American culture. While cultural pluralism on the global and local levels has become a part of our regular experience—at least our knowledge of it—the consequences for ethical thinking have not always been understood. In that regard the failures of ostensibly moral crusades to instill a Western vision of democracy in lands that do not share that heritage seem to provide a good example of that shortfall in cultural sensitivity. We are often oblivious to the lingering reality of our prejudices and can easily underestimate their staying power.[12]

Women who have sought to have their concerns fully represented in the theology and life of the church have also found that the problem is not only a matter of equal representation but also a problem of simply being understood and having people open to their ideas. That is to say, when they try to speak of how the Christian faith should lead us to thinking differently about the role of women and men in the church and society there is a great deal of resistance to even considering such ideas. Thus, many feminist theologians felt the need to focus their efforts on confronting injustices to women, some of which still persist in Christian communities. Only recently, then, have more feminist theologians begun to do constructive theological work addressing the main themes of the Christian faith.[13]

All of us are aware of the fact that artists have depicted their impressions of what Jesus was like in a wide variety of ways. Several recent and well-known examples of artistic renditions of Jesus make this point very neatly. Countless numbers of Christians have learned to see Jesus through the eyes of the artist Warner Sallman, whose portrait of Jesus enjoyed widespread popularity a generation ago. It is a picture of a serene Jesus with gentle features bathed in a heavenly glow. The portrait had a strong appeal to more than one generation of Christian people whose piety was founded on an understanding of Jesus that was deeply spiritual, a Jesus whose personal holiness was the inspiration of his followers. In contrast to this is the more recent portrayal of R. Hook's *Laughing Christ*. Not only is the style of the artistry more contemporary and infused with vitality, but the Christ is more robust, emphasizing the humanity of Jesus as one who participates fully in our joys as well as our sorrows, one who has experienced all our emotions. For an even sharper contrast, we might choose to examine the sculpture of the crucified Christ by the Peruvian artist Edilberto Merida. This is a picture of Jesus whose features are gnarled and distorted. It is a vision of the suffering Christ, reflecting the sufferings of oppressed people in Latin America and a statement concerning the solidarity of Jesus with their suffering. We could engage in a considerable analysis of what lies behind these different pictures of Jesus and why they are significant for the artists and for the people who relate positively to them. Simply noting the contrasting styles, however, makes the point that our experiences in life and our cultural backgrounds are something that we read into our portraits of Jesus. Our images of Christ express the different insights of the Christian faith that are born of a variety of human experiences.

It should surprise no one that these different portrayals of Jesus can easily offend those who have not experienced Jesus in quite the same way. For some, Sallman's Christ is hopelessly sentimental and out of touch with the humanity of Christ and Jesus' participation in the full range of human experience. For others, Hook's *Laughing Jesus* could easily be considered almost profane. A colleague of mine tells the story of how a pastor friend of his in Texas hung a picture of the *Laughing Jesus* on the bulletin board outside his office door. A parishioner, not knowing that the pastor had put it there, was so deeply offended that she took the picture down and tore it into pieces. She presented the pieces to the pastor, confident that she had done a service! Still others would be very likely to find Merida's crucified Christ a distortion and a caricature of Jesus, ugly beyond words and insensitive to the sensibilities of many Christians. Yet Merida's crucifix and the other portrayals of Jesus are authentic expressions of the Christian experience in the universal church throughout history. However we judge their artistic worth, we cannot gainsay their validity as representative of the extraordinary variety of Christian faith experiences.

In a similar fashion, the manner in which we give voice to the Christian story is colored by our experience, our culture, and the particular histories we have been a part of. If we try to say that the way with which we are familiar is the only way of looking at the faith, we will fail to realize the catholicity of the church and we will fail to benefit from the spiritual insights and the Christian witness of others whose experience and cultural background are different from our own.

There is, however, a strong tendency among us all to shut out that which is unfamiliar and uncomfortable. We prefer security rather than openness to others. This drive for security is characterized by a deep need to keep things under control. In our need to control we feel threatened by that which is new and different and fearful of anything that might challenge our long-established ideas and comfortable ways of doing things.

I still remember the lesson I learned about myself years ago on a trip to India. I was exposed to a good bit of the overwhelming poverty and wretchedness that besets so many there. I went, I thought, with the spirit of openness and concern. I went with the expectation that I would learn and grow as I became involved in the lives of the people. However, I was gripped by a sense of shame at how quickly my main impulse became one of surviving the experience and returning without mishap to the relative health and order of my middle-class Western world. One may, of course, grant oneself the benefit of doubt by observing that such anxieties are simply culture shock, which would be overcome with adequate time for adjustment. However, the point is that our anxieties for security easily cause us to recoil from the world around us and turn us in upon ourselves.

At least one theologian has described this drive for security as a manifestation of human sin. It is one particular way of expressing selfish concentration on our own concerns. It stands in contrast to the trust of faith that relies solely on the promise of God. Such trust and openness to God's leading enables true openness in love to our neighbors and their needs.[14]

The trust of which we speak here characterizes poverty of spirit. The poor in spirit place no trust in their own resources; they are not preoccupied with the drive for security or control. Rather, their security resides in the promise of God in Jesus Christ. Thus the poor in spirit are open to God and the neighbor. In poverty of spirit we are able to receive the ideas and experiences of others in the faith and be enriched by them rather than threatened by notions that are different from our own. In such an atmosphere of trust the virtue of poverty of spirit makes catholicity possible. As such it is a virtue essential to the spirituality of the people of God if they are to give faithful witness to the all-inclusive unity that is the promise of God and the hope for the world, the promise and hope that the people of God are set apart to proclaim in what they are, in what they do, and in what they say.

Poverty of Spirit and the Problem of Justice

While the church, in its catholicity, may model equality as the pattern for a just society, the realization of justice in society requires more than simply the recognition of the equality of all persons. Certainly the recognition of the equal dignity and worth of all persons is the foundation of a just society. However, for this to be meaningful, the notion of equal worth must be wedded to the ideas of equality of opportunity and equality of outcome.[15]

Equality of opportunity by one definition is that "people of equal need and ability desirous of a scarce resource not available to everyone should have an equal opportunity to obtain it."[16] This means that factors such as race, marital status, or gender would not normally disqualify a person for consideration. Such a principle has become well established in our society, even though it has not been consistently applied.

Equality of outcome takes matters a step further. Let us imagine, for example, a person who is well qualified in computer science but who is disabled and confined to a wheelchair. A policy of equal opportunity would suggest that the person should not be disqualified from competing for a job in the field of computers along with other persons of similar skill simply because he or she is disabled. Yet assuring that the outcomes in job competition for the disabled will be similar to the outcome for those without disabilities requires special efforts, such as providing access to the workplace and educating people to understand disabilities in more appropriate ways. This is the purpose of the Americans with Disabilities Act (1990), which protects persons with disabilities from discrimination in hiring because of their disability. Among other things, it also requires employers to provide access to their facilities and make reasonable accommodations in the workplace so that qualified persons with disabilities will be able to fulfill their potential in competing for a job or in the performance of their job.

Policies like the Americans with Disabilities Act, designed to foster what we have been calling "equality of outcome," are responsive to two material principles of justice for the distribution of goods and opportunities: (1) to each according to their merit; (2) to each according to their need. We shall look more closely at these and other principles of distributive justice in chapter 10. For now it is sufficient to note that persons with disabilities have a "need" for the accommodations that level the playing field so that they too can compete for opportunities on the basis of their "merit," their ability to do the job or meet the standards of a given opportunity.

Insofar as poverty of spirit fosters a community where equality of worth prevails, it makes a contribution to building a more just society. In its openness to the various gifts that all the people of God bring, poverty of spirit can be construed to contribute to equality of opportunity as well. However, in the struggle for justice in society, equality of outcome is far more difficult to achieve. It is here that tough decisions of public policy must be made in order to meet the needs of all people in all circumstances. It is here that tough legal sanctions must be hammered out in situations of confrontation to ensure that racism, sexism, the neglect of persons with disabilities, and the exploitation of the poor are not allowed to deprive some people of their fair chance in life.

Affirmative action programs have sought to overcome long-held prejudices based on race, creed, color, national origin, or gender that have kept certain people at a disadvantage in our society. President Kennedy coined the term "affirmative action" in a 1961 executive order establishing the President's Commission on Equal Opportunity Employment. However, affirmative action as we know it today did not become a matter of public policy until the Labor Department guidelines of 1970. These guidelines interpreted the 1964 Civil Rights Act to require large employers to make special efforts to include, hire, and select for positions of leadership and trust persons from underrepresented groups. Employers are also expected to upgrade the skills of the underrepresented.[17]

Affirmative action seeks to make equality of worth and opportunity real by providing a means to equality of outcome. At the same time, affirmative action illustrates the difficulty of sustaining such tough measures; it has become one of the most controversial initiatives of the past half century. Many hold the cynical belief that those hired under affirmative action wouldn't have qualified otherwise, even though the law does not require employers to hire those who are unqualified. Charges of reverse discrimination have been filed by persons claiming that they were better qualified than the underrepresented persons who got the job or gained entrance to the school. Even those the law was designed to benefit are not of one mind as to whether it helps by providing opportunity or harms by adding a further stigma.

It is in this sort of tough struggle for justice that some might question the value of poverty of spirit as a virtue that can help us toward a just society. Once again, poverty of spirit, like self-sacrificing love, summons up an image of passivity. Those who are on the short end of an unjust situation are not likely to be impressed, some would argue, by the encouragement to cultivate the virtue of poverty of spirit. It sounds too much like being asked to humbly accept a bad situation and patiently wait for a better world to come. The words "For theirs is the kingdom of heaven" tempt us even more to such an interpretation. However, such is not the case.

This beatitude announces the possibility of reliance and trust in God that accompanies being infinitely valued by God as the children of the promised future. In this blessing we are empowered to extend that promise to others by promising to take up their cause, even if that is done in taking up our own. Poverty of spirit does not preclude involvement in the struggle for justice for oneself among others. Rather, poverty of spirit signals the kind of trust that is able to give of the self in the struggle on behalf of the needs of one's own group or those of another because of the faith and hope that the fulfillment of those needs is ours in the promise of God. For poverty of spirit, the struggle for justice is an anticipation of the promise in which we live as a people of hope.[18] That is the key! Our hope does not reside in the struggle or our success in pursuing it. Our hope resides in the promise of God that energizes us in the quest for justice. Thus, we do not fight for justice in the pride of purpose but in the hope of promise.

I shall have more to say about the subject of justice in a later chapter. For the present time, it is sufficient to make the connection between the virtue of poverty of spirit, nurtured in the faith and life of the Christian community, and the cause of justice in society that the Christian community is called to advocate as an anticipation of the perfect justice of the coming reign of God.

Poverty of Spirit and Dedication to the Truth

Poverty of spirit is without pride or pretense. It is an attitude of complete trust in the promises of God that places no reliance on our own merits. It is a spirituality that can be sharply contrasted with the desire to justify oneself. The desire to justify oneself is a first cousin to the drive for security or control. If we can make a case for our own worth before God and before others, we can rest secure in the conviction that we are okay. This desire for self-justification is an attitude that Jesus continually confronted in his ministry. In Matt. 23:27-28 Jesus utters the following condemnation: "Woe to you, scribes and Pharisees, hypocrites! For you are like whitewashed tombs, which on the outside look beautiful, but inside they are full of the bones of the dead and of all kinds of filth. So you also on the outside look righteous to others, but inside you are full of hypocrisy and lawlessness."

This passage opens up for us a further dimension of poverty of spirit. In that we are free from self-justification through trust in God's acceptance of us, we are also free to be honest with ourselves, free to overcome the kind of hypocrisy Jesus condemns. In this we understand that poverty of spirit involves freedom to face and seek the truth, even about ourselves.

Poverty of spirit and Luther's "theology of the cross" go hand in hand. "A theologian of glory calls evil good and good evil. A theologian of the cross calls the thing what it actually is."[19] These are Luther's familiar words from the Heidelberg Disputation. Theologians of glory were in that context the authoritarian and presumptuous church leaders Luther believed to be distorting the gospel with false and burdensome demands for works prescribed by the church. For theologians of the cross who have seen the truth of their own brokenness in the reality of the crucified, there can be no such pretense concerning our ability to contribute to our salvation. There is only the open-armed gratitude of poverty of spirit for the blessing of God's mercy.

If the cross of Good Friday is foundational for the truthfulness that goes with poverty of spirit, so is the hope of Easter. Without hope, it is more than likely that an appreciation of truth as meaningful, as of intrinsic value, will be diminished. Without a promising future in which to hope—a future that addresses the truth of our lives revealed by the cross—life becomes a matter of *management* rather commitment. In the absence of a transcendent, value-laden future in which to trust, we have only our finite personal plans that we hope to realize if we manage things properly and have some luck. Under these conditions the value of truth becomes relative to our own designs amid the contingencies of an uncertain life. We manage it rather than face it or serve it.

Whether we are speaking of justice or of some other principle of healthy relationships in human community, truthfulness is necessary for its realization. As with individuals, nations unable to face the truth about themselves cannot be open to the kind of constructive change necessary for a more responsible relationship to their neighbors. Instead, they will continue to perpetuate lies in the interest of what they consider to be their own security, and, in so doing, will perpetuate the hurts and injustices of which they are guilty. A society that will not face the truth of its own racism will perpetuate racism. An individual who refuses to face the truth of his or her own selfishness will continue to be insensitive to those nearby. An economic system that refuses to acknowledge the truth that it fails to provide sufficient opportunities and for the needs of all the people will be incapable of adjusting to meet those needs. As anyone knows who has ever worked with people who are addicted to alcohol or drugs, the first step toward recovery is to acknowledge that there is a problem in the first place.

Poverty of spirit in its commitment to truthfulness bears a family resemblance to at least one dimension of the classic virtue of prudence. In the classical discussion of the virtues, Christian thinkers have often associated prudence with a radical capacity for honesty. The prudent person is able to give up all self-centered impulses to confirm his or her own goodness or rightness at all costs.[20] The desperate need to defend oneself, the fear of losing control or the security of a good reputation in the eyes of others, leads to self deception, cover-ups, and outright lies. The utter importance of its commitment to truthfulness has made prudence first among the so-called natural virtues in the classical tradition.

However, poverty of spirit in its dedication to the truth is not a natural virtue in the sense of being a virtue that we can attain by our own natural capacity for goodness. As should be clear by now, our ability to be truthful is only a possibility for us because of the grace of God in Jesus Christ. Dietrich Bonhoeffer put it beautifully in these words: "The truthfulness of the disciples has its sole basis in following Jesus, in which he reveals our sins to us on the cross. Only the cross as God's truth about us makes us truthful. Those who know the cross no longer shy away from any truth."[21]

I have tried to look at poverty of spirit as refracted through the lenses of several different ethical issues. My hope is that by this means we begin to appreciate how this disposition of the life of love in the gospel is so essential to our other virtues.

Questions for Discussion

1. Review the quote from Henri Nouwen at the end of the first section. How does it help to explain what that first section sets forth? Do you think Nouwen is correct in his judgment?

2. Is it clear why "poverty of spirit" is a virtue that should lead the church to be more inclusive? What specific fears do you think people have when it comes to being inclusive in the church? Does the promise of your acceptance in Christ help you accept others, or is it still sometimes hard to do?

3. Is it possible for Christians who want to affirm the virtue of this beatitude in their lives to still disagree on affirmative action? Can you say why or why not?

6

SOLIDARITY IN SUFFERING

Blessed are those who mourn, for they will be comforted.

—Matthew 5:4

Jerzy Kosinski's famous novel *The Painted Bird* tells the nightmarish story of a young boy abandoned by his parents during World War II. It tells the story of the cruelty and brutality experienced by the boy as he moves from one village to another in Eastern Europe. The cause of his suffering is revealed in the following episode, which provides the title of the book.

At one time during his odyssey, the young boy stayed with a man named Lekh, who was a trapper and seller of birds. Lekh was also highly respected by the local farmers because of his ability to build storks' nests that never failed to attract a stork. The farmers believed that having a stork's nest on their roof was a promise of good fortune, and therefore, they were willing to pay high prices for Lekh's services. However, despite Lekh's love of birds and his skill at handling them, he had his dark moments when he would use the natural cruelty of which the birds were capable to express his own rage and brutality. He did this by choosing a bird that he would paint with many brilliant colors. He and the young boy would then go out into the forest, and when the sound of the painted bird's chirping attracted others of the same species, the bird would be let go to fly to its flock. The painted bird would eagerly try to establish community with the other birds. The other birds, seeing the brilliant colors, would be confused and seemingly dazzled, but before long each of the other birds would begin to attack the painted bird until, finally, it would fall to the ground dead or near dead from the attack of those who were its sisters or brothers.[1]

The incident of the painted bird is a parable for the story of the young boy. Dark-skinned and different looking, he was a stranger to the peasants of that region whose fear, suspicion, and hostility were awakened and who often

61

reacted to him with acts of brutality. The parable of the painted bird is, of course, a parable for all of us. So often in human society, those who are different, who are strangers, who threaten us, are avoided or driven off and even destroyed.

Certainly there are many applications for this message. However, what I want to focus on has to do with the way in which those who are suffering and those who are dying often appear as strangers to us. Their suffering or their dying is somehow a threat to us. The disposition and ability to be with the suffering and the dying in significant ways is a virtue of love signaled by the beatitude, "Blessed are those who mourn." For Stanley Hauerwas this virtue of being present with the suffering and the dying should be part of the essential character of the community we call the church. It is an expression of faithfulness to each other that reflects the faithfulness we experience from God who is with us in our pain and in our death. His comments help us set the stage for our discussion: "Only a community that has pledged not to fear the stranger—an illness always makes us a stranger to ourselves and others—can welcome the continued presence of the ill in our midst."[2]

The Meaning of Mourning

Martin Luther in his sermon on this beatitude maintains that people in general want to have joy and happiness and avoid trouble at all costs. Jesus, Luther points out, says exactly the opposite when he calls those who sorrow and mourn blessed. Thus Luther concludes that Jesus' statement is "aimed and directed against the world's way of thinking, the way it would like to have things. It does not want to endure hunger, trouble, dishonor, unpopularity, injustice, and violence." However, "a Christian must count on sorrow and mourning in the world."[3] This comment fits well with one of Douglas John Hall's observations of Luther. In reflecting on Luther's theology of the cross and the understanding of the human situation embedded in it, Hall sees in Luther "a deep sympathy with human weakness and wretchedness—a sympathy, alas, that is nearly unique in the history of Christian scholarship, including the scholarship of the Reformation."[4]

The background for our text is once again Isaiah 61, specifically verses 2 and 3, which speak of comfort to the people of Israel who mourn in their state of exile. The mourning implied here is that of a people with a keen sense of their own loss, their own failure and sins before God, which have driven them into exile from their promised land. Theirs is a sense of grief and helplessness with the knowledge that only God can deliver them; there is nothing they can do for themselves. Thus, mourning would appear to be a reference to persons in all ages who sorrow for sins, their own and others, the grief that sin has produced and the despair into which it would lead without divine help.[5]

Of course, mourning as sorrow for sins should not be understood too narrowly as simply remorse for one's misdeeds. More broadly, it is sensitivity to the sorrow of life in a fallen world. In this sensitivity there is a note of empathy for the grief, the suffering, and the dying of those around us. The capacity to mourn is the capacity to be in touch with and to be touched by the human situation. In this there is an echo of Jesus' own compassion for human need.

In Mark's Gospel we read of this compassion on several occasions. In the first instance, the Gospel speaks of how Jesus is moved to pity when approached by a leper who asks for healing (Mark 1:41). Later Mark tells us that Jesus is moved by compassion for the crowd whom he describes as sheep without a shepherd (Mark 6:34). Finally, in another account of Jesus' feeding miracle, Mark describes Jesus as having compassion for the crowd because they had been three days with nothing to eat (Mark 8:2). In each of these instances, the Greek verb for pity or compassion is the same, one that conveys strong feelings from Jesus' depths. There is in these accounts an expression of deep caring for human need in various forms.

As in the case of Jesus, then, those who mourn are those who, like their Lord, are continually moved by the needs of those around them, by all manner of suffering and pain—whether from hunger, oppression, despair, or dying.[6] This note of compassion suggests that mourning involves the capacity "to be with" others in their need and in their suffering, just as Jesus is *Emmanuel*, "God with us," in our flesh, in our sin, in our sufferings, and in our death.

To summarize, then, the heightened sense of one's own situation of sin, suffering, and utter dependence on God leads to compassion for others and a readiness, like that displayed by our Lord, to be with them in their trial. That is, it leads to that capacity when we know the promise of comfort that is also part of the beatitude. To know the comfort of divine forgiveness and salvation is to be free to be with the other in his or her trouble. In the gospel we are empowered to do as the apostle commands, "Bear one another's burdens" (Gal. 6:2). This comfort of the gospel also enables us to know joy despite sorrow, to live the contradiction that the apostle Paul presents: "in honor and dishonor, in ill repute and good repute. We are treated as . . . dying, and, see—we are alive; . . . as sorrowful, yet always rejoicing" (2 Cor. 6:8-10).[7]

The spirit of mourning, the virtue or capacity for empathetic and compassionate solidarity with others in their sufferings and need, can also be described by what Kosuke Koyama has called the "crucified mind." In *No Handle on the Cross*, Koyama draws a contrast between carrying the cross with a handle and without a handle. To carry the cross without a handle is the way Jesus carried it, with all its bulky, heavy, and demoralizing reality. Jesus did not try to place conditions or limits on his entry into human suffering. He did not try to manage it or control it. With open arms he submitted to the cruelty, suffering, and death that are the burden of human sin. He endured the terrors of a humiliating and excruciating execution, which in all its intentional violence and brutality brought to a head the horror of humanity's estrangement from God and hatred for one another.

Others who claim to follow Jesus often try to put a handle on the cross in order to carry it more easily, in order to manage it more comfortably. By placing a handle on it, they can carry it as one might carry a briefcase containing the tools of one's trade. Koyama writes of those Christians who do not have the "crucified mind" but the "crusading mind." The crusading mind is an aggressive brand of evangelism and outreach that approaches others with an attitude of paternalistic superiority, using or *handling* the cross to manipulate and intimidate the people. The attitude is one of detachment rather than solidarity with the burdens of others. The crucified mind does not display such arrogance. Rather, the outreach of the Christian community, when characterized by the crucified mind, is a message from sinner to sinner, a message of those who are dying in hope to those who are dying. There is not the slightest whiff of detachment in all of this; there is rather a spirit of mourning bearing a message of joy.[8]

On the Care of the Dying

Our reflections on the virtue signaled by this beatitude seem to lead us to a consideration of the contemporary ethical discussions of euthanasia and the relevance of Christian character to this area of concern. How does love in its solidarity with the suffering and the dying respond to the dilemmas modern medicine has created in the treatment of the terminally ill?

Euthanasia is a Greek word that literally means "good death." It normally refers to how we treat dying persons in such a way that they might die with the least amount of suffering and in the most peaceful way possible. Ethicists often make a distinction between active and passive euthanasia in this regard. The former refers to direct and deliberate action to end the sufferings of a painful death by ending life itself. This is often spoken of as *mercy killing. Passive euthanasia,* by contrast, refers to the practice of withdrawing or withholding life-sustaining treatments from patients who are irreversibly dying in order to concentrate on keeping them as comfortable as possible and letting death come naturally.

Since active euthanasia is usually considered morally and legally unacceptable, most of the ethical debate concerns acceptable decisions about passive euthanasia. When is it right to cease further life-support measures? Are we obligated to continue so-called ordinary measures of life support but free to withhold or withdraw treatments that might be considered extraordinary or heroic? If so, what is ordinary? For example, must we give antibiotics to a dying cancer patient who has contracted pneumonia, or may we allow the more peaceful death from pneumonia to proceed undeterred? If the ordinary-extraordinary distinction is not useful and morally binding, is it even permissible to stop tube feeding and hydration of those in irreversible coma or persistent vegetative state? When the patient is unable to decide, who decides? These very questions recently became the center of public attention as the media played out the drama of Terri Schiavo's last days.

Terri Schiavo had been in what her doctors firmly believed was persistent vegetative state (PVS) for fifteen years. PVS is a state in which the brain no longer has cognitive function, but that part of the brain that governs automatic functions like breathing and circulation continues to operate. Through the use of feeding tubes for nutrition and hydration, persons in PVS can live indefinitely but with no apparent awareness. Public attention was focused on the court battle between her parental family, who wanted the feeding tube to remain in and her husband who wanted it removed in what he believed was faithful to her desires. Side by side with this unfolding story of bitter estrangement between spouse and in-laws, we saw religious leaders choosing up sides based on what they believed were basic articles of faith. Even Congress and the president entered the lists on behalf of keeping Terri alive while the courts upheld the right of her husband's request to allow her to die in peace.

These are some of the questions that arise in ethical reflections on euthanasia. They are important questions that test our decision making to the utmost. We will look at some of them further as issues of Christian decision in a later chapter. For the present I want to focus on the further questions they raise about the dispositions we bring to the situation of decision. The ethic of Christian love is not merely a matter of doing the "right thing" in a narrow legalistic sense of what is permitted and what is prohibited. The Christian love ethic has a depth that takes us beyond "rulings" to connect with the human needs that are involved.

Sometimes operating on the basis of a rigorous adherence to principle, as conscientious and responsible as this may appear, can get in the way of connecting with human need. James Nelson and Jo Anne Smith Rohricht give us a good example of this. They report the case of a seventy-three-year-old man who, having gone through a number of surgeries and the pain of other ailments, refused his surgeon's request to do exploratory surgery for the removal of an intestinal polyp. He reasoned that if the polyp was benign, it was doing him no harm, and that if it was cancerous, the cancer had probably spread. Why, then, should he endure the suffering of yet another surgery? He was right. It was cancerous, and the cancer had spread. He died as a result within a year. The remarkable thing about this case, a fellow physician observed, was that this patient's doctor became so angry with him for refusing the surgery that he was very limited in the comfort he could give to the patient and family, comfort they obviously needed.[9] This man's physician was so rigorously committed to the principle of his medical code that everything possible in medical science must be done that he was blinded to the human needs of his patient.

Concern for all the human needs of the terminally ill years ago prompted the great ethicist Paul Ramsey to emphasize the "care of the dying." Ramsey reflects on the difficult questions of what should or should not be done for persons who are dying. However, the basis for his views on these questions is not a hard and fast set of principles, even though principles of moral responsibility are certainly involved. Rather, Ramsey's basic outlook is expressed in the following statement: "Attending and companying with the patient in his (her) dying is, in fact, the oldest medical ethics there is."[10] Attending to the patient means expressing sensitivity to human values and personal needs in making choices about treatment rather than simply following the dictates of medical science. Companying with the dying means actively "being with" persons in their suffering and death and choosing the course of action that will create the greatest opportunity for human community with the dying person. Constant and useless medical interventions can be a way of denying the reality of approaching death and, thereby, keeping the dying one at a distance from our care.

To keep company with the dying means to share fully in their lives, even the end. It means caring enough to tell them the truth of their circumstances, for such truth-telling requires sharing in their need to deal with that truth. Withholding the truth from those who are dying can be a way of avoiding them! To care for the dying means to overcome our contemporary inclination to avoid what is unpleasant by keeping people in unpleasant circumstances at a distance from us in institutions like hospitals.[11]

It is heartening that so much interest has developed in recent years for hospice care. The hospice movement provides a counterpoint to prevailing impulses to avoid the dying. It is an avenue for attending to and companying with the dying. Hospice care is a program for terminally ill patients designed, first of all, to keep the dying at home as long as possible. It relies on the family as the primary unit of care. Hospice seeks the most effective means of pain control possible and seeks, thereby, to enable patients to live as normal a life as possible with the highest degree of human community possible during the waning days of life. The program is committed to these values even when care can no longer be given at home. Hospice seeks to meet the physical, social, emotional, and spiritual needs of the dying.[12]

Obviously, the Christian virtue of solidarity with the suffering and the dying is the very sort of disposition that can transform the ethical discussion of death and dying from one that is narrowly legalistic to one that is concerned to care for the dying.

Is There a Limit to Compassion?

Community with the dying is hard for many to deal with, but there is at least recognition that they deserve our compassion and our care. By contrast many people find it hard to feel compassion for and be in solidarity with those whose suffering and dying seems to be a result of their own misdeeds. The spirit of mourning is often overcome by the spirit of prejudice and judgmentalism. Let's look at two examples.

AIDS and Attitudes

During the early years of heightened public attention to AIDS and its increasing incidence, there were disturbing reports of physicians and even hospital departments who, having little sympathy for persons with AIDS or those believed to be HIV infected, refused to serve them.[13] Physicians and other health-care workers who demonstrated this prejudice did not represent the majority of dedicated and self-giving health-care professionals, and I trust that this sort of aversion has dissipated as we all have gained greater understanding. However, those who did betray their prejudice in their practice were simply reflecting attitudes shared broadly in our society. Such attitudes remain in place even today among many of our fellow citizens and fellow Christians.

AIDS is caused by the HIV virus, which does not discriminate between types of people. In other countries, HIV/AIDS° is found predominantly in the heterosexual population, and in our country it has also spread to the hetero-

---

°The designation HIV/AIDS refers to all who are infected with the HIV virus, which includes those who already display the symptoms of AIDS and those who are likely to manifest them in the future.

sexual population. It is now found among all age groups, all racial and ethnic groups, all varieties of sexual orientation, a wide variety of sexual practices, and all socioeconomic classes.[14] However, in this country the majority of persons with HIV/AIDS are gay men, followed by intravenous drug users who share contaminated needles and forms of promiscuous and risky sexual behavior. Since many in our society regard these practices as evil or abnormal, the painful reality of AIDS is often compounded by the painful reality of prejudice and the isolation from needed help and support that follows in the wake of prejudice.

This sort of stigmatization and discrimination is global in scope according to a recent report published by the World Council of Churches:

> Almost everywhere, HIV/AIDS remains associated with stigma and discrimination. Stigma and rejection lead to individual suffering for the persons against whom they are applied. . . . Often, HIV-positive people experience rejection and exclusion in families and communities, through refusal of care, loss of living space, neglect, physical violence, and the collapse of partnerships and marriage.[15]

Donald E. Messer's book about the global crisis of HIV/AIDS adds further substance to the analysis from the World Council of Churches. With specific reference to the situation in the United States, Messer speculates on how dramatically his life would be changed by the professional and social consequences of being diagnosed as HIV-positive. To begin with, he says, people would care for him conditionally, depending on how he got it; was he an innocent victim or guilty of some unsavory behavior? By contrast, if he were diagnosed with cancer, he judges that people would care for him unconditionally regardless of how he got it. Far too many in our society with HIV/AIDS have faced discrimination, hatred, and rejection from families, friends, government, and even the church. "When the famous tennis player, Arthur Ashe, learned he was infected due to a blood transfusion, he so feared discrimination against himself and his family that he lived with the knowledge for three and one-half years before revealing he had the disease."[16]

The kind of prejudice we are discussing here is a classic case of "blaming the victim." In this reasoning, people identify homosexual conduct, drug usage, and sexual promiscuity as moral sickness. One sickness leads to another, they argue. Therefore, they conclude persons with AIDS are only getting what they deserve! Thus, some years ago a church leader in one of the largest church bodies in America was quoted as saying, "AIDS is God indicating his displeasure with homosexuals." Today one seldom hears public pronouncements quite that blunt, but the sentiment remains in some quarters of the churches where aversion to homosexuality and especially gay male sexuality runs very deep. The identification of AIDS with male homosexual practices makes compassion for gay persons with HIV/AIDS almost impossible for some. Public debates over gay rights to full and equal participation in society, the professions, churches, and the customary protections of the law for married people serve their cause but also fuel the resentment and alienation of the disapproving. Solidarity with those suffering the ravages of AIDS and slowly dying, as well as ministry to and with those who are HIV positive requires that Christians sort out ambiguous feelings about sexuality in the soul searching spirit of mourning.[17]

Attitudes of prejudice are often supported by fear. James Nelson has noted that HIV/AIDS combines two of the most anxiety-ridden dimensions of human life: sexuality and death. He contends that more fear is touched off by these aspects of life than any others.[18] The power of these fears is such that it drives people away from persons with HIV/AIDS and their needs; it even drives them away from discussing the problem and becoming responsibly involved in educational programs that can help to combat the spread of the disease.

The fact that some persons with HIV/AIDS may have contracted the virus through activities that many Christians would consider to be immoral does not remove them from our care. Our previous discussion of agape love reminds us that love is not conditioned by the characteristics of the persons who are in need of our love. We may debate the morality of some behaviors but not the obligation of love to the needs of our neighbors. The fact that many of those neighbors are a part of the church, the body of Christ, has prompted the claim that "the church has AIDS." The salient passage is from Paul's discussion of the body of Christ: "If one member suffers, all suffer together with it" (1 Cor. 12:26a).[19]

Jesus was no stranger to prejudice. He was challenged and condemned for keeping company with tax collectors and sinners. But he stood staunchly with them, healing their ills and bringing them the good news of God's forgiveness and acceptance. In so doing, he embodied the virtue he has made possible for us as well, the spirit of mourning.

It is a possibility with a promise, a promise especially for those who place no conditions on the call to solidarity:

> "They shall find consolation," says the New English Bible, but the older, "they shall be comforted," is just as true, the more especially because "comforted" originally meant "fortified." We need both versions: they shall be consoled and fortified. They seek no such favor, or their sympathy might become selfishness. They ask no explanation of sorrow; they know

there is none for our poor mortal minds. They believe that patience for oneself and love for one's neighbor will yield their own answer.[20]

The Suffering Homeless

The suffering and dying of those with AIDS can make them strangers to us, as we have observed suffering and dying in general can do. We have also seen that, to many, persons with HIV/AIDS may seem to be strangers even more distant from our affections and care because of their sexuality and/or their behavior. The situation is similar with the suffering and needs of the homeless, who also strike many as strange, maybe even repugnant or scary, and somehow implicated in their own downfall and misery.

One researcher concerned about the spiritual needs of the homeless, believes that when we are overtaken by such feelings and fears, those very real needs suffer a lack of awareness and concern:

> For many people who are homeless, their disconnectedness from the world is made worse by the actions of the non-homeless. People who are homeless often have strong, unpleasant body odors, may be dirty and unkempt, and exhibit a host of negative physical conditions and actions that are generally offensive to persons who might normally approach them about their spiritual needs. Thus, most homeless people are not approached, and their spiritual needs are not addressed. Homeless women, for example, have been unfairly judged and shunned because they often exchange sex for drugs.[21]

A recent study of two different organizations serving the homeless and the impact of the experience on the moral development of their volunteers provides some additional insights. The two organizations, Loaves & Fishes and the Salvation Army are the primary providers of food for the poor and homeless in the city of Sacramento, California, where the study was done.[22]

Loaves & Fishes is a charity born of the Catholic Worker movement. It practices a "personalist hospitality" that stresses the innate dignity of every person. Loaves & Fishes treats everyone who comes for food as a "guest" or Ambassador of God, and accepts each without condition, expecting nothing in return, not even expressions of gratitude. This is the sort of radical vision of charity that one might say is the very embodiment of the spirit of mourning. It expresses the unconditional character of agape love of which solidarity with the suffering is a specific virtue. Yet, even for the volunteers who have stepped forward to serve, there is often a moral dilemma as they struggle to treat all guests as deserving:

> The difficulty evidenced among some of the routine volunteers in extend-
> ing charitable love to all guests can best be understood when situated
> in historical context. American society has historically demarcated the
> deserving poor from the undeserving poor. . . . At Loaves & Fishes the
> routine volunteers participated in a progressive vision of charity that
> worked against this tradition. . . . Although the volunteers occasionally
> lapsed into victim blaming "cloaked in kindness and concern" . . . when
> they sanctioned those wanting seconds or made inquiries of the guests
> deemed inappropriate by staff.[23]

One volunteer spoke of his inability to actually serve meals to the homeless or
look them in the eye. Instead, he settled for serving in the kitchen "behind the
ovens."[24]

The Salvation Army vision of charity opens up another dimension of what
it means to be in solidarity with those who suffer in homelessness. The Salvation Army corps of volunteers was almost totally comprised of "drafted volunteers": in-house homeless residents and persons performing court-ordered
community service. The Salvationist vision stresses hard work, discipline, and
self-transformation in service to others. Given the substance abuse of many of
its residents, the moral rhetoric was also heavily salted with the language of
Alcoholics Anonymous.[25] For those who serve and for those who are served in
this setting, there are common needs and a common goal of discipline, self-
transformation, and self-esteem.

Regardless of how one thinks about the respective merits of the two organizations, they represent complementary aspects of what the spirit of mourning requires for compassionate solidarity with those who suffer: unconditional
loving acceptance, response to essential material needs, and a ministry for
renewal. Solidarity with those suffering the fatal ravages of AIDS and those
who suffer the manifold miseries of homelessness as an expression of agape
love does not rule out the additional obligation to work with individuals on
both prevention and recovery. In that regard, a final word on the ministry to
the homeless:

> Soup kitchens and shelters may be operated or sponsored by faith-based
> organizations, but actual time spent addressing the spiritual needs of the
> homeless is very little, if any. People who are homeless are often socially
> shunned and are denied admission to worship services or placed into an
> "inferior status that does not allow them to participate in activities such as
> Bible study, prayer meetings and so forth. By denying the homeless access
> to faith support that could provide the encouragement to escape home-
> lessness, homeless services are missing an important link.[26]

The Church and the Suffering God

In ancient times the church condemned the theological position called *patri-passionism,* which it considered heretical. This teaching held that God the Father suffered in the sufferings of Jesus. This was condemned because the church reasoned that Jesus suffered according to his humanity not his divinity. Therefore, God the Father, as one with the Son in divinity, did not suffer. It deemed this reasoning to be important since if God could suffer as mortals do, then God would be less than God. Undoubtedly, there was an important theological point at stake in this decision, and I shall not attempt to review it or debate it here.[27] I would only say that, when we look at God through the eyes of the Bible, there is another side to the story. The Bible depicts God as having an intimate relationship with humanity and with the whole creation. It is a relationship of love. All that we have observed about the character of God's love, as the Bible teaches it and as Jesus exemplifies it, tells us that that divine love is marked by compassion and solidarity with human suffering. In light of the biblical witness, it is hard to think about a God who is detached.[28] "If God were incapable of suffering in every respect, then he would also be incapable of love."[29]

Theologians following this biblical lead in thinking about the union of divinity and humanity in the Christ in relation to the intimacy of sharing in the divine life of the Trinity are led to speak of the reality of God's suffering in solidarity with humanity and the world in its sufferings. Ted Peters speaks of *theopassionism.*[30] If the crucified Christ is truly God with us, then "the Christian God must be seen as a suffering God."[31]

In the life of the congregation, the festival half of the church year is a narrative of God's intimate involvement in the life of our world. In Advent and Christmas we know that God is present to us as our promised future as well as part of our flesh and history in the mystery of the incarnation. Epiphany further reveals God in our midst. Lent is a catalog of God's solidarity with the human situation culminating in Christ's passion, born of compassion, and the triumph of love over sin and death in the victory of Easter. Pentecost then tells us that the life-giving spirit of God remains with us and for us. This story told and lived in the community of the faithful instills in the people of God the spirit of mourning and quickens them with new resolve to bear one another's burdens. We act it out in intercessory prayer for the needs of all people, in the support we offer each other within the community, and in the multitude of ministries spawned in the congregation by the powerful presence of a loving God.

Questions for Discussion

1. This would be a good discussion for a guest who is involved in hospice work. People might also share their experiences of companying with the dying. How does this information about hospice and/or the stories shared add depth to our discussion of solidarity with the suffering? How does the beatitude add meaning to those experiences?

2. Read James 2:1-10. As we think of how illness, dying, AIDS, and home-lessness can make people strangers to us, how do these verses from the Epistle of James speak to solidarity with the suffering?

3. Do you find the discussion of God suffering—theopassionism—disturbing or comforting? Can you say why in either case?

7 / MERCY AND PEACE

Blessed are the merciful, for they will receive mercy.

—Matthew 5:7

Blessed are the peacemakers, for they will be called children of God.

—Matthew 5:9

Years ago, when I was a college professor, I team-taught a course on sexuality and marriage with a psychologist. Oddly enough, a thoroughly secular psychology text, which my colleague chose as required reading, provided one of the best insights to a Christian approach to human relations. The author captured the vital importance of forgiveness. His point was that healthy, intimate relations with one's marriage partner are based on the sort of trust that enables each to be open and relaxed with the other, to share freely, to just "be yourself." However, trust will sometimes be severely tested because, he said, "We can be confident that at some time those we love will be the following: indifferent, inconsiderate, selfish, deceiving, difficult, demanding, exploitative, and unappreciative—in short, imperfect. Each of us is human."[1] He continued, saying that the trust needed is dependent on our readiness to forgive each other. And that forgiveness is possible when we care as much about the happiness and well-being of the other as we care about our own. "With such caring, their forgetful deeds, their unkept promises, or their failures are dismissed because the focus of our attention is on their difficulties, their feelings, or their needs."[2]

Blessed Are the Merciful

The readiness to forgive, rooted in caring for the needs of the other, is at the very heart of the virtue of mercy signaled by this beatitude. Mercy is linked to compassion in Jesus' teaching.[3] It is a reflection of God's own disposition in dealing with humankind. Undeserving though we are, a merciful and forgiving God, out of compassion for us, supplies our needs and continually renews the divine promises of wholeness and life. In the Old Testament the word for God's mercy is *hesed,* sometimes translated "kindness" or "loving-kindness." It is used to describe God's deliverance, the bounty of nature that God provides, the hope, joy, and assurance of divine love for humanity, and God's gracious ordering of the events of history to continually reaffirm the covenant with Israel and, ultimately, with all of humanity.[4]

In the New Testament the idea of God's *hesed* is carried forward by the Greek word for "mercy," *eleos,* and is connected with the heart of the gospel message:

> God is rich in mercy (Ephesians 2.4), and it is that mercy which saved us (Titus 3.5). It is that mercy which we find at the throne of grace (Hebrews 4.16); it is that mercy which gives us hope through the Resurrection of Jesus Christ (1 Peter 1.3), and through which Jesus Christ confers eternal life upon us (Jude 21). A particularly significant usage of it is that Paul connects the mercy of God with the giving of the gospel to the Gentiles (Romans 9.23; 11.31; 15.9). The outgoing love of God has gone even further out and has embraced, not only the people of the original covenant, but all humankind.[5]

God is merciful, forgiving, and kind. This is the source of the mercy required of us. In Luke 6:36 this point is made clearly: "Be merciful, just as your Father is merciful." As one commentator has put it, "the merciful are those who demonstrate the Godlike conduct of offering pardon to those in the wrong. . . . Thus, this beatitude is addressed to those who have recognized their failure before God, have experienced [God's] forgiving mercy and reflect it in their relationship toward others in the wrong."[6]

This, of course, runs counter to our tendencies much of the time. We want mercy and forgiveness from others but may be grudging about giving it ourselves. Thus, we nurture our hurts and punish others for what they have done to us. The psychologist I quoted at the beginning of this chapter is aware of this human tendency also. He observes, "If we are going to share that which we are with another we have to have some certainty that they are going to be forgiving of us. Self-disclosures, for those needing ammunition for getting even or winning a point, can easily become bullets which the discloser may wish that he had kept to himself."[7] Another counselor, writing from a Christian perspective, makes much the same point: "We need to forgive those we love because grudges get in the way of intimate connecting. Holding on to grudges limits our ability to love ourselves, our partner, and life itself. . . . Grudges keep us stuck in the past."[8]

How many of us have not had a conflict with a spouse or another family member only to have that person dredge up the memory of a past hurt we caused and throw it in our face anew? How many of us have not done that ourselves?

There is, of course, nothing new in this behavior. Jesus told the parable of the unforgiving servant in order to reveal just this tendency among us. You may remember the story. A certain servant owed the king ten thousand talents. He begged the king to have mercy on him. The king, having pity on the servant, forgave him the debt instead of selling him and his family into slavery as he might have done in those times. The same servant soon came upon a fellow servant who owed him a hundred *denarii*. When his fellow servant asked him for time to repay, he refused and had him thrown into prison (Matt. 18:33-30). Jesus exaggerates to make the point. A talent was worth about ten thousand dollars! The debt of ten thousand talents was astronomical. And yet it was forgiven. A *denarius* was worth about twenty cents. So the debt he would not give his fellow servant more time to repay was a mere twenty dollars.

The contrast is between God who, like the king, is forgiving of our astronomical debt of sin, and the human heart which is so often grudging. We are appalled at the behavior of the unforgiving servant until we suddenly see him in ourselves.

Though we feel the sting of judgment in this parable, the promise of God's forgiveness still stands out. This is a parable of the reign of God. The mercy shown by the king in the parable is a sign of the promise of God's forgiveness in the future consummation of that divine dominion, a promise revealed and assured even now in the forgiveness brought about by Jesus' victory over sin and death. This promise is present in the beatitude itself. When the beatitude says, "Blessed are the merciful, for they will receive mercy," it points us to the assurance of God's mercy on the day of judgment.[9] Thus, once again, when the people of God are set free by the mercy of God to be merciful to others, they anticipate the promise of God's ultimate reign by their attitudes and actions. They bear witness to the hope that is within them. They are not, in contrast to those who hold grudges, "stuck in the past."

The virtue of mercy as an expression of love is conceived, born, and nurtured in the gospel-life of the gathered community of faith. It is there in the waters of Holy Baptism, proclaimed in the words of absolution, consumed in the Eucharist, and continually reiterated in the mutual acceptance of each other in community as broken lives are brought together by grace in the wholeness of Christ's body.

Justice Again

If the disposition of mercy is linked to compassion and provides the corner-stone for healthy relations between people, it is not surprising that it is also linked to justice as the cornerstone for healthy relations in society as a whole. Mercy born of compassion not only signifies a readiness to forgive, but it is also the biblical way of responding to the needs of people. That is what it means to seek justice.[10]

The biblical understanding of justice is not presented in terms of an abstract set of principles and laws designed to provide a canon of fairness for society. Rather, it recognizes that in a sinful world such schemes break down or are manipulated in such a way as to cause suffering for many. Thus, as we observed in the chapter on poverty of spirit, the poor or the oppressed are at the top of God's agenda. Principles and laws are important and necessary, but they are only fulfilled when infused with mercy and compassion. This is the implication of Jesus' confrontation with the Pharisees, "Go and learn what this means, 'I desire mercy, not sacrifice'" (Matt. 9:13). Strict adherence to religious codes and practices (the Pharisees), like strict adherence to civil law or theories of justice, is a shallow righteousness if it lacks the warm blood of mercy and compassion. A further analogy may help to make this point more fully.

I am a great fan of Sherlock Holmes. I have read all the Sherlock Holmes stories over and over again, spacing them out in my recreational reading over the years so that I can savor them and enjoy them as though they were fresh and new. I am fascinated by his faultless reasoning, his indestructible energy, and his ingenious methods. But at least one story of his adventures is recounted by Holmes himself without the benefit of Watson as his chronicler or dialogue partner. It is my least favorite story. Something is missing when Watson is not telling the tale. Perhaps Arthur Conan Doyle included this piece to help his readers understand that Holmes without Watson is not that attractive a personality. Watson provides the human element, the warmth, the surprise, the depth of feeling and caring, that complements the utter competency of Holmes the detective. And Watson alone draws out in Holmes what human features can be discerned in his personality. So it is with justice. The most ingenious theory of justice, however precise in its logic and rationale, is like Holmes without Watson if not blended with mercy and loving kindness.

The biblical understanding that justice must be fueled by mercy in a cruel and sinful world is made vivid in the Old Testament tradition of the *jubilee* and the use of that tradition in the New Testament. In recent years a number of biblical scholars and ethicists have taken an active interest in the meaning of this tradition for the Bible's understanding of justice and its connection, in turn, with the central message of God's promise ultimately revealed in Jesus, the Christ. According to Sharon Ringe, the Old Testament traditions of the jubilee year come to focus in Lev. 25:8-10:

> You shall count off seven weeks of years, seven times seven years, so that the period of seven weeks of years gives forty-nine years. Then you shall have the trumpet sounded loud; on the tenth day of the seventh month—on the day of atonement—you shall have the trumpet sounded throughout all your land. And you shall hallow the fiftieth year and you shall proclaim liberty throughout the land to all its inhabitants. It shall be a jubilee for you: you shall return, every one of you, to your property and every one of you to your family.

This kernel of the jubilee decree has its background in the sabbath year provisions, which were part of the Sinai covenant tradition. The Sabbath year had four basic provisions:[11]

1. The soil would be left fallow every seventh year, trusting that God would provide, and allowing the poor who had no land to harvest the crops that grew spontaneously during that year.
2. Debtors would be forgiven.
3. Those sold into slavery for their debts would be set free.
4. Lands sold due to economic hardship would be restored to the families who once owned them and families would be reunited again on their land.

Karen Lebacqz, along with Ringe, sees in this tradition an image of biblical justice in which people are set free from oppressive economic and social circumstances to begin life anew. The image is one of liberation or deliverance. It demonstrates the fact that the Bible views justice from the vantage point of those who are in need.[12] That is, the biblical concern for justice begins with the mercy of God and the merciful actions God demands of the people and for the people.

It is not surprising, then, to find that the jubilee tradition has connections with some of the central themes of God's merciful promise. Most importantly, the laws underlying the jubilee requirement can be found in the covenant code, the laws of God's covenant with Israel recorded in Exodus and later in Deuteronomy. The covenant code spells out the obligations of Israelites to release their kin from slavery and debt incurred through economic setback. It is a way for Israel to imitate God who brought them out of slavery in Egypt and made a covenant with them. In this covenant, born of God's merciful deliverance and sustained by divine loving-kindness, God is the true ruler of Israel and Israel is to bear witness to its sovereign by embodying that same mercy in its national life.[13]

Israel knew God as its ruler in the here and now. Insofar as Israel responded to the provisions of the jubilee and the covenant codes, it acknowledged that rule. But, in so doing, it also anticipated the promise of God's future reign. In a passage we have already seen related to the first beatitude, the prophet of Isaiah 61:1-2 echoes the spirit of the jubilee as a hope for the ultimate reign of God:

> The spirit of the Lord GOD is upon me, because the LORD has anointed me; he has sent me to bring good news to the oppressed, to bind up the brokenhearted, to proclaim liberty to the captives, and release to the prisoners; to proclaim the year of the LORD's favor, and the day of vengeance of our God; to comfort all who mourn.

When we see Jesus applying this prophetic hope to his own person and work in Luke 4, we can begin to connect the Old Testament hope of the jubilee with the New Testament promise of God's dominion as revealed in Jesus. Jesus' message of God's forgiveness of sin is woven together with the promise of deliverance from bondage in all aspects of life and punctuated by his care and concern for outcasts and sinners, his works of healing, and his teaching of compassion. The New Testament hope in the Christ fills out the picture, begun in the image of the jubilee, of the final, future reign of God when God's mercy will be realized in all its fullness.[14]

The jubilee traditions of the Bible concretize the virtue of mercy, combining the closely knit meanings of mercy as these relate to the whole of human need: forgiveness of sin and forgiveness of debt, freedom from physical and economic bondage, and freedom from bondage to evil and, ultimately, death.

In the final anlysis, the jubilee traditions are not a set of divine prescriptions amounting to a systematic scheme for achieving justice in our time.[15] Yet the moral force of these traditions gave impetus to the Jubilee 2000 campaign to provide debt relief to the world's poorest countries. Begun in England in anticipation of the new millennium, Jubilee 2000 had the support of church leaders, including the archbishop of Canterbury, the pope, and a variety of poverty activists. The deliberate application of Leviticus to global economic realities of the twenty-first century predictably aroused skepticism. Remarkably though, the movement took hold among the governments of the more prosperous nations and many of their leaders with the result that significant gains were made in debt relief. It would be naïve to think that even the measurable success of this campaign will deal adequately with the dramatic economic disparities among nations. Economic justice will require a far more comprehensive approach to the manifold issues of globalization.[16] The realities of life in a fallen and ambiguous world are likely to be fragmentary and riddled with compromise. Nonetheless, "the mediocre realities of our present . . . are to be nurtured for the intuitions of the ultimate they possess."[17] We give thanks for all that anticipates the promises of God's future.

In their modeling of mercy, the jubilee traditions help us to understand how the compassion and grace of God, working in and through people, can create new beginnings from the devastation of a sinful and unjust world. Mercy as forgiveness and the compassion for human need that fans the fires of justice is a witness to the gospel. Imagine a family broken apart by conflict and hopelessly mired in its feelings of hurt and anger being granted a brand-new life by the discovery of forgiveness so deep and caring that it wipes the slate clean! If you can imagine such a thing, you can begin to imagine the joy that comes with knowing the mercy of God. If only our broken families could have a jubilee. If only our societies could have a jubilee to provide new beginnings for the starving and the homeless, all the poor and all the oppressed. The virtue of mercy has glimpsed this vision in the mercy and promise of God and, in its "thirst for action," is restless in its seeking for moments of jubilee.[18]

From Mercy to Peace

Mercy, in its commitment to renewal of relationships through forgiveness and justice, is closely linked to peacemaking in the ethics of love. When relations are renewed and alienation is ended through the exercise of mercy, peace is made and community is created. Where community is created, the separated are reunited and love's goal is attained, as we saw in our earlier discussion of agape love. Both mercy and peacemaking are founded on the giving of oneself to the neighbor out of regard for the neighbor as coequal with oneself and all others.

The disposition of the peacemaker is thus one of commitment to actively work toward reconciliation and wholeness where there is conflict and estrangement. It involves a readiness to engage in conflict when it is necessary to reconciliation.[19] It involves struggle to reorder and renew relationships when they are broken and marked by hostility.[20] It involves respect for the neighbor that precludes behavior that contributes to alienation.

Peacemaking and Truthfulness

In Luther's discussion of this beatitude, it is interesting to note that he moves back and forth between admonitions to the rulers to promote peace instead of war and admonitions to individuals to speak well of each other and promote peace and harmony in personal relationships instead of creating suspicion and hatred through spiteful talk.[21] The weaving together of these admonitions reminds us that there is a direct relationship between our personal and political lives. Though the problems of international peacemaking may be vastly more complex and impersonal than making peace and harmony in the household, the attitudes and commitment that inform both are not unrelated.

For Luther, strife and conflict in personal relationships are often created by our sinful propensity to slander each other and the enjoyment we derive from hearing and telling the worst about our neighbors. He gives these commonplace examples. "If a woman were as beautiful as the sun but had one little spot or blemish on her body, you would be expected to forget everything else and to look only for that spot and talk about it. If a lady were famous for her honor and virtue, still some poisonous tongue would come along and say that she had once been seen laughing with some man and defame her in such a way as to eclipse all her praise and honor."

Lies and mean-spirited speculations create suspicion and conflict where there is no reason for these to exist. Luther contrasts this with Augustine's testimony to his mother: "St. Augustine boasts that when his mother Monica saw two people at odds, she would always speak the best to both sides. Whatever good she heard about the one, she brought to the other; but whatever evil she heard, that she kept to herself or mitigated as much as possible. In this way she often brought on reconciliation."[22]

Luther's concern about the damage we do through twisting the truth and speaking the worst about each other is pertinent to virtually every venue of life. Certainly, efforts to discredit opponents, competitors, or adversaries are commonplace in politics, business, and legal maneuvering. Perhaps, such behavior is most poignant, even tragic, when it happens in the context of church conflicts. It is not unheard of in such disputes for those who take an absolutist stance on their theological and ethical convictions to seek to discredit those of a different view. Often this is done not by theological argument but by casting aspersions on the integrity of the opponent through a distortion of the truth or even outright falsehood. Apparently, when one is convinced that he or she is absolutely right, the end justifies the means; truth takes a backseat to winning. As a result, conflict and division are fostered instead of the peacemaking art of respectful dialogue and the spirit of reconciliation that should mark Christian community. Church members and leaders who have been on the receiving end of unjustified defamatory remarks can relate to Luther's lament:

> I suppose I should respond to everything while I am still living. But then again, how can I alone stop all the mouths of the devil, especially those

(for they are all poisoned) who do not want to listen or pay attention to what we write? Instead they devote all their energy to one thing: how they might shamefully twist and corrupt our words down to the very letters.[23]

The close connection between truthfulness and peacemaking that we are exploring is certainly clear in the realm of public policy. A quarter century ago, after a lengthy and technical discussion of nuclear diplomacy and the politics of disarmament, Alan Geyer called upon the religious community to be a force for truthfulness in order to foster a more effective politics of peace. Thus, he said, "The nuclear arms race has become this generation's severest test of truth. It is zealously promoted with false words, deceptive jargon, pretentious dogmatics, hateful propaganda, and arbitrary bars on access to the truth. No realm of public policy is more corrupted by untruthful speech than national security."[24] Americans at the time of this writing could certainly be forgiven for seeing in Geyer's statement a very real application to present circumstances. Substitute "war in Iraq" for the words "nuclear arms race" and the statement seems totally appropriate in the minds of many who languish over this war as one after another of the reasons for being there appears to be discredited by the facts. Moreover, the celebration of military exploits in our society as an expression of national pride, even in the face of unanswered questions, leaves us open to the dangers of hubris and militarism. History will finally pass judgment on this bloody episode, but it clearly presents Christians with a case study in the relationship of truthfulness and peacemaking, both of which are activities of love's character.

A Christian witness marked by the spirit of peacemaking can be a force for the kind of truthfulness that contributes to authentic peace. It can call into question the false claims of peace. Furthermore, children of the biblical tradition know that peace is more than the absence of war. In the Bible, peace is defined by the Hebrew word *shalom,* which has the meaning of wholeness and well-being in all of life. Thus, the spirit of peacemaking is in league with zeal for justice. To begin with, the injustices of this world are breeding grounds for the hostility that shatters peace. Beyond that reality, however, is the troublesome truth that in armed conflict and other forms of hostility and aggression (such as those played out by national and private sector forces in the fierce competition of economic life, it is the poor who suffer. They are the ones who do most of the fighting in war. They are the ones who do not have the resources to withstand the vicissitudes of economic strife.

Peace begins with you and me. It begins with the spirit of peacemaking born of our faith and hope in God's ultimate shalom. It is a durable virtue ready to endure conflict for the sake of peace. It is neither naïve nor cynical. It is a spirit ready to take on the hard work of reconciliation whether in personal life or public policy.

No "Cheap Peace"

We have already noted some of Luther's comments on the kinds of attitudes and behaviors that contribute to peacemaking in everyday life. After that lengthy admonition, Luther recognizes that some may question his behavior by asking why he attacks the pope and other church leaders instead of being himself a peacemaker. Luther's response reveals another aspect of peacemaking and reconciliation. In answer to his imagined critics, Luther says, "A person must advise and support peace while he [she] can and keep quiet as long as possible. But when sin is evident and becomes too widespread or does public damage, as the pope's teaching has, then there is no longer time to be quiet but only to defend and attack, especially for me and others in public office whose task it is to teach and to warn everyone."[25] Peace does not come cheaply when parties are in conflict and wrongs have been done. The process of reconciliation is not one of papering over the hurts and the wrongs with a too-easy forgiveness. Neither is it a matter of overlooking those wrongs and allowing them to go unchallenged. Rather, reconciliation requires acknowledging wrongs, repentance, and a commitment to change. This will often involve confronting persons with the role they have played in creating a situation of conflict or estrangement.

James Cone has made this point forcefully in his discussion of a Christian approach to black-white relations in our society and globally. Too often, he maintains, whites expect blacks to forgive past wrongs done to them, forget the injustices under which they have suffered, and be reconciled to them while they have still done very little to change the situation of injustice for which they, the white community, are responsible.[26]

Reconciliation for the Christian begins with God's action in Christ to break down the barriers of sin that have divided humanity from God. This reconciling love of God is not only spiritual in nature. It has implications for our lives in the here and now. As God has broken down the barriers of sin that separate us from God, so we are called to break down the barriers that separate us from one another. God's reconciling activity through the people of God, who live in Christ's reconciling love, is a matter of making the social and political changes that correct the injustices African Americans and others have suffered under racial and ethnic discrimination. This reflects God's willingness in Jesus Christ to participate in our history and to confront the reality of human evil to the point of death and thereby overcome it to the end of reconciliation.

Cone describes this understanding of the full implications of reconciliation in terms of *justification* and *sanctification*. We have been reconciled to God in Jesus Christ by the forgiveness of sins. As a reconciled people of God, we are freed from slavery to sin to be the people God intends us to be. That is our justification. However, justification by God's grace always involves growth in grace as the people of God or sanctification. As people freed from slavery, we are committed to the freedom of all. That is the implication for our sanctification.[27] For the white community this will mean the hard work of understanding our racism and being schooled by the African American community concerning the changes in attitudes and public policy needed to overcome oppression. That there is much hard work to do has been brought home once again in a most graphic fashion by the devastation of Hurricane Katrina in August 2005. Natural disasters are no respecters of persons, but Katrina uncovered the stark reality that human societies are. When the levees broke under the force of Katrina and most of New Orleans was flooded, those stranded without means of escape, languishing miserably in makeshift shelters or on roof tops and in attics, were the poor, mostly working poor, mostly African Americans. Day after day the television cameras recorded this fact, reminding us in a most painful fashion of the sorry, lingering disparities of our society.

How hard will it be for white people to participate in the incomplete process of reconciliation? Cone echoes the radical language of the New Testament: "When Whites undergo the true experience of conversion wherein they die to whiteness and are reborn anew in order to struggle *against* white oppression and *for* the liberation of the oppressed, there is a place for them in the Black struggle of freedom."[28] Such a conversion comes as a gift of God through the black community, and it involves a radical change of lifestyle and value whose authenticity is measured by those who have been wronged. As we discovered in the previous discussion of poverty of spirit, the oppressed become our teachers; there is no room for paternalistic superiority on the part of the majority. In the ethics of reconciliation there is no cheap peace just as, to recall Dietrich Bonhoeffer's well-known point; there is with God no cheap grace.

From Formation to Decision

Two beatitudes with which we have not yet dealt provide a good concluding perspective on all the virtues of love's character that we have been discussing:

> Blessed are the pure in heart, for they will see God. (Matt. 5:8)

> Blessed are those who are persecuted for righteousness' sake, for theirs is the kingdom of heaven. (Matt. 5:10)

I suggest that these two beatitudes, taken together, point us in the direction of the classical virtue of *courage*.

The first of these beatitudes, "purity of the heart," in Jesus' proclamation is being placed in contrast to the ritual purity so much a concern of the Pharisees. In the Sermon on the Mount in general, we observe Jesus adding depth to the law by forcing his listeners to consider what is in their hearts, not merely their actions. It is a call to radical transformation. This would seem to be the case with this beatitude as well. Matthew 15:10-20 helps us understand Jesus' intent in contrasting purity of the *heart* with mere *ritual* purity. The Pharisees were questioning why Jesus' disciples did not wash their hands before eating as ritual tradition required. Jesus' response was that is not what goes into one's mouth that defiles, but what comes out of it from the heart. "From out of the heart come evil intentions, murder, adultery, fornication, theft, false witness, slander. These are what defile a person, but to eat with unwashed hands does not defile" (vv. 19-20). This brief summary of those actions and intentions that violate the prohibitions of the Decalogue suggests immediately that purity of heart embraces the first of the commandments, which governs all that follow, "You shall have no other gods before me" (Ex. 20:3), or, in Jesus' words, "You shall love the Lord your God with all your heart, and with all your soul and with all your mind. This is the greatest and first commandment. And a second is like it: You shall love your neighbor as your self" (Matt. 22:37-39).

Søren Kierkegaard picked up the meaning to which we've been led by the texts. Purity of the heart is to will one thing. That one thing is the Good, for its own sake alone, and to will the Good is have one's will be one with the will of God. "If a man should will one thing, then he must will the Good. . . . He must be willing to do all for the Good, or he must be willing to suffer all for the Good."[29] In a concluding prayer of repentance, Kierkegaard prays that he may "have the courage to once again will one thing."[30]

The second of these beatitudes speaks to us of a readiness to suffer for the sake of righteousness. This refers not only to persecution on behalf of the Christ as spoken of in the final beatitude (Matt. 5:11), but of persecution for all just causes. Bonhoeffer was very forceful in making this point. The target of his assertion in this regard was those Christians who argued that, while they had an obligation to stand up for the survival of the church, they had no such obligation of faith and conscience in the civil arena. His pointed comments in that context have enduring relevance for Christian ethics and Christian character in all times and places:

> With this beatitude Jesus thoroughly rejects the false timidity of those
> Christians who evade any kind of suffering for a just, good, and true cause

because they supposedly could have a clear conscience only if they were to suffer for the explicit confession of faith in Christ; he rejects, in other words, the kind of narrow-mindedness that casts a cloud of suspicion on any suffering for the sake of a just cause and distances himself from it. Jesus cares for those who suffer for a just cause even if it is not exactly for the confession of his name.[31]

As Bonhoeffer's life would reveal, he had, in the words of Kierkegaard's prayer, the courage to will one thing and, therefore, the readiness to suffer for the sake of a just and humane cause in his opposition to the Nazi regime.

Whatever else we might say concerning these two beatitudes, taken together, they point us in the direction of courage. Purity of heart in its single-minded trust is ready to risk all in identifying totally with the Christ. Courage requires risk, and the risk here is not only the physical risks we often associate with courage or bravery, but the risk of one's very being and destiny. Only this kind of Spirit-given, grace-based courage can face suffering for righteousness' sake, for only utter trust that God's promise in Christ is true is willing to run that risk. Thus, in Paul Tillich's well-known book, *The Courage to Be*, Tillich speaks of the courage displayed in the confidence of the Reformers, as courage and confidence possible only when one ceases to base it on oneself. The courage of confidence is based solely on God and nothing else.[32]

Why, then, do these two virtues, which are suggestive of the classic virtue of courage, provide us with what I have called a concluding perspective on all the virtues rooted in the Beatitudes? I have said that "poverty of spirit" is foundational for all the virtues of love's character; it is the spiritual core. The virtue of courage is the dynamic core, the gift of grace that powers the life of love and all its virtues. Ethicist Robin Lovin speaks of the cardinal virtues of the classical tradition: "What makes courage a cardinal virtue is that we cannot act on any of the virtues for very long without it. . . . Courage enables us to put all of our other virtues as the service of the good we hope to do."[33] Daniel Maguire points out that "Thomas Aquinas says that courage is the precondition of all morality and virtue. If you don't have it, your commitment to persons and the earth is specious. Courage is love ready to risk. Where there is not readiness to risk, there is no love."[34]

We can see from our discussion of the Beatitudes that there is a certain overlapping character to their meaning for us. At the same time, each of them has its own nuances for expressing specific characteristics of the virtues of love's character. Furthermore, we have observed that these virtues are not just spiritual qualities but are geared to the fundamental relationships of life and to the fundamental needs of people. As such, we have observed their thirst for action. In fact, even though we have been addressing the ethics of being, we have seen all along the implications of character and virtue for the ethics of doing, the positive actions of Christians in the world. Thus, though there is more to say, we are ready to move on to discuss how we are not only *formed* by love but *informed* by love in the life of Christian decision. The challenge of decision will need to find its spiritual depth in the virtues of love's character, including courage in the face of uncertainty and conflict.

Questions for Discussion

1. In what way does this chapter's discussion of mercy and forgiveness speak to your relationships and experiences in life?

2. Can the Christ-centered virtue of mercy really make a difference in the harsh world of economic life where you always have "haves" and "have nots"? Does economic life simply run on a separate track while the works of mercy belong to the realm of personal relationships?

3. Can you think of your own examples of the connection between truthfulness and peacemaking or reconciliation?

4. What are the things in our lives and the ethos of our society that stand in the way of peacemaking at the personal, social, and political levels? How does our Christian faith speak to these barriers?

PART THREE
Decision

8

DIALOGICAL ETHICS

Sin boldly, but believe and rejoice in Christ even more boldly, for he is victorious over sin, death and the world.[1]

—Martin Luther

Christian life may be described as the ongoing experience of God's approach to us in law and gospel, God's word of judgment and grace. The desperation of the human situation is revealed in the law: how far we have come from God, how far we have come from our neighbor, how far we have come from that which is life-affirming. The choice of self-centeredness with its rejection of God and the other person is a choice to be alone and dying. The law tells the truth of that choice. In the gospel we experience the acceptance of God and the forgiveness God offers through Jesus Christ, even though we are unworthy of that favor. In this forgiveness there is reunion with God. Reunited with God and secure in the knowledge of God's acceptance of us, we are free *from* concern for self, free *for* the self-giving love that brings reunion with the neighbor. Experiencing gospel grace by the trust of faith, energized by the Spirit, enables us to reach out in love to the other as God has reached out in love to us. This is the new possibility of those who are a new creation in Christ (2 Cor. 5:17).

Still, as we live in the newness of grace with all its possibilities, we continue to struggle with all that remains "old" about us: that lingering desire to serve the self and its desires first rather than the will of God and the good of the neighbor. Again, we can identify with St. Paul when we read his words:

> For I know that nothing good dwells within me, that is, in my flesh. I can will what is right, but I cannot do it. For I do not do the good I want, but the evil I do not want is what I do. (Rom. 7:18-19)

Biblical scholars have differed over whether or not Paul is describing life before faith or after faith in this passage. However, I know of few Christians who would not acknowledge that it is, in fact, a good description of their own experience. Luther, in particular, was very vivid in his description of this ongoing struggle with the "old Adam" that remains in us and the new person that we are in Christ.[2]

Although these thoughts are a reiteration of what has been elaborated in the preceding chapters, it is important to state these fundamentals of the Christian outlook on life in order to emphasize that any theory of decision making that we adopt will need to faithfully reflect this experience. Any method of ethical decision making that simplistically assumes we can justify ourselves by using that method to demonstrate how we have done the right thing beyond a shadow of a doubt would not be true to the reality of life as we experience it in judgment and grace. In having a method for making decisions as Christians, we adopt the means by which we justify the decisions we make in the sense of having good reasons for those decisions. But this "justification" is not to be confused with the justification of the self. In the final analysis, it is God who justifies us by our acceptance in Jesus Christ, and it is God who gives us the freedom in Christ to make those decisions in the confidence of the Spirit's ministry, despite our ambiguous motives and our limited vision.

It is important to build into our understanding of decision an awareness that the word of God in law and gospel also illumines the human situation of life in a fallen and imperfect world and provides us with the courage to act even in the face of tragic choices. Indeed, the hard and often tragic choices serve to illustrate this point. Consider as an example the following case recorded in a prominent journal:

> A 32-year-old woman with multiple sclerosis became pregnant despite use of a diaphragm. She and her husband had two children, four and six years old, for whom she was the principal caregiver. Although the couple were generally opposed to abortion, both were extremely concerned that continuation of the pregnancy would further compromise the woman's health. Previous pregnancies had resulted in permanent aggravation of her condition, to a point where she required a wheelchair. One week after learning she was pregnant the woman requested an abortion. She hoped, she said, to preserve her ability to care for the children she already had.[3]

The brief clinical description of this case omits any description of the couple's religious faith or the struggle they may have had in making that decision. We can only imagine that their general disapproval of abortion, their evident care for their existing children, and their concern for the values involved in the lives of all members of the family created a terrible moral dilemma for them. We can only speculate on the grief that must have been involved in the final decision to end the pregnancy. Even when our motives and intentions appear to be at their noblest and we have done our best to make a good decision, ethical dilemmas are often so intransigent as to leave us with no sense of moral certitude. Thus, in and through the process of applying ethical principles to perplexing questions of decision, the truth of what the law reveals about the human predicament is often apparent, and we are forced to recognize and live with the radical ambiguity of some of our decisions and the tragic character of a world whose full redemption is not yet consummated.

In the pain of moral choice, we appreciate ever anew our desperate need for the new life that is ours in Christ Jesus. Our method of decision making will need to have built into it an appreciation for these realities and for the power of God's grace to grant us the courage and freedom to make these choices even when the choice can only be the lesser evil and even when there is no certainty as to what the lesser evil might be. When confronted with these more difficult choices, we need to remind ourselves that our confidence in the moral life is not rooted in certainty of our judgments but in the assurance of God's promise to deal graciously with us in all things.

With these observations in mind, I sketch a method of Christian decision making in the following chapters that I trust will be consistent with the account of the Christian life that has been elaborated in the first two parts of the book. I have called that method dialogical ethics.[4] The reason for referring to it as a "dialogical" method should be clear as we go along.

In approaching this task, two things need to be noted. First of all, Christians have differed and do differ on how one decides the right. We cannot survey and critique the wide variety of ethical methods in the Christian tradition. Space allows only for an occasional contrast. Second, it is also clear that the different approaches Christians have suggested for deciding what is right have their counterparts in non-Christian ethics. Moreover, it is frequently the case that Christians and non-Christians share some of the same moral principles and arrive at some of the same answers to specific moral questions. Again, I will not take the space to illustrate these points of correspondence between Christian and non-Christian ethics. It simply needs to be acknowledged in order to emphasize what was hinted at above: the distinctiveness of Christian ethics is not primarily to be found in its methods of decision making, or even in the conclusions it reaches on specific problems, but in the foundation of the ethic that is God's grace in Christ as the key to the meaning of all things and the dynamic of the moral life. Therefore, one need not be disturbed by the similarities that exist between Christian and non-Christian ethics, as though these rob Christianity of its uniqueness and authority. Also, it is not necessary to discredit the achievements of non-Christian ethics or of non-Christian people of high moral sensitivity in order to buttress some notion of the superiority of the Christian way. Our understanding of God's universal rule should lead us to expect that, outside as well as inside the community of the faithful, the purposes of God are served through all kinds of people in manifold ways. We rejoice at the right and the good wherever we find it (Phil. 4:2). In constructing and living the Christian ethic, as in all endeavors of life, the Christian witness is finally to the triune God, who is with us as our future, a future made present in the promise of the Christ, who incarnates, inspires, and energizes our life by the work of the Spirit.

Informed by Love

In chapter 4 we discussed the nature of agape love and how the Christian community and individuals within it are formed by love. This was foundational to our understanding of how the Christian character and its virtues are shaped by the love of God in Jesus Christ. It is consistent with this understanding of an evangelical ethic that we are not only formed by love in our moral character but that we are also *informed* by love in our decision making. Thus, it follows that love is the fundamental principle for Christian decision making and the cornerstone of our method of decision making.[5] However, it is important to note that not all Christian thinkers and traditions operate with agape love as the central premise of all Christian ethics. Two examples of different outlooks—one based on "natural law," the other on a separation of love from justice—help to focus more sharply on the particular nature of our love-based ethic.

Natural Law Ethics

In my judgment, the most prominent alternative to *agape* ethics is the natural law ethics that we normally associate with Roman Catholic tradition. When looking at this tradition, we need to be cognizant of the twofold way in which the term *natural law* is used in Catholic moral thought. The primary sense of natural law is the belief that there is a set of moral propositions, expressing the eternal will of God, that are universally known to natural human reason. Because all people are created in the image of God with reason and the capacity for goodwill, they should be able to know and do the will of God revealed to them in the natural law. This is a general revelation. The second sense in which natural law is used as a basis for ethics is when it asserts that there is an order and purpose that God has created in nature that can be the source of moral rules that govern our conduct. According to this perspective, human reason can discern the purposes of God in nature, and people ought to act in accordance with them. This commitment is neatly illustrated by the traditional Catholic moral argument against artificial birth control. It is maintained that God's primary intention for sexual intercourse is to create children; therefore, to intervene by using contraceptives is to violate natural law. Another illustration of this reasoning is the consistent opposition of the Catholic Church to artificial insemination. Procreation by other than "natural" means is regarded as contrary to the law of nature that God intends for us to follow.[6]

While most Protestants do not operate with natural law ethics, they do recognize that there is a natural law in the limited sense that people have an innate appreciation of right and wrong and can freely choose between good and evil. They take seriously the biblical statement that the law is written on the hearts of all humankind (Rom. 2:14-15). Some who are not consistent practitioners of natural law ethics often fall back on a kind of natural law argument when they condemn certain acts as immoral because they appear to be "unnatural." This kind of argumentation is particularly prominent among many who condemn homosexuality or who consider various other sexual behaviors to be perversions. Still others would reject as immoral certain practices of modern medicine, such as *in vitro* fertilization, because they believe such procedures violate God's natural order of things. There is a strong residual appeal to a natural law basis for deciding right and wrong even among those who do not consistently follow the tradition of natural law ethics.

Such appeals to the sanctity of the "natural" notwithstanding, most Protestants are critical of natural law ethics because they maintain that sin has so corrupted the human will and reason that any system of natural law is imperfect, inconsistent, and unreliable. In fact, the history of disagreement among natural law advocates over the content of what God teaches us through nature tends to support that concern. Furthermore, there is a related concern that natural law ethics places too much emphasis on human reason and will to know and do the right as God commands it and too little emphasis on the necessity of God's grace in Jesus Christ as the real force of the Christian ethic. Finally, the Reformation emphasis on Scripture as the norm of faith and life stands in contrast to the natural law tradition's heavy reliance on human reason.[7] On the matter of the role of Scripture, however, it is fair to say that, since Vatican II, scriptural resources have played a far more normative role than in the past. Moreover, at least some apologists for Catholic natural law tradition would argue that it has also tempered its optimism concerning human reason and paid more attention to the reality of sin in the pursuit of the moral life.[8]

Our commitment to the primacy of grace and the manner in which it shapes us in a love reflecting the love of our Lord and Savior leads to the choice of *agape* as the premise of Christian decision making rather than natural law.

Moreover, the tendency of natural law ethics is to emphasize the conformity of human reason and decision to divine law given in nature rather than focusing on the needs of the neighbor, which is the thrust of agape love. A gospel-centered ethic of love focuses on relationships as the heart of ethical decision—our relationship to God and our relationship to the neighbor in his or her needs. However, this distinction is important but not absolute. Catholic moral theologians like Richard McCormick understand the natural law to be in the service of the life of love in Christ and not a morality separate from that existence in the gospel.[9] I would certainly affirm McCormick's stance in that regard as a salutary outlook. However, it is still possible to lift up the problematic tendencies of natural law and offer an alternative to that tradition without condemning it entirely and without being unappreciative of its most sensitive advocates. As we move on to a discussion of rules in Christian decision making a little later in this chapter, we will consider further how natural law works in practice. That discussion should serve to underscore some of the points I have just made.

Love and Justice

One of the great appeals of natural law tradition, to which I have already alluded, is that it represents a general revelation providing moral guidance for all people, Christian and non-Christian alike. Those outside the natural law tradition have often been eager to assert that such a general revelation does indeed exist and can be affirmed as a basis of general morality without entailing a commitment to natural law ethics. This position has sometimes taken the form of asserting that there are two basic ethical principles ordained by God: love *and* justice. Love is understood to be the principle central to the personal ethics of believers, whereas justice is a principle of general revelation central to the governance of human affairs in the civil and political arena. In their personal lives believers should aspire to the ideal of love in their dealings with other individuals. In their public life believers, along with nonbelievers, should subject themselves to an ethic of justice for the common good. The presumption is that justice and law are necessary as an expression of God's providential ordering of a world in which not all are Christians and not all adhere to the ideal of love.

While justice and law are certainly necessary to provide order in an imperfect and often evil world, separating justice from love easily leads to two divergent ethical systems in which the concerns of justice are not related to the concerns of love and in which the church is often tempted to neglect the concerns of justice. Justice is too readily left to the realm of secular reason without being critiqued or influenced by the ethics of love.

In the foregoing chapters, we have already made a number of connections between love and justice. We have said that the values of God's promised dominion, toward which the people of anticipation strive as a witness to the hope within them, include concerns of justice, such as equality and freedom among people. We have connected this concern for equality and justice with the virtues of love as integral to the character of the people of God. Thus, we have already laid the basis for connecting justice to love rather than separating the two as distinct principles representing differing ethical systems.

Many years ago, a Christian ethicist from Princeton named George F. Thomas offered this succinct statement concerning the relationship of justice and love. I think it still holds true in the present discussion.

> Social justice, though an indispensable, can never be a complete and adequate expression of love. The reason lies in the nature of social justice itself: social justice is concerned with the *general* or *common* good shared by all the members of a group but it pays no attention to the *special* needs of the members. But love is concerned with the needs of persons, special as well as common. Therefore, love must seek social justice for all but must also go beyond this to seek the welfare of *each* as an individual.[10]

Thomas's statement is helpful because it distinguishes justice in society from love but does not separate the two principles. Rather, it suggests that justice is an expression of love in public life and policy.

Reinhold Niebuhr also distinguished love from justice without separating the two. Niebuhr points out that justice is required by the reality of sin and remains an imperfect expression of a sinful world, even in serving as the conduit for love's concern for the neighbor. Thus, love criticizes various expressions of justice from time to time and place to place. Love seeks to influence governments and public policy toward a more adequate justice. In the end the fulfillment of the ideal of love in the coming reign of God is at the same time the fulfillment of justice and, therefore, the eclipse of all the penultimate and imperfect efforts of justice throughout history.[11] We will have another chance to look at the relationship between love and justice in chapter 10.

General Rules of Love

We have already said a great deal about the content of agape love. We have noted that it is self-giving, that it regards all equally as the object of its care and concern, and that it strives toward union within the self and communion and union among persons who are alienated or estranged from each other. We have spelled out some of the implications of these characteristics of love in terms of the virtues it displays, as revealed in the Beatitudes. However, there is more that can be said about the nature and obligation of love. These characteristics of love can be further delineated as they are embodied in general rules that give the specific direction for deciding the right in a variety of circumstances. This means that as we enter into a decision-making situation, we do so with a clear sense of what our obligations in love are. We bring to that situation more than an attitude or an orientation of character; we bring a general idea of love's duty. It is necessary to note that the decision to operate with rules of love that state in advance love's duty as a basic guide to decision making distinguishes this approach from that taken by those who believe that the consequences of our actions should be the determining factor in deciding right and wrong.

Those who stress consequences as the key to ethical decision making believe that deciding the right is basically a function of the choices we have in any given situation. When faced with a moral problem, I have only so many alternatives from which to choose. The alternative that appears to produce the greatest good as an outcome is the alternative that is right. If we look back to the example of the pregnant woman with multiple sclerosis cited earlier in the chapter, we can illustrate this approach to ethics by observing that her decision to abort, if she were a follower of this theory, would have been based on her judgment that the preservation of her life and health and the care of her existing family amounted to a greater good than the preservation of unborn life. By contrast, if she stood in the natural law tradition, an evaluation of the consequences would not be a part of her decision. Rather, she would simply have to obey the natural law duty to preserve that unborn life regardless of the outcome. Were she operating with the pattern of dialogical ethics and the general rules of love that we are now in the process of presenting, her approach to the decision would differ from both these alternatives regardless of the outcome, as we shall soon see.

Consequentialism is probably best represented in our history by utilitarianism, a philosophical theory associated with John Stuart Mill and Jeremy Bentham. Utilitarianism states that we should make our moral choices based on the principle of utility: what will produce *the greatest good for the greatest number.* This approach has been very influential in economic life and public policy as well as other arenas of human endeavor.

An ethic of consequences can also work with the principle of love. Joseph Fletcher, still the best-known consequentialist in Christian circles, has done that.[12] For him, doing that which produces the greatest good as a consequence is to do "the most loving thing." He recognizes no other rule of obligation as binding. Thus, in a given situation, we may theoretically choose to lie, break a promise, or even take a life if it will produce the greater good, which represents the most loving thing. Such an approach has often been criticized as being highly subjective, leaving the content of love basically up to the individual. When only consequences count in determining what is right, it becomes too easy to set aside other obligations that seem compatible with love, such as truthfulness, promise keeping, and preserving the sanctity of life. Critics of consequentialism in general and Fletcher's version of it in particular fear that this theory provides too little direction for sinful people in a sinful world. They fear that behaviors that would otherwise be considered immoral could be too easily rationalized on the basis of good consequences. As we shall see, concern for understanding our choices in peculiar situations and concern for consequences both are important to good ethics. For the present, I am primarily concerned simply to point out the manner in which our commitment to operating with general rules of love marks this approach off from the ethics of consequences. All good ethics is concerned about the consequences of our actions, but not all ethical systems make the calculation of consequences the basis for making and justifying one's decisions.

The general rules of love are *general*, first of all, in the sense of being *universally valid*. The logic of the love commandment is that it is God's commandment and, therefore, the absolute, universal ideal for all humankind. Because the general rules of love faithfully embody this love commandment, they participate in its universal validity. They are concrete instances or examples of how that love behaves in various arenas of human activity.

In the following chapters, I offer some examples of general rules of love based on the Ten Commandments. It is important to maintain that the general rules of love have their validity in that they faithfully embody love, not only because it provides a basis for their universality as expressions of the love commandment, but also because this grounding in love distinguishes them from rules as they are commonly used in a legalistic approach to ethics. In a legalistic approach, rules tend to form a code stating what we ought to do and ought not to do. Each of the rules in the code is valid in its own right and should be obeyed for its own sake. The stress is, then, on our obligation and our ability to obey those rules. However, when rules are embraced because they express love in some tangible way, our response to the rules is the response of love for the neighbor directly related to the power of the gospel at work in our lives. The rules then become statements of possibilities for those created anew in the life of love rather than simply statements of duty and judgment. To be sure, the general rules of love, as the love commandment itself, spell out duty and can convey a sense of judgment in our failure to respond to them. However, in contrast to legalism, their direct connection to the new life of love in the gospel keeps alive the tension of judgment and possibility, the tension of law and gospel that is characteristic of life in the "not yet" situation that we described earlier.[13] I believe the relationship between the love command and the general rules of love based on the Decalogue with which we will be working are consistent with Saint Paul's comments in Romans 13:8-10:

> Owe no one anything, except to love one another; for the one who loves another has fulfilled the law. The commandments, "You shall not commit adultery; You shall not murder; You shall not steal; You shall not covet"; and any other commandment, are summed up in this word, "Love your neighbor as yourself." Love does no wrong to a neighbor; therefore, love is the fulfilling of the law.

The second sense in which I am using the term *general* is that of *broad*. General rules are characterized by *generality* rather than being highly specific and narrowly limited in their frame of reference.° The decision to work with general rules in this sense distinguishes our approach from methods of ethics that operate with an elaborate set of specific prescriptions designed to cover, as much as possible, all conceivable circumstances of decision. Historically, this approach is sometimes referred to as casuistry.

Casuistry expands upon basic principles (general rules) by deriving additional rules that spell out how these principles apply to specific cases. In some instances, rules are created to govern exceptions to the rules. Some of the law codes in the Old Testament illustrate casuistic reasoning, and casuistry was also characteristic of the Pharisees in Jesus' time. Casuistic reasoning is amply illustrated in secular law codes or in the precedents of case law. Casuistry has also been a prominent feature in the tradition of natural law.[14]

An example of natural law casuistry is the well-known rule of double-effect, usually attributed in its inception to the writings of Thomas Aquinas. To illustrate the use of this rule, imagine the case of a pregnant woman who receives a diagnosis of uterine cancer. The physician attending her determines that she must have this cancer surgically removed in order to save her life. When the operation is done, there is, of course, a double effect: the surgery not only results in the removal of the cancer, it also results in the abortion of the fetus. According to natural law, abortion is considered wrong under all circumstances.

°The notion of "generality" may suggest to some that the term "principle" is preferable to "rule" because the former often connotes something general in scope whereas the latter may suggest greater specificity of direction. In the actual practice of ethical discourse the terms tend to be interchangeable.

However, in this case it is morally acceptable because the primary purpose of the surgery that caused the abortion was to save the woman's life and not to do an abortion. The abortion was simply a secondary, unintended consequence that was unavoidable. This was a case of indirect abortion legitimated by a rule designed to cover exceptions to the absolute rule that we ought never to terminate innocent life at any stage of its development.

Rule ethics endeavoring to prescribe action for as many circumstances as possible and even to provide rules to cover exceptions to the rules through casuistic extension of basic principles tend toward legalism. This legalistic tendency is seen in the emphasis on prescribing behavior rather than inviting decision. It is further evident in the stress on our capacity to demonstrate the rightness of certain actions on the basis of their conformity to rules or their acceptability under a rule covering exceptions to those rules. To be sure, ethical systems that operate with rules of any kind will need to interpret the appropriate application of the rules in dialogue with situations or individual "cases." Furthermore, as in casuistry, the discoveries and decisions made in one case will inform future deliberations and decisions in similar cases. My concern here is not to ignore this necessary practice. Rather, my concern is when casuistic reasoning becomes a legalistic drive toward certitude. This claim of certitude involves a presumption that is simply out of sync with our "not yet" reality.

To put the matter in a somewhat different fashion, operating with a legalistic or casuistic approach to rule ethics is like being given a coloring book. The picture is printed out for you in black and white; the moral life is a matter of coloring within the lines. To operate with the general rules of love, by contrast, is more like being provided with an empty canvas, colors, and brushes. We are not unequipped, and we have a vision of what the moral picture should be, but to paint the moral picture will require some struggle, some insight, and some courage for decision. This leads us to our next point: general rules need to be interpreted in dialogue with the situation of decision.

In Dialogue with the Situation

In this system of ethics, the word *dialogical* comes from the observation that moral decision can happen only after love's general rules are brought into dialogue with the situation of moral choice, whether that is a personal encounter or a matter of social concern. Because love's general rules are broadly stated or characterized by generality, they do not present us with a clear prescription in many cases. Because moral choice in a complex and imperfect world is often highly particular from one case to the next and frequently ambiguous, there is no getting around the need for good ethics to take careful account of the situation. Indeed, this process of dialogue with the situation is a natural extension of what has been a basic premise of our discussion to this point. As the community of faith gathers around Word and Sacrament, it is always in dialogue with the world. In that dialogue, faith sheds light on the nature of the world and our hopes for it, and the world situation opens up new dimensions of the meaning and significance of the faith.

Appreciating the Facts

Since appreciation for the situation is so important in ethical decision, good ethics will strive to understand facts of the situation. Thus, in the realm of bioethics, decisions on abortion, euthanasia, genetic control, and so on, we will need to be as sure of the medical and scientific facts as possible. Similarly, moral choices involving social and political solutions in the interest of justice will often entail working out a way through a maze of sociological, political, and economic realities. However, there are two pitfalls to avoid in our quest for the facts.

The first danger is to become so entangled in our fact-finding that feelings of frustration at not having adequate knowledge of the facts paralyze our ability to make decisions. In teaching ethics or conducting workshops in which I have groups discussing cases that pose an ethical dilemma, I find that groups frequently fall into this trap. It is common for them to complain that the account of the case with which they are working does not include enough facts about the problem for them to reach a definite conclusion. Sometimes they have a good point. However, often they are expressing the mistaken notion that, given enough facts, the facts will virtually make the moral choice for us. Ultimately, the facts can only set some parameters for our decision. It is the moral discernment of those deciding under the impulse of love and the guidance of its rules in dialogue with the situation that must finally determine the right and the good in a given case.

This brings us to the second pitfall involved in our attempt to appreciate the facts of the situation, namely, the failure to recognize that facts are not always simple and straightforward matters. The details of any life situation usually come to us clothed in the interpretations given to them by the people with whom we are involved and viewed by us through our own interpretive lenses. Thus, appreciating the situation requires of us not simply that we ask, "What are the facts?" but rather, "What's going on?" in the minds and feelings of all involved, including ourselves.[15] Let me illustrate with an experience from my own life.

Some years ago my oldest daughter talked with me about her interest in going to college and her aspirations for a career in the theater. At issue was the choice between two universities, both of which had strong programs in theater. The difference was that one required theater students to have a strong general liberal arts background for their degree whereas the other offered a program that was almost totally concentrated on the disciplines of theater and acting. In responding to her situation, I treated the facts of her choice as being rather clear and simple and interpreted that choice in terms of my own academic background and rather traditional approach to future planning. Consequently, I argued that she should choose the university with the strong general liberal arts requirement as providing a broader educational background for a greater variety of options in the job market while yet satisfying her interests in theater. This almost brought the discussion to a halt. It took me some time to reengage her on the subject since my initial response had alienated her. I failed to see clearly that my own response was conditioned by influences on my outlook that were not part of her life experience. I simply interpreted the choice in my own terms and failed to ask, "What's going on?" What was going on was that she had already made up her mind. Her passion for the theater was so strong that she wanted to immerse herself totally in preparation for that career. She was not in the least interested in mixing that with a general liberal arts program. What she really wanted was my support and encouragement. Had I tried to appreciate her thinking, my response could have been more fitting and more helpful.

Although this illustration is not strictly a case of moral decision, I think it makes the point we are working on. It also alerts us to an element of ethical reflection that has become more and more prominent in the minds of ethicists in our time. I am referring to the idea that much of what we know and the way we think about things is a product of our social location. We discussed this to some extent in chapter 5 when we observed that different groups within society will think about issues differently and understand those issues differently because of their social experience and history. Thus, women, persons of color, or persons of different economic classes may interpret moral issues and situations differently from white middle-class males, for example. Their experience under oppression provides them with a different agenda that is socially conditioned by their participation in a history of injustice and discrimination. An example helps to make the point.

Shortly after the *Roe v. Wade* decision in 1973, in which the Supreme Court essentially legalized abortion, there was a wave of public policy initiative to provide free or subsidized legal abortions for the poor. The liberal support for these programs was led by a sincere conviction that this kind of public service was a morally responsible way to relieve the desperate situation of poor families who could not afford more children. However, some leaders of the African American community responded in a decidedly negative fashion by charging that this liberal program was a veiled effort on the part of the white majority to lure poor blacks into a legalized program of genocide. Since African Americans represented such a high percentage of the poor and such a high percentage of the black population was poor, the appeal of free or subsidized abortions to poor black women was seen as an effective tool for preserving the minority status of the African American community while failing to address the sources of that community's poverty.

Appreciation for the facts of the situation—asking the question, "What's going on?"—requires all of those involved to have a keen sensitivity to the social realities that shape the interpretation of issues. Recognizing these differences and their enormous importance for responsible and effective ethics is a first step toward dealing with them in the decision-making process.

Forms of Dialogue

Within the framework of these concerns about appreciating the facts of the situation and how those facts come to us in interpreted form, I would posit that there are three forms of dialogue between the general rules of love and the situation of ethical decision.

First, the most basic form of the dialogue might well be termed *direct interpretation*. It is a form of dialogue involved in the other two forms yet to be named even though it represents a separate category of deliberation. It is probably true that most of the day-to-day moral decisions we make are fairly straightforward and require little or no reflection. It takes little interpretive effort on our part to know that, normally, we should tell the truth, keep promises, help a neighbor in need, and respect human life. Still, there are many choices that do require a good deal of direct interpretation in the situation to determine how to act upon love's rules. Lewis Smedes puts it nicely in his helpful book *Mere Morality,* as he discusses positive interpretations of the Decalogue:

> As love turns negatives into affirmatives, it pays the price of imprecision. We venture into uncharted regions with the Commandments as a compass, not a map. It isn't difficult to understand what it means to refrain from stealing; but helping other people get enough property to survive as human beings is a loose-jointed mandate. Staying out of a neighbor's bed is simple; creative fidelity to one's spouse in the boredom and agony of a bad marriage is complicated. In short, as love translates the law into affirmative directions, we are left with greater responsibility but less precision.[16]

That I am obligated to respond to my neighbor's needs when she comes to me distraught and suffering is clear. But what is required? Sympathy? Confrontation? Referral elsewhere? Material assistance? Some combination of these? I know I have an ongoing responsibility to the health of family life, but how, as a parent, do I implement this in shaping my children's lives and values? Some things are clear; others are not. Direct interpretation, then, is a process of discerning how the general rule of love takes concrete shape in a given situation. It is in some respects artful and intuitive.

The second form of dialogue is *resolution of conflict*. It is often the case in hard cases that two or more rules of love, or more than one person's claim on our love, will be in conflict. In such cases it often seems that no choice is possible without some compromise. I alluded to such decisions earlier as matters of choosing the lesser evil. We recognize a seemingly unavoidable encounter with the tragic in human existence. How does a mother deal with the knowledge that she is pregnant with a severely defective fetus? To abort is to prevent suffering. However, to abort is to take life. How do physician and family respond to a terminally ill patient when relieving his or her suffering appears incompatible with preserving his or her life? How many apparently conflicting claims can one identify throughout society as one seeks to design a more just and humane policy of national health care? How does a small-business owner balance the conflicting claims in the needs of family, employees, and customers at a time of serious downturn in profit?

We can recall again the case study of the pregnant woman with multiple sclerosis that we have been discussing in this chapter. I have already commented on the different forms her decision might have taken had she been a consequentialist, on the one hand, or a practitioner of natural law, on the other hand. Approaching her problem from the vantage point of dialogical ethics, her situation is one of conflict resolution. She has a general rule obligation of love to preserve life. But there is more than one claim under that obligation: her unborn child's life and her own life. In tandem with that conflict is her obligation in love to care for her husband and children in what is already a considerably debilitated state of health. Her resolution of the conflict by deciding on an abortion in order to preserve her own life for the sake of her family involves the tragic compromise of sacrificing unborn life. While her decision may be responsible, it is not justified by the argument that the good consequences outweigh the bad or by any claim that the decision conformed to a specific and overriding rule of obligation. She and her family must simply live with the compromise. The resolution of conflict is agonizing work for the morally sensitive. In chapter 11, I consider how we can analyze the process of resolving conflicts in the dialogue between general rules and the situation.

The third and final form of the dialogue between rules and the situation occurs in the process of formulating *middle axioms.* In certain specific areas of ethical concern, it is sometimes possible to construct what have been called middle axioms. These are a somewhat more specific set of moral directives that spell out the implications of general rules for a special area of immediate concern. They say more by way of interpreting love's obligations than do the general rules from which they are derived, but they pull up short of prescribing specific decisions. Thus, while their guidance in our decisions on the issues they address is more detailed, they do not deliver us from the further efforts of direct interpretation or even, in some cases, struggle with the resolution of conflict. They occupy a position midway between general rules and prescriptive judgments; hence, the term *middle* axioms.

A great many statements adopted by church bodies on specific social issues are characterized by enunciating a number of middle axioms. In this way a church can address public policy issues in light of its Christian principles without, on the one hand, restricting itself to empty generalities or, on the other hand, becoming mired in the support of specific political solutions, not that the latter should never be done. A recent church body social statement on environmental responsibility provides an example of a middle axiom. First, the statement defines the principle of *sustainability* as the obligation to provide a good quality of life for present generations without compromising that of future generations. The general principle of sustainability is then further developed by the following middle axiom:

> Protection of species and their habitats, preservation of clean land and water, reduction of wastes, care of the land—these are priorities. But production of basic goods and services, equitable distribution, accessible markets, stabilization of population, quality education, full employment— these are priorities as well.[17]

Middle axioms, like our direct interpretations and our resolutions of conflict, are relative; they come and go as the circumstances that give rise to them appear, change, and disappear. They too must be applied through further dialogue with the situation to which they are addressed. This is clear in our sample statement when, immediately following the above middle axiom, the statement goes on to recognize the potentially conflictual interpretive struggle that lies ahead:

> We recognize the obstacles to sustainability. Neither economic growth that ignores environmental cost nor conservation of nature that ignores human cost is sustainable. Both will result in injustice and, eventually,

environmental degradation. We know that a healthy economy can exist only within a healthy environment, but that it is difficult to promote both in our decisions.[18]

The Church and Moral Deliberation

Our reflections on the development of middle axioms in the formulation of social statements by various church bodies, reminds us of an important aspect of any account of Christian ethics: the church is a place of moral deliberation. In part 1 I laid out the theological rationale for the church's ethical witness as an integral part of its gospel witness. This is an overarching premise of all that follows. Individuals engaged in the dialogue of ethical deliberation and decision share that same calling. However, as I pointed out at the end of chapter 1, we need each other in the journey of moral deliberation. Ethical reflection in the community of faith gathered around the Word helps to equip each of us as we confront the ethical challenges of daily life. At the same time, the combined insights of individuals gathered in the faith community are needed to shape the corporate ethical witness of the church and direct its advocacy and practices.

The church has from the very beginning been a community of ethical discourse, facing the challenge to define the good and the right in a host of circumstances just as it faced the challenges that led to establishing the biblical canon and the formulation of the ecumenical creeds.[19] My colleague, Mark Allan Powell, has shown how the "binding and loosing" passages in Matt. 16:19 and 18:18 give us a glimpse of the early church at work in moral deliberation. The majority of scholars, he points out, now regard the terms "to bind" and "to loose" as a reference to the church in the process of determining how scriptural commands apply to present situations. Matthew's Gospel, then, provides a number of examples of this binding and loosing, notably in the manner in which Jesus applies the law in the "antitheses" statements of chapter 5. While these statements deepen and expand the demand of the law beyond what was traditionally taught, other passages demonstrate a loosing of the law as in the case of 12:9-14, where Jesus drops the prohibition of work on the Sabbath when it comes to works of healing.[20]

Often the process of ethical deliberation in the church can achieve a high degree of consensus. While there may be disagreement about what behaviors or policies constitute racism or what steps are needed to counteract it, there is no disagreement that it is a moral evil that Christians are conscience bound to oppose. While there may be some disagreement about how we achieve sustainability, to recall our previous example, Christian responsibility to promote care for the creation is not in doubt. Disagreements of this kind are usually understood as disagreements we can live with in community as long as we are sincerely committed in conscience and practice to the general principles. At the same time, these disagreements signal the need for constant dialogue with each other and the situations we face.

More vexing is the fact that some areas of deliberation within our faith community seem resistant to anything approaching consensus. This is the case most often when there is not only disagreement over the facts of the matter but over what the Bible says to us in that regard. The lingering debate over abortion is a case in point. People disagree over the facts of when life begins and whether or not the Bible's prohibitions of murder apply to abortion. The current debate among Christians over stem-cell research that uses "fetal tissue" is an extension of the abortion controversy. Another possible illustration of this problematic in ethical discourse is the morality of homosexual conduct. There is disagreement over the facts in that some Christians refuse to believe that this sexual orientation is a "given" rather than a choice. There is further disagreement over the facts in regard to whether or not or to what extent homosexual orientation can be changed through therapeutic intervention. In addition, then, we have disagreement as to what the Bible really says about same-sex conduct and the extent to which those texts are applicable in light of present understandings.

These more recalcitrant disputes over moral matters usually raise the question of biblical authority or how the Bible shapes our ethical positions on a host of issues. The ensuing debate is sometimes made even more difficult by the fact that the Bible is silent on many of the problems we face in our scientific age. The wisdom we require is there, but it has to be discerned, and once again, this is the vocation of the community, gathered around the Word, confident of the guidance of the Spirit (John 16:13), and prayerful in demeanor. Unfortunately, hard cases involving differences over facts and the way in which the Bible speaks to the present situation often lead some to accuse others who disagree with them of refusing to accept the authority of Scripture. The real difference is not usually over the authority of the Bible at all but over its interpretation.

I shall not be providing a lengthy discussion of the authority and use of Scripture in Christian ethics. I hope, instead, that the way in which Scripture is used throughout the book will itself make a clear statement in that regard.

The relativity of our decisions in whatever form of the dialogue between general rules and situation is, as we have observed, a product of the way in which the lingering reality of sin clouds our judgment and our motives as well as a product of the ambiguous decisions forced upon us by the conflicts of life in a tragic and imperfect world. Beyond that, we live with relativity also because we are finite or limited creatures. We have already alluded to our finitude in discussing the influence of social location and personal experience on the way we interpret the issues confronting us. As human beings and even as societies we are limited by contingent factors that make us what we are: our genes, our parental influence, the variables that shape our personality, our native intelligence, our education, our culture, our economic and social circumstances, and so on. We cannot do and see everything we need to do and see. The choices we must make and the forms they take are not entirely within our control. The relativity of ourselves and our circumstances lend relativity to our moral decision, and deny us the absolute certitude we covet.

At the same time, love and the general rules of love abide; they are always our obligation. More important, they are always our possibility. They are rooted in God's gracious love in Jesus Christ in which we are formed and by which we are informed. They express obligations that are directly correlated with the values God has revealed and promised for the future of humankind in the victory of Jesus Christ. Thus, our decisions, however relative or imperfect, are, nonetheless, acts of anticipation as a witness to the hope within us.

We began the chapter with Luther's admonition to "sin boldly" as the superscript. It seems good to close with a brief summary of Dietrich Bonhoeffer's insightful comment on that famous statement. If we take Luther's statement as a *premise*, he wrote, it becomes a license for "cheap grace"—sin boldly, do as you please, God will forgive you. If, however, we see the statement as Luther did, as a *sum*, it looks very different. As a *sum* it indicates that, being sinners, even our best efforts in life's tangled circumstances will add up to sin, but at the same time God's gracious promise attends us and calls us to live boldly and with courage and trust in that assurance.[21]

Questions for Discussion

1. Can you give examples of decisions made in accord with consequentialism in people's personal lives and in public policy matters? How do you evaluate these decisions and the consequentialist approach when looked at through the lens of the love commandment?

2. Does the dialogical method offered in this chapter differ from the way you approach ethical decisions? If so, how? Try to be specific, and even use concrete examples to show how your approach has either been different or much the same.

3. Discuss the case of the pregnant woman with MS. How might you counsel her in her decision if she were to seek your counsel?

4. What are some of the examples of conflict resolution that people commonly face? Do you think this chapter is helpful for people of faith who face such tough choices? Why? Why not?

9

AUTONOMY

You shall have no other gods before me.

—Exodus 20:3

You shall not make for yourself an idol.

—Exodus 20:4

You shall not make wrongful use of the name of the LORD your God.

—Exodus 20:7

Remember the Sabbath day, and keep it holy.

—Exodus 20:8

Before we begin the formulation of the general rules of love based on the Ten Commandments, a word needs to be said as to why we are focusing on the Decalogue in particular. Certainly it is possible to draw from a much broader range of scriptural material as a basis for our general rules.

The first reason might be called a practical reason. Not only are the Ten Commandments prominent in the Bible, but in practice they are and have been prominent in the life of the church and the congregation. I refer, of course, to the place of the Ten Commandments in church catechisms, which have traditionally enjoyed a central place in Sunday school teaching, catechetical instruction, and adult education. Tapping into a major resource in the educational ministry of the church enables us to reinforce again our emphasis on congregational life as the seedbed of Christian ethics.

Closely associated with this practical concern is the further observation that the Ten Commandments also enjoy a relatively high visibility in cultures like our own that have developed under the influence of the Judeo-Christian tradition. Moreover, the substance of the commandments readily can be formulated in language familiar to ethical discourse beyond the context of religious ethics. Thus, working with the Ten Commandments enables us to build a conversational bridge to those in our society who are dealing with ethics in the framework of secular thought. In my formulation of general rules, I have tried to pay attention to this potential.

It is important to note that both these claims are disputed. Some would say that the Ten Commandments have lost much of their influence in our secular world, which believes itself emancipated from their quaint-sounding requirements. Others would claim that a similar loss of prominence has occurred in the life of the church itself. They point out that the Ten Commandments are a pre-Christian text that is out of step with moral life lived in the freedom of the gospel. This, together with the fact that the church is not immune to the influences of secular thinking, places the commandments in a position of rather questionable authority.[1]

Are these claims true? Have the commandments lost influence in our contemporary society and in much of the church? These are ultimately very speculative questions. One might view the practices of our society as indicators that the commandments have lost their force. Violence and sexual promiscuity not only appear to be a major part of life but are regularly portrayed in the media without explicit or even implied censure. Lying appears to be endemic. A search of the word "lying" on the Internet turns up an almost endless supply of references expressing concern for children's lying, corporate lying, government lying, lying in marketing, and media lying. We also have scientific studies to consult about physiological indicators of lying and even some sites to help one lie effectively and persuasively! The spirit of covetousness is readily fueled by the public celebration of greed and ostentation. Are these phenomena merely more evidence that people have broken the commandments from time immemorial, or do they signal that the tradition of the Decalogue has itself been tacitly rejected and the churches' moral grip on the ethos of society has weakened?

Recent efforts to have the Ten Commandments prominently displayed in public places have not only been the subject of court battles, but the significance of the commandments is also open to varied interpretation. Is this a sign that we are having a resurgence of moral concern in our supposedly secular world? Or, is it rather a desperate prophetic effort by the religious right to protest the morally corrosive forces of secularism inside and outside the church and, as such, a sign that we do have a problem?

Regardless of the interpretation one gives to this state of affairs as to the abiding influence of the Decalogue tradition, the matters dealt with in the commandments are matters of constant deliberation in our society and our world. They are matters of what it means to be fully human in humane community.[2]

Walter Harrelson has contended that we need to build upon the influence that the Decalogue and the Judeo-Christian understandings of Scripture already have in the society of most Western countries. "We should not underestimate the present impact within our lands of the Decalogue and of the religious understandings that produced it in ancient Israel," he says. "Already the secular members of the community are likely to give assent to the import of the set of prohibitions, when they are presented soundly and sensibly."[3]

Harrelson goes on to demonstrate that the commandments can be reformulated in terms readily understood in our contemporary world. He argues that such a newly devised list of prohibitions and obligations can be supplemented or correlated with the Universal Declaration of Human Rights adopted in 1948 by the United Nations. He calls upon the church to reaffirm the tradition of the commandments and to make these connections for the modern world.[4]

Harrelson's proposal that a bridge of understanding can be built between the biblical tradition of the commandments and the ethical sensibilities of modern society contains dangers about which Stanley Hauerwas has consistently warned. His concern is that the radical distinctiveness of what it means to be a Christian and the Christian ethic will be swallowed up by liberal humanism.[5] There is no doubt that history has shown that danger to be real and, if there is such a thing as a "Christian" ethic, it is first and foremost about the radical reality of life in Christ rather than merely a set of principles with which all reasonable people would agree. Nonetheless, with all due vigilance and devotion to the integrity of the faith, the Christian community seeks paths of dialogue that contribute to the common good in anticipation of the final good.[6]

In order to proceed along the path of Harrelson's proposal, then, we must ask how we understand the commandments as an integral part of the Christian ethic of love and as a powerful resource for the gospel witness of the people of anticipation. My own answer to that question forms the second set of reasons for choosing to work with the commandments. It is a theological rationale undergirding the practical reasons stated above.

First of all, the Ten Commandments in general and the first table of the Decalogue in particular reflect the basic commitment of faith as a way of life with God. This is the direction Luther took in his discussion of the First Commandment, which set the tone for his understanding of all the commandments. Luther points out that to have a God is nothing else than to trust and believe in that God with our whole heart. When this is understood and the heart is right with God, not only is the first commandment kept but the fulfillment of all others will follow of its own accord.[7] Thus, the commandments are a function of the trust of faith inspired by the grace of God.

Second, Harrelson helps us further by making the connection between the Decalogue and the commandment to love. He says, "The Decalogue is the negative counterpart of the commandment to love God and the neighbor, and both the negative and positive forms of the commandment are essential for human beings. Taken together, they sum up for Judaism and for Christianity what it means to belong to the family, the household of God."[8]

Finally, taken together in their positive and negative formulation, the commandments are an expression of love in its anticipation of the promised values of the reign of God.[9] In chapter 2 we observed that the good toward which love strives is understood in terms of the values promised in that ultimate future of God: life, wholeness, peace, equality among all, community, unity, joy, and freedom from bondage. The commandments as expressions of love, like the virtues that express love, orient us toward the anticipation of those values in the witness of our moral striving. In like manner, taken in the context of the promise we have in Jesus Christ, Paul Lehman sees the Decalogue as "paradigmatic for what God is doing in the world to make room for the freedom and fulfillment that being human takes."[10]

Terence Fretheim's reflections on the law of God in the Old Testament fit here as well. These laws "are a gracious gift of God for the sake of the life, health, and well-being of individuals in community." Citing Deuteronomy 5:33, he adds, "God gives the law in the service of life." Moreover, the law reflects the very trajectory of God's purposes in creation (to which I would add, God's purposes in the values of creation's fulfillment in the coming future): "Positively, the law is a means by which the divine ordering of chaos at the cosmic level is actualized in the social sphere and thereby brought into conformity with the creation that God intended. The law is given because God is concerned about *the best possible life* for *all* of God's creatures"[11]

In sum, the commandments fit into our lives as a people of anticipation. How that works in specific terms is the question now before us beginning with the ethical implications of the first table of the Decalogue cited in the verses at the start of this chapter.

The Image of God and Love for the Neighbor

By now the reader may be wondering how a discussion of the first table of the law is related to the title of this chapter, Autonomy. Do not these first several commandments deal with our relationship to God? Would not a requirement to respect the autonomy of persons refer instead to our relationship to our neighbor?

Certainly the straightforward meaning of the first table of the law deals with right relationship to God. But this relationship to God, which the commandments imply is fundamental to authentic human existence, is grounded itself in a biblical anthropology to which the commandments are related. When we look at what the Bible says about what it is to be human in the fullest sense, we not only see the background of what the first table of the Decalogue says regarding our relationship to God, we also gain some insight regarding our obligation in love to uphold the authentic humanity of our neighbor. Our obligation to the humanity of the neighbor, implied in the first table's reflection of biblical anthropology, will eventually lead us to assert a general rule of love respecting autonomy.

In the Bible and in the history of Christian thought, the understanding of what it is to be human is dealt with in the doctrine of the image of God. The biblical teaching that human beings are created in the image of God and the development of that idea in Christian tradition is a subject I dealt with in another book some years ago.[12] For our present purposes, I think we can summarize several of the key points of both the Old and New Testaments on the doctrine of the image of God.

1. The creation account in Genesis 1 tells us that humanity is a special creation. It is distinguished from all other living things by having an immediate relationship with God. This relationship we might well describe as personal. Humanity is "on speaking terms" with God, as George Forrell once put it. In the command to represent God in the care of the earth (Gen. 1:27), we see reflected the marks of personhood: freedom and responsibility. Responsibility is inconceivable without freedom, and freedom is inconceivable without responsibility.

2. However, humanity is not God but the *image of God.* Our being is dependent on God. We are not to find the meaning of our existence or the fulfillment of our existence either in nature or ourselves. To be God for oneself or to find the ultimate in other things is to rebel not only against God but also against our own true selves by stepping outside that intimate personal relationship with God that constitutes our very being. This betrayal of God and ourselves is the meaning of the fall story and the notion that underlies the all-encompassing sin of idolatry.

3. Although in sin we are alienated from our true being as image of God, God, through the redeeming work of Jesus Christ, seeks to perfect us, according to all the image implies. Indeed, our perfection in the image

of God is a promise of the resurrection when God's promise for the future is realized in all its fullness.[13]

Two things follow from this portrait of our humanity as created and redeemed in the image of God. First of all, the first table of the Decalogue, which commands that we have no other gods and that we spurn idolatry, respecting and upholding the name of God in worship, essentially commands us to be what we are: persons whose existence is constituted by an intimate relationship of personal communion with God. We remain in this relationship to God despite the alienating effects of sin because our fulfillment in this image is the promise of Christ's victory. The command to be what we are suggests the mandate to respect our neighbor's need to live authentically as well.

Second, and more specific, genuinely personal existence with God is characterized by freedom and responsibility. This is involved in our fundamental relationship to God and in our responsibility for the world and each other that God built into our creation in the image. This specific focus on our freedom and responsibility calls up the requirement that respect for other persons involves respect for their autonomy as integral to love's commitment to the good of the neighbor. The manner in which this is so should become clearer as we discuss this requirement.

Respect for Autonomy

Nora Helmer is a doll living in a doll's house that her husband, Torvald, maintains as their home. He calls her his "little lark," his "little squirrel." He heaps affection on her. He plays with her. In an unsurpassed attitude of male chauvinism, he gives her no credit for being intelligent, free, or responsible but, instead, controls her entire life as her father did before him. This is the picture with which we are presented in Henrik Ibsen's play *A Doll's House*. It is the story of Nora, who has been disenfranchised as a person and whose whole life revolves around pleasing Torvald.

As the play unfolds, the one thing Nora *has* done on her own initiative proves to be the turning point in their lives. Some time ago Nora had secretly borrowed from a moneylender of dubious reputation. Her purpose was to finance a trip to Italy that the doctor said was essential to Torvald's health. The holiday saved his life. Now Nora is about to make the last payment, and Torvald, in good health, will soon begin his new position as bank manager. Things look bright. That is, they do until the moneylender, Krogstad, gets into the act. Krogstad, who also works at Torvald's bank, learns that Torvald will be dismissing him and hiring Nora's friend Christine in his place. He attempts to blackmail Nora into interceding for him with Torvald by threatening that he will expose the fact that she has not only borrowed money from him but also forged her father's signature as cosigner on the note. When Nora's efforts to save Krogstad's job fail, he sends a letter revealing Nora's indiscretion to Torvald.

When Torvald reads the letter, he becomes angry with Nora because he fears for his own reputation and for the hold that Krogstad will have over him, compromising his position and authority at the bank. However, in the midst of his tirade, another letter arrives from Krogstad returning the loan note and repenting of his actions. Suddenly, everything is fine again, and immediately Torvald reverts to his former behavior, forgiving Nora and expressing his affections for her once more. With this sudden reversal of behavior, Nora realizes the true character of their life together and the emptiness of her own life. Torvald had failed to stand behind her and had thought only of his own problem. She was a plaything to him. As soon as things looked right again, Torvald wanted to resume that kind of relationship. It is then that Nora determines to leave him and the children in order to become a person in her own right.

She expresses the situation in these words: "Our home has been nothing but a games-room. I've been your doll-wife in exactly the same way as I used to be my father's doll-child. And the children have become my dolls, in their turn. I used to enjoy it when you played with me, just as they did when I played with them. That's what marriage has meant for us, Torvald." Torvald objects to her leaving by accusing her of renouncing her most sacred duties to husband and children. But Nora responds, "I have other duties just as sacred. My duties to myself."[14]

Philosophical discussions of the concept of autonomy and what is entailed in respect for autonomy are very complex, as one can imagine. I think, for our purposes, we can operate with a commonsense notion of autonomy in formulating our general rule of love to respect the autonomy of others. Respect for autonomy by our definition involves the respect for and protection of the freedom of other persons to make their own judgments and decisions, particularly in matters of morality, and to take responsibility for those judgments and decisions. In other words, in matters of moral consequence, we want to give each person the right to be his or her own person provided it does not harm others or deny others their own freedoms.

It is precisely respect for autonomy that Nora has been denied by Torvald and by her father before him. She seeks to acquire this sense of autonomy or being her own person by her drastic decision to leave both Torvald and the children. Radical as it may seem in the face of Torvald's protest that she is denying her responsibilities, she is so convinced that her life and their lives are empty and that she is nothing and, therefore, has nothing to give to them, that no other course of action seems possible. It might be interesting to debate whether or not Nora's response is morally justifiable. However, although the play suggests the ways in which respect for autonomy might be applied in family relationships, my primary purpose in using Ibsen's work is to illustrate the concern of respect for autonomy by providing a dramatic portrayal of its opposite in the life of Nora Helmer.

Respect for autonomy, then, can be further understood by yet another discussion of its opposite, *paternalism*, or, if we prefer a more inclusive term, *parentalism*. Paternalism or parentalism has been a concern for James Childress, a distinguished thinker in the field of biomedical ethics. Specifically, Childress addresses the paternalistic treatment of patients as an ethical problem in the practice of medicine. He tries to help us understand the situation of the patient in what one sociologist has called the "sick role."[15] Sick persons are understood to be victims of illness, usually through no fault of their own. In their debilitated circumstances, they are excused from many of the daily responsibilities that they would otherwise be expected to perform. Instead, they come under the care of health-care professionals who are characterized by competence, ability, skills, and authority. In this situation the patient is afflicted with an illness that is bad and the professional has the wherewithal, if restored health is possible, to give treatment that will restore that person to health, which is good. In this situation the patient as debilitated victim is easily seen as passive in the face of the competent professional who dictates the terms of the treatment for the patient's own good.[16] Thus, the relationship between patient and physician is likely to be characterized by the dictum, "The doctor knows best." This is a version of the old paternalistic formula, "Father knows best." And we are reminded again of Nora Helmer who, as they are preparing for a costume party, says to Torvald, "Torvald dear, won't you make up my mind for me and decide what I'm going to be and what I'm to wear?"[17] Torvald always knows best.

Childress is convinced that the relationship of the patient to the doctor and other health-care professionals is such that patients are vulnerable to a loss of autonomy, and health-care professionals are strongly tempted to exercise some form of parentalism in their treatment of patients. If patients are to be responsible participants in their own health care, we need continually to guard against the temptations of parentalism and lift up the responsibility to respect autonomy.

There has certainly been a growing awareness of this need in the medical profession. Respect for patient autonomy is clearly one of the obligations involved in the legal and moral insistence that physicians must obtain the free and informed consent of patients before they proceed with significant therapeutic measures or experimental procedures. In other words, patients should know what they are getting into before they give their consent. They need to know the risks and the benefits, the pain and the possibilities. These risks and benefits need to be explained in terms that the patient can understand so that the patient really knows what his or her decision involves and can make it in a genuinely uncoerced fashion. This legal and moral constraint institutionalizes the value of the person as person in the practice of medicine. It also points us in the direction of further interpretation of what respect for autonomy might mean in the general relationship that exists between the patient and his or her physician.

During the last few decades, there has been extensive discussion of the ethics of physician-patient relationships in the burgeoning literature of bio-medical ethics. To illustrate, we will look at an article written early on in this contemporary discussion by Robert M. Veatch. It provides a brief treatment of the matter that is helpful for our present purpose. The article is still discussed in current literature. Veatch approaches the subject with the presumption that in modern medicine health care has become a right. In order to preserve that right, all persons must be treated by the health-care profession equally with respect to their dignity, freedom, and individuality. He then asks which approaches to the patient-physician role relationship will serve this purpose. In answering that question, Veatch analyzes and critiques four different models for thinking about those roles.[18]

The first of these models is an engineering model in which the physician is styled as a pure scientist possessing some technical information and skills. It is then incumbent upon the doctor simply to provide the patient with the essential facts of the situation, free of any moral judgments or value consider-ations, and allow the patient to make all the decisions of any moral significance regarding his or her own treatment. While this view may purport to respect the autonomy of the patient in a very strict way, it is an unrealistic approach. It dehumanizes the physician by presuming falsely that a doctor can present medical facts in a value-free fashion and by assuming that the doctor's view of things is not a part of the decision-making dynamic confronting the patient. Preservation of patient autonomy does not require that the personal values of the physician are not a part of the discussion.

The next model is the priestly model. In this model the physician possesses an almost sacred authority in deciding what might be beneficial and what might be harmful to the patient. The notion of the physician in a priestly role, says Veatch, is a parent-child image as an analogy for the physician-patient relation-ship that has a long tradition in the literature of medical sociology. "It is this paternalism," he says, "in the realm of values which is represented in the moral slogan 'Benefit and do no harm to the patient.' It takes the locus of decision making away from the patient and places it in the hands of the professional."[19]

Neither the engineering nor the priestly models pay adequate attention to the protection of individual freedom or the preservation of individual dignity. Different models are needed to preserve and enhance those values and to promote respect for autonomy.

Some have suggested that a collegial model would be more helpful. In such a model the patient and the physician understand themselves as equal partners in the treatment of illness and the restoration of health. They are colleagues, collaborating on a mutually agreed upon course of action. In this way the moral integrity of the physician comes into play as it does not in the engineering model, and the autonomy of the patient is preserved as it is not in the priestly model. However, Veatch observes that this is a rather idealistic and unrealistic approach to what we might reasonably expect in most physician-patient relationships. There is no reason to assume in many cases that there is the kind of mutuality and common set of goals between the physician and patient that would be necessary for this model to really work. Differences in cultural background, class, and personal values make this model impossible to commend as a general rule.

A more realistic approach is found in the final model Veatch recommends, the contractual model. In the contractual model the physician and patient enter into a covenant in which it is intended that, despite their possible differences, both the patient and the physician will retain their moral integrity, freedom, and responsibility to the benefit of each. "With the contractual relationship there is a sharing in which the physician recognizes that the patient must maintain freedom of conscience over his or her own life and destiny when significant choices are to be made. Should the physician not be able to live with his or her conscience under those terms the contract is not made or is broken."[20] In this model there is a real sharing of decision making without either party being required to sacrifice integrity or autonomy.

It is worth noting that Veatch's contractual model has been received with both appreciation and criticism. One of the major criticisms made is that the contractual model is a bit cut and dried. Some view it as a transaction not necessarily involving the building and nurturing of a relationship between patient and physician that is important to the multidimensional nature of healing. William May has offered the biblically based notion of "covenant" as having all the benefits of the contractual model in the protection of patient autonomy, but it is richer in the relational dimension.[21] Howard Brody proposes a "deliberative" model as an alternative to the contractual model. In the deliberative model, the physician is also a teacher and friend trying to help the patient sort out values and choices in advance of decisions on a plan of care. This is then supplemented by the consideration of the virtues physicians need to cultivate, reminding us, as I have stated in part 2 of this book, that virtues underlie the application of principles and rules in the act of decision.[22]

Greater detail would be required to fully elaborate Veatch's recommendation for the contractual model and the alternatives proposed. However, to stay with Veatch for the sake of illustration, we can safely say that the outline of his concern is clear enough for us to understand what he intends. Without suggesting that Veatch is self-consciously operating with the kind of moral reasoning we are discussing here, it seems appropriate to say that he has provided us with a good example of direct interpretation of our general rule of obligation in love to respect the autonomy of others. As we look at Veatch's discussion, we see him bringing the concern for autonomy into dialogue with the specific situation of physician-patient relationships. He attempts to ascertain the relevant facts and to ask the question; "What's going on here?" The end product of that dialogue is to commend a specific interpretation of how respect for autonomy might best be implemented in situations of this kind. In this instance, direct interpretation involves the analysis of role relationships and results in a specific recommendation for the kind of role relationship that should prevail. Because Veatch does not operate with a specific case or cases, his discussion is abstract and his conclusion is general guidance rather than a recommendation for specific action. Most often, direct interpretation is a dialogical process that happens in concrete situations. A real-life story will give us further insight into the direct interpretation of respect for autonomy.

One of the most frequently cited cases in the literature of biomedical ethics is the case of Donald C., a burn victim. Childress discusses this case in his treatment of autonomy and paternalism. I first encountered the case in an article by Robert B. White,[23] and later saw the videotaped interview with Donald C. He was an active young man who had been a jet pilot in military service and an athlete who loved sports and the outdoors, particularly rodeos, in which he often performed. The world of this active, competent, and independent young man went up in flames when he and his father started up their car near a leaking propane gas line. The ensuing explosion set the whole area on fire, killed his father, and sent Donald to the hospital with second- and third-degree burns over 68 percent of his body. Most of his burns were third-degree burns. His eyes were blinded by corneal damage, his ears were mostly destroyed. He suffered severe burns to his face, upper extremities, body, and legs. For months, Donald underwent repeated skin grafting, treatment of his eyes, and amputation of portions of his fingers on both hands. To control infection in many areas of his body and keep him alive, he had to be bathed daily in what is called a Hubbard tank. The process of tanking, which included removal of dressings, was excruciating.

From the time of the accident onward, Donald insisted that he did not want to live any longer. However, he did accept treatment until, finally, he refused to give permission for further corrective surgery on his hands and insisted that he be allowed to go home and die. Nonetheless, the tankings continued, despite his protests.

His mother found his demands very upsetting. She feared for his well-being; she found the idea of bringing him home to die with puss-covered sores on his body more than she could bear. She also feared for his spiritual life because he had left the church some time ago. It was at this juncture that Robert B. White was asked to see Donald as a psychiatric consultant.

As White tells it, his first reaction was one of sympathy for Donald and his desire to refuse further life-sustaining treatment. He thought that he might wish the very same thing if he were in Donald's position. He found him coherent and competent to participate in decisions about his own life. He recognized that respect for Donald's autonomy was at issue in considering his right to refuse further treatment. And that issue was all the more vexing because it was clear that Donald would survive if he continued treatment, albeit in a highly debilitated state. This was yet one more incidence of how the marvels of modern medicine are able to keep people alive under dire and undesirable circumstances. Had Donald had his accident earlier in history, he never would have survived to face this decision.

White decided, first of all, that he would assist Donald in seeking legal counsel and subsequently had a number of sessions with Donald and his attorney. The upshot was that the attorney finally agreed, reluctantly, to represent Donald's wishes in court. However, White also confronted Donald with the decision that he and the other doctors involved would not immediately agree to his demands to leave the hospital and die. He could not expect the doctors to participate in his suicide. Moreover, he reminded Donald of the unfair burden that his going home would place upon his mother. For this reason he arranged that Donald could remain in the hospital without further life-sustaining treatment if the court agreed to his petition. He would be kept as free of pain as possible and allowed to die.

With these decisions in place, Donald apparently felt that he had won his case and suddenly decided to continue treatment. He went forward with the surgery on his hands and remained in the hospital for five more months before returning home. Donald regained a considerable measure of self-sufficiency and, seemingly, a new lease on life. His decision confirmed White's initial intuition that the demand to die was the only way that Donald could regain his sense of independence and self-determination. Once that was possible, it was also possible that Donald would want to live.[24]

White's dialogue between the rule of respect for autonomy and the situation at hand is an excellent example of direct interpretation under very difficult circumstances. He artfully perceived that what Donald needed most was to regain autonomy—the freedom to decide for himself—but also that he needed to responsibly respect the needs and rights of his doctors and his mother. Thus, White showed respect for Donald's autonomy not only in giving him the legal recourse to take charge of his life but also in reminding him of his responsibility to others. His intuitive sense that Donald would choose life if a measure of autonomy were restored is a prime illustration of the need to interpret what is going on in the lives of the people with whom you are interacting and the facts as they present them.

Notwithstanding the apparent success of White's response in this case, we are not left without questions. Some may wish to argue that other obligations of love on the part of the health-care team to preserve his life may have been in conflict with their respect for Donald's autonomy. In that analysis we would be engaged in a dialogue of resolving conflict between competing obligations to Donald and competing claims: Donald's claim to self-determination and the doctors' claim to their obligation to preserve life. Others may argue that, although Donald's initial demand to die was free and coherent, it may not have been an authentic expression of his true orientation to life, given what we knew of his convictions.[25] If such were the interpretation, autonomy might best have been served by refusing any cooperation, at least at first, and forcing him to explore his motives and desires more deeply and responsibly. There is some evidence that White attempted to do this. In any case, it might have turned out differently for White and Donald. He may have chosen to die after all. Thus, White had to proceed with a measure of uncertainty and risk. This further illustrates my earlier observations about the ambiguity of decision and, from a Christian view, the need to operate in the freedom of the gospel to "sin boldly" or make ambiguous decisions with courage and confidence. Perhaps we also need further reflections on the idea of autonomy before we close.

Autonomy and Christian Conscience

We have sampled Childress's defense of autonomy against its potential abuses in the practice of medicine. However, elsewhere Childress has written a caution to the effect that a Christian account of autonomy will need to be severely limited by a number of other factors. Christians recognize that people are both finite and sinful. They are conditioned by experience and culture. They are limited in their capacity to reason and often do not act rationally. The natural egocentricity of our sinful nature can easily distort the concept of autonomy and turn it into a form of selfishness in an independent nature that is insensitive to the needs of others. Thus, Childress says, the principle of autonomy must be constantly placed under the criticism of the New Testament norm of love.[26]

This caution underscores the need to keep in mind that the obligation to respect autonomy with which we are working here is an obligation of love that finds its place among the other obligations of love to respect the needs of our neighbors. Thus, not all behavior is acceptable simply because we invoke a claim to our autonomy. While we may be sympathetic to Nora Helmer's plight as Ibsen presents her extreme state of affairs, the play reminds us of the many broken marriages that occur because one partner feels that her or his personal freedom and self-development have not been well served. There is no denying that the complaint is often valid. Undoubtedly, spouses have failed in not respecting their partners' autonomy as persons. But the freedom for self-development they desire is also a freedom balanced with responsibility to the marriage covenant and to the needs of the family. It is a responsibility to examine one's own motives and reasoning and to examine the ways in which counseling and communication may help improve the relationship and preserve the covenant. It is a responsibility that requires the virtue of truthfulness or honesty that we discussed in our previous section. Consequently, it is important not only to lift up the obligation of love to respect the autonomy of others, but it is also important for those who claim that respect to examine the basis of their claim in light of their own motives and their own obligations to those around them. This is precisely what White forced Donald to do in his attempt to respect Donald's autonomy by not only enabling his freedom to decide but also by reminding him of his responsibility to others in that decision.

I have argued that our creation in the image of God is a biblical and theological doctrine that provides us with a basis for love's obligation to the autonomy of each person. At the same time, in the biblical story of the fall, original sin is depicted as humanity's decision to step outside the dependent character of that existence in the image of God. That is, Adam and Eve chose to be *autonomous* in its literal meaning of being a law unto oneself. The serpent beguiled them into thinking that they could be as gods if they ate from the forbidden fruit. They could be independent instead of being merely the *image* of the divine. Thus humanity's sin is understood in terms of a distorted view of autonomy with its denial of the dependent relationship implied in our creation as image of God. In this way a theological and biblical warning is built into the theological and biblical basis for love's obligation to respect autonomy.

Similar thoughts are possible when we consider the concept of Christian conscience as it has been developed throughout the tradition. Conscience is akin to the notion of autonomy in that it presumes a sense of moral responsibility that comes from relationship with God. Therefore, tradition has always asserted that one should not be forced to act or act against one's conscience. We should respect the consciences of others, and we should respect our own conscience even as we respect the autonomy of others and affirm autonomy for ourselves. But Christian tradition has also been equally clear that conscience can err. This is true of Christian conscience as well as the conscience of non-Christian or nonreligious people, who also have a right to conscience even as they have a right to autonomy.

The danger of a distorted view of autonomy or an erring conscience brings us back to the need for the community of the church as a place where faith, formation, and decision are shaped and clarified in the light of the promise. Here the obligation to respect autonomy is clarified in the understanding of sin and grace. Here the conscience may be educated as the people of God gather around word and sacrament to discern the meaning of their faith for practical living and as a witness to the world. Here the power of God's grace is at work. Here we discover that the obligations of love and the human good sought by love are neither laws imposed from outside by a dictatorial god nor the products of our own subjectivity but are instead insights, urges, and impulses that grow naturally with the growing intimacy between God and ourselves, which our merciful and promising God enables out of divine love for us.

In the final analysis, the doctrine of the image of God, which we have viewed as a resource for understanding the worth and dignity of each individual, is also a doctrine that teaches us that we are created for community with God and each other. This recalls a point made in chapter 5. There I spoke of how theologians have helped us see that the unity and harmony among the persons of the Trinity are a pattern for our understanding and living out of our creation in the image of the triune God. The fact that we are constituted both in individuality and in community presents us with an ongoing challenge to moral discernment: we can neither abrogate the rights of the individual nor undermine the good of community. This twin danger of distortion is present in most of our moral deliberations. It is certainly a matter at the very heart of our concern for justice to which we now turn in the next chapter.

Questions for Discussion

1. Think back on what you have been taught about the Ten Commandments or what you have thought about them. Have you understood them to be a part of God's loving purpose for our good or simply a list of prohibitions that finally condemn us? What difference does it make to see the commandments as related to the promised values of God's future?

2. What new ideas about the "image of God" arise from the discussion in this chapter? Why do you think it is an important doctrine for Christian ethics?

3. Most, if not all of us, have had a variety of experiences in physician-patient relationships, our own or that of loved ones we have attended. Can you characterize those experiences in terms of the various models proposed by Veatch and others? What difference did the approach taken make in care for the patient?

   Are there times when you think that patient autonomy may need to be compromised or rethought in the interests of the best possible medical care? What specific conditions might require this?

10

JUSTICE

Honor your father and your mother, so that your days may be long in the land that the LORD your God is giving you.

—Exodus 20:12

You shall not steal.

—Exodus 20:15

We have already discussed the link between love and justice and looked at it in several different ways. It is now time to take that connection a step further by asserting that justice may be considered a general rule of love, embodying love's drive toward equality and freedom as values that express the ultimate good of God's promised future reign. In considering the command of love to practice justice, we focus in this chapter on justice as *a rule of social order* designed to maximize freedom and equality for all.

> [Y]ou cannot play off justice and love against one another. God's justice is his love in action, to right the wrongs of his suffering world by taking their weight upon himself. God's love is the driving force of his justice, so that it can never be a blind or arbitrary thing, a cold system, which somehow God operates, or which operates him.[1]

As we look at the way in which the commandment to honor our parents illumines our understanding of love's commitment to justice, I would like to follow for a while the discussion of this commandment in Jan Milic Lochman's work. Lochman makes the point that the purpose of all the divine commandments is to give order to the fundamental concerns of human life. Within the framework of that purpose, this commandment presents the family as a basic model for human society and includes in its implications the order of human society as a whole.[2] This reading is consistent with interpretations traditionally given to this commandment in a variety of catechisms, which expand the scope of the commandment's meaning to include a respect for not simply parents but other figures in authority who provide for the common good through that authority.

According to God's loving design, order in society exists to protect and promote the freedom of all and the fullness of life in a community of love for all. Lochman arrives at this conclusion by considering the fact that, first of all, the commandments in general were established in the context of God's liberating deliverance in the exodus of the people of Israel from captivity in Egypt. They exist to govern the people's lives in accordance with God's liberating purpose to make of Israel a free people under God rather than a slave people under the Pharaoh. Second, the promise associated with this commandment for long years of life emphasizes God's loving purpose that all should have fullness of life in that new society born of divine love. This life is, in Lochman's mind, an anticipation of the ultimate life of perfect community with God and each other in love revealed as the promise for the future in the triumph of Jesus Christ.[3] From this we may readily infer that that life in freedom and the communion of love involves the equal dignity of all persons, which agape love entails and God's future promises. Though the commandment clearly intends a specific focus on parents and family life, this broader focus on a just society, ordered for freedom and equality in the interest of the fullness of life, is surely intended as well.

The commandment against stealing adds further depth and texture to our understanding of love's concern for justice, particularly when we set it in the framework of the Bible's general witness to God's concern for the well-being of the poor. Certainly, the commandment forbids simple theft of property. However, scholars are agreed that this narrow interpretation is too limiting and can even be utilized in a distorted way by the rich to insist on the protection of their property and their right to amass wealth at whatever cost to the poor of society.[4]

The emphasis of the commandment in the biblical ethos is not on the protection of property but on the protection of persons. Its concern is that property be used for the well-being of all. People must be understood as more important than property. The commandment targets those who amass wealth by unjust means and therefore oppress the poor. To the extent that the wealthy make victims out of those with lesser means, they diminish the dignity, opportunity, and freedom of those who have little. Just as a theft can destroy the well-being of an individual or a family by depriving them of something vital to their lives, so the manipulation of the economic system for unjust gains can damage the common good. "The commandment not to steal means, in effect, that persons are not to whittle down, eat away at, the selfhood of individuals or of families or communities."[5]

We have already encountered in our discussion of the beatitude on mercy (Matt. 5:7) some indication of how divine justice is understood in terms of God's merciful concern for the needs of all people. In the eyes of God, justice is done when mercy reaches out to people in their need. We gave an illustration of that in the biblical provision of the jubilee laws, which, at least symbolically, expressed God's concern that those captive to economic disaster might find freedom and renewed opportunity to meet the basic needs of life.

One Old Testament scholar has offered the following summary of the Old Testament perspective on this commandment in terms of the jubilee laws and other provisions of Israelite society:

> Consideration of Israel's legislation concerning simple theft, loans, slaves, gleaning, and tithing reflect the strong concern with human need. Unlike neighboring cultures Israel tended to place the priority on people rather than property. Legislation frequently provided for the restoration of status, people received their freedom after debt slavery, and property returned to its original owner. In this way the egalitarian nature of society was maintained.[6]

As we saw in our discussion of poverty of spirit, this concern for the poor in the Old Testament is echoed by the teachings of Jesus. The prophet's concern for the poor and the captive, as expressed in Isaiah 61, forms the backdrop of Jesus' teaching of the beatitude on poverty of spirit (Matt. 5:3) as well as being the text he chose for the inauguration of his public ministry in Luke 4. The ideal of concern for the needs of all people is perhaps most concisely expressed for the New Testament ethos in 1 John 3:17, "How does God's love abide in anyone who has the world's goods and sees a brother or sister in need and yet refuses help?"[7]

To summarize, our brief consideration of these two commandments and their biblical background reveals once again God's concern for justice as a merciful concern for the needs of all people. Justice as a general rule of love seeks a social order that is designed to maximize freedom and equality as the universal obligation of society to the well-being of each of its members. Though justice is not mentioned specifically in the texts of the Decalogue, it is by no means absent; it underlies all that the commandments point to in their concern to safeguard the humanity of all in this world of God's creation.[8] This egalitarian vision of justice is consistent with the universal outlook of agape love as I discussed in chapter 4.

In a sense, the Bible and Christian tradition do not take us beyond that point. They do not provide a specific system of justice for a situation of limited resources and competing claims and for a world in which people are inclined to injustice for their own gain. The implementation of justice requires further deliberation in practice. We had a hint of this in our discussion in chapter 5 of how equal worth and equal opportunity need to be complemented by special efforts to ensure equal outcomes in order to provide a truly just state of affairs.

Along this same line, Lochman, in his discussion of how the second table of the Decalogue is designed to give order to human life, stresses the fact that, while God gives us direction, God does not establish a specific social order but ordains that all social orders exist to serve divine justice in its concern for freedom and equality. Thus, with regard to the implications of the commandment to honor parents for the social order as a whole, he says:

> This means that if a specific form of human life in society, in marriage and the family (and even in the wider community and society as a whole) contradicts the fundamental concern of the Decalogue with human liberation—if, for example, one group, one sex, one generation is oppressed by another (and how often this is the case in the history of civilization and the church)—then this structure can never be justified by appeal to the divine commandment. On the contrary, it must be changed.[9]

What we have, then, in the biblical foundations of love's commitment to justice and in terms of our developing theory of dialogical ethics, is another example of a general rule that needs to be interpreted in dialogue with the situation. The dialogue in this case involves the struggle to deal with the various competing and conflicting claims that arise within society as we work to maintain the maximum of freedom and equality for all people. The task of working this out comes under what ethicists refer to as distributive justice. People have proposed a number of competing theories for how we justly distribute the goods of life in society with respect to the rights and needs of every person. This is a very complex discussion involving a special set of terms and definitions along with fine distinctions and elaborate argumentation. It is an area of discussion involving the expertise of ethicists, philosophers, economists, political scientists, and others. Obviously, we do not have the space in this kind of book to cover all this ground. However, we can look at three particular issues of justice in our time that I hope will shed further light on the connection between love and justice and on the workings of dialogical ethics as Christians become involved in justice decisions.

Justice, Love, and the Delivery of Health Care

During the 1960s and into the early '70s, it seemed certain that Congress would enact some form of national health-care insurance. A number of different proposals were in circulation and the battle lines were drawn between those who advocated such a national health-care system and those who feared socialized medicine. However, it seems that two developments combined to stall progress toward national health insurance. The first of these developments was the recognition that Medicare was costing the American public far more than many believed we could afford. Unless there could be serious containment of constantly rising medical costs, it was hard to see, some argued, how we could continue with Medicare and Medicaid, let alone extend national health insurance coverage to all people in our society.

Worry over the prohibitive costs of national health insurance then paved the way for the second development, a shift of focus to preventive health care. In the '70s and '80s the federal government shifted its efforts away from consideration of a national health-care policy to the encouragement of preventive measures designed to improve the health of the general public. As a result, we have seen and continue to see campaigns against smoking, alcohol, drugs, cholesterol, and various practices that adversely affect the health of many Americans, including more recent concerns over the growing problem of obesity. Coupled with these efforts were government programs to improve fitness, highway safety, and more responsible prenatal care.

No one can gainsay the value of such preventive health maintenance measures, and, clearly, the benefits of such programs to the national health are of considerable value. Historically, the greatest progress against morbidity and mortality has been the result of public health measures. Nonetheless, the cost of health care has continued to rise, and large numbers in our society find themselves at a disadvantage in gaining access to needed care. Businesses and institutions increasingly find that they can no longer afford to provide health insurance or at least not at a desirable level of coverage. The estimated forty to forty-three million people in the United States without health insurance underscores the fact that we have a great deal of unfinished business. Therefore, despite the failure of efforts to establish a national health-care policy early in the first Clinton administration, the issue of national health insurance or a national health-care policy to provide coverage for all people is not yet dead.

Daniel Callahan, a highly respected thinker in the field of ethics and medicine, has argued that we will never provide adequate basic health care for all Americans unless we are ready to set limits. Individual consumers of medicine and much of the medical profession itself are greedy for health care and more and more medical science, respectively. If we set no limits on what individuals can or ought to consume and what medical science can or ought to pursue, we will be unable to serve the needs of all. There is only so much in the way of medical resources to be distributed and developed, given the fact that other necessary social goods compete for the resources required. Thus, the question of the freedom of individuals and professions to go after as much as they can in medical care and research is in tension with the basic needs of the whole community.[10] As a result, mortality and morbidity rates in the United States are not nearly as good as those of other developed countries that spend a great deal less on health care per person but cover all persons.[11] The advent of "managed care" has demonstrated that there are more efficient and cost-effective ways to deliver health care. However, the savings are not being invested in decreasing the numbers of uninsured.

Health care is surely one of the essential goods of human life, and the manner in which it is made available to people in a society is definitely an issue of distributive justice.

Ethicists Tom Beauchamp and James Childress have identified a *formal* principle of distributive justice attributed to Aristotle as common to all theories of justice: equals ought to be treated equally and unequals unequally. The principle is formal, they explain, "because it states no particular respects in which equals ought to be treated the same. It only says that no matter what respects are under consideration, if persons are equal in those respects, then they must be treated equally. More fully stated in negative form, the principle says that no person should be treated unequally, despite all differences with other persons, unless it has been shown that there is a difference between them relevant to the treatment at stake."[12]

Since the formal principle is abstract and difficult to understand and work with in that form, Beauchamp and Childress explain that material principles are needed to specify the relevant respects in terms of which people are to be treated equally or unequally. Material principles stipulate the basis on which the good should be distributed equally or unequally as the case may be. Debate over which material principles are valid is where most arguments about competing theories of distributive justice arise.[13] Here is a list of material principles commonly advocated:

1. To each according to merit or desert.
2. To each according to societal contribution.
3. To each according to ability to pay.
4. To each according to need.

Beauchamp and Childress further explain that theories of distributive justice are commonly developed by systematically elaborating one or more of these material principles, often in conjunction with other moral principles believed to provide the needed support or foundation.[14] That is, indeed, what we will be doing here, at least in part. We will examine the material principles listed above as they relate to justice in the distribution of health care in the light of our moral principle of agape love in order to determine which of these material principles finds the most support in the principle of agape. In this way, we further exemplify the connection between love and justice.

Material Criteria and Distributive Justice

Some years ago I was a faculty member team-teaching an inter-professional course on social values at Ohio State University. The class brought together students and faculty from various helping professions, including law, medicine, nursing, education, and those preparing for ministry. In one particular session, the discussion turned into a debate over national health-care insurance. Those who opposed the idea cited first the cost of such a project. However, the discussion soon turned to the question of whether or not it was fair for the public to pay insurance costs covering the health care of those who were in some way responsible for their own health problems. A number of the class members argued that it was unjust to tax everyone in order to pay the high costs of illnesses associated with smoking, alcohol, drug abuse, and other irresponsible behaviors. In addition, some contended that we should not be forced to pay for injuries sustained by motorcyclists who refuse to wear helmets or drivers who refuse to use their seat belts. Since that time I have heard this kind of commentary in a variety of forums. The issue of covering AIDS patients whose problems were brought on by high-risk behavior has been added to the list. As the knowledge of how self care or the lack of it contributes to disease and disability, the opportunities for blaming the victims increase. We already have met this question in chapter 6 in our discussion of attitudes toward persons with HIV/AIDS and the homeless.

The kind of objections raised in that class and others since are arguments that the benefits of health care should be allocated according to the first material principle of distributive justice listed above: to each according to merit or desert. Leaving aside for the moment the fact that we are already paying for these cases through our private health insurance premiums, the argument seems to have a certain compelling logic as an argument for justice.

Yale ethicist Gene Outka wrote an important article at the height of the national health policy debate, commenting on this approach to justice in the delivery of health care and the other material principles listed above as well.

Outka's purpose was to look at these principles in the light of agape love and ask what guidance that provides in our choice of an approach to national health care.[15] As we pursue this issue, I will draw upon Outka's article, which remains pertinent to the discussion today.

Outka acknowledges that the distribution of the good according to merit may be appropriate in many situations. For example, those who work hard and excel on the job deserve promotion and higher pay. Similarly, students who excel in their schoolwork are worthy of their high grades and academic honors. This is not necessarily incompatible with agape love in these restricted cases. However, in the case of health care, Outka rejects the criterion of merit for the distribution of the good.

To begin with, he considers the process of distinguishing between those deserving of treatment and those undeserving to be highly impractical in the context of medical crises. Although we might adopt partial measures such as taxing alcohol and tobacco and allocating those funds for health-care services, this is a somewhat arbitrary and inadequate measure. In the end, health crises are not issues of merit or desert. They happen often for reasons beyond our control and our ability to predict. "They frequently fall without discrimination on (according-to-merit) just and unjust, i.e., the virtuous and the wicked, the industrious and the slothful alike."[16]

One may also infer from Outka's argument that it is virtually impossible to determine in every case the extent to which we are responsible for our own health problems. As an example of our uncertainty in this regard, we might cite illnesses related to alcohol abuse. While I do not wish to debate the issue, alcoholism and other forms of chemical dependency are now commonly regarded by many health-care professionals as themselves being a disease rather than a simple matter of moral weakness, as they were once considered to be. Furthermore, speculation and research on genetic predispositions to alcoholism and other health problems continues to increase. This does not eliminate responsibility for self care, but it forces us to rethink past judgments as more evidence accumulates.

The criteria of societal contribution and ability to pay suffer a similar fate under Outka's critical scrutiny. Discriminating between relative values of social contribution among persons is notoriously subjective. Access to health care simply on the basis of ability to pay turns health care into a mere commodity sold by physicians at the going rate. This view has a number of problems associated with it, not the least of which is the intuitive sense we have that the urgency of dealing with a health crisis is in a different category from shopping for other goods and services, most of which might be considered options.

To Each according to Need

In all the three material principles mentioned thus far, the most telling argument that Outka makes from the standpoint of agape love is that all of those criteria operate by discriminating between people according to certain characteristics they possess. When it comes to the essential needs of human life, agape is universal in its outreach and regards all as equally the object of its concern and ministrations. It does not stop to ask regarding merit, social contribution, or ability to pay in its response to basic human need. For this reason Outka settles on "to each according to need" as that material principle of distributive justice most compatible with *agape*'s outlook when the benefits of health care are the issue.[17]

In my earlier discussion of *agape*, I took note of its universal outlook in meeting the needs of all people regardless of any qualities they may or may not possess. If we accept the analysis Outka offers and conclude that agape is most compatible with the equalitarian principle of each according to need in the area of health care, then two further observations are in order. First, love's rule of justice when brought into dialogue with a question of equal access to health care in our society has led us to the creation of what might be termed a *middle axiom;* a middle axiom, we recall, is a rule of ethics to cover the middle ground between a general principle or rule, on the one hand, and a specific and detailed policy on the other hand. To assert that justice in the delivery of health care should be according to the principle of each according to need is more specific than our general rule of justice, which guarantees love's commitment to equality, and less specific than a policy proposal, such as some form of national health insurance, whereby we implement our concern for equality in access to health care.

The second observation that follows, then, is that in applying the middle axiom of "to each according to need" in the delivery of health care, many policy options need to be considered. Is our ethical commitment in this regard best achieved by some form of national health insurance? If so, what kind of structure or system needs to be established in the most effective way possible to accomplish this goal? To establish genuinely equal access to health care will it be a practical necessity to define what is "fundamental health care" that all people ought to be guaranteed and to recognize thereby that some forms of medical service are simply too costly to guarantee for the whole population? These and other related questions constitute the hard work of fulfilling justice in this area of human concern. Practical limitations may require a variety of compromises in the process. However, I contend that it makes a difference to the moral health of society if we begin with the equalitarian principle of each according to need rather than refusing to deal creatively with that need because the practical problems of cost and implementation are too difficult for us to entertain.

Justice in Economic Life

Issues in the just delivery of health care are but one perplexing instance of justice in economic life. Plenty of hard work is needed to resolve the inequities of life between rich and poor, and many of the measures proposed are certainly painful for the prosperous and the near-prosperous. We are reminded of the main thesis of one of Reinhold Niebuhr's best-known books, *Moral Man and Immoral Society*. While morally sensitive individuals may be moved to consider the needs of others as well as their own, this is "difficult if not impossible for human societies and social groups."[18] In my own work, I have spoken of how those who benefit from an economic system generally have the economically based power to sustain that system against changes that would be to their disadvantage.[19]

Indeed, in the area of economic life our difficulty in securing justice is in large measure due to the fact that economic and political systems frequently bring freedom and equality, the two goals of justice, into conflict with one another.[20] Modern capitalism stresses the freedom of individuals to acquire wealth by legitimate means in the free market for goods and services. But this freedom also leads to severe inequities within society and among nations because many cannot compete on an equal footing due to various disadvantages not entirely within their control. Socialist solutions, at least in theory, have attempted to equalize wealth but often do so at considerable cost to freedom. Furthermore, in the absence of incentives that freedom provides, restrictive socialist economies have struggled to grow and provide the jobs they were supposed to guarantee. However, the classic battle between capitalism and socialism is now a thing of the past. The success of capitalist economies has all but driven the socialist alternative out of existence. Nevertheless, the question of individual freedom and the common good remains.

How can a biblical notion of justice as loving concern for the needs of all people pursue both freedom and equality in the economic life? At bottom I am convinced that this is first of all a matter of moral commitment to the vision of God's justice as concern for the poor, and second, that the agape love we are called to live dictates that the limits of personal freedom and ambition are set by the needs of our neighbors. Christians, who are the recipients of God's rich and undeserved love, are called to embody a sharing spirit and work toward a sharing society.[21] Reflecting on Acts 4:32-35 and 5:1-12, Daniel Maguire sees an enduring message in this account. The nub of this perspective is that *"poverty must be eliminated by appropriate modes of sharing, and the burden of ending poverty falls on the economically secure."*[22] However, while the virtues of Christian love must underlie and inform our approach to the question of balancing freedom and equality for the sake of justice, further direction is needed as a guide to advocacy and action.

One noteworthy effort in our time is the lengthy proposal made by the Catholic bishops of the United States in 1986.[23] The pastoral letter produced by the bishops is paralleled by similar attempts to make statements on economic justice on the part of other church bodies or ecumenical groups. However, none is quite as extensive as this document and none has received as much public attention and discussion. We cannot undertake here a discussion of all its parts or even a general criticism of its basic approach. There is considerable published commentary on the pastoral letter that attempts to do this.[24] We shall have to content ourselves with lifting out a few features of the document that fit into the present discussion.

The section on "Ethical Norms for Economic Life" begins with the affirmation of the love commandment as the true foundation for human community and community with God. Recognizing that the fullness of love and community is ultimately a hope for the fullness of God's future reign, the bishops nonetheless assert that we are committed to pursue justice as an expression of that love and community that are both commanded and promised.

Biblical justice is the goal for which we strive. This rich biblical understanding portrays a just society as one marked by the fullness of love, compassion, holiness, and peace. On their path through history, however, sinful human beings need more specific guidance on how to move toward the realization of this great vision of God's kingdom. This guidance is contained in the norms of basic or minimal justice. These norms state the minimum levels of mutual care and respect that all persons owe to each other in an imperfect world.[25]

Basic justice, emphasizing respect for the equal dignity and freedom of all persons, can be described as an instrument of love in an imperfect world. Basic justice is concerned with basic human concerns, including fair economic transactions and contracts, the meeting of basic material needs of life, and full participation in society.[26] When the bishops take this notion of basic justice and apply it to the current economic situation in our society and world, they come up with further and somewhat more specific statements of obligation, which I would consider to be in the nature of middle axioms, although the document itself does not use that designation.

The moral norms or middle axioms needed in a Christian vision of economic justice, as the bishops see it, might be condensed for our purposes in the following way, with basic justice understood to require:[27]

1. *Minimal levels of participation in the life of the human community for all persons.* This requirement draws special attention to overcoming the exclusion and powerlessness of the poor, the disabled, and the unemployed within society. On the international level, similar efforts must be made to correct the exclusion of least-developed nations from full participation in the economic order.

2. *The protection of human rights for all.* These rights include freedom of speech, worship, and assembly, as well as rights to life, food, clothing, shelter, rest, medical care, and basic education.

3. *The urgent needs of the poor are such that the meeting of those needs should have the highest priority.* "Personal decisions, policies of private and public bodies, and power relationships must all be evaluated by their effects on those who lack the minimum necessities of nutrition, housing, education, and health care. In particular, this principle recognizes that meeting fundamental human needs must come before the fulfillment of desires for luxury consumer goods, for profits not conducive to the common good, and for unnecessary military hardware."

4. *Economic and social policies—along with the organization of the work world—should be continually evaluated in light of their impact on the strength and stability of family life.*

The concern throughout this discussion is to ensure human dignity through economic justice, recognizing that physical, spiritual, and family well-being are tied directly to economic viability. Although these statements and the extensive commentary they are given in the actual document may suggest to some a policy bias on the part of the bishops, the bishops clearly intend for their remarks to be middle axioms. "These priorities are not policies. They are norms that should guide the economic choices of all and shape economic institutions. They can help the United States move forward to fulfill the duties of justice and protect economic rights."[28] To use our language, the bishops have carried the dialogue between the general rule of biblical justice and the economic situation of our time to the point of giving further and somewhat more detailed comment on what would constitute a Christian vision of economic justice. This vision serves both as a witness to the world at large and as guidance to the Christian community for its participation in public policy initiatives and personal practices related to matters of economic justice.

Presumably these statements of the bishops and other similar social statements by various church bodies would also inform the practice of those church bodies in the conduct of their own affairs as organizations in society who must conduct business, make investments, deal with fair employment practices, and consider other measures of affirmative action urged upon all institutions of society.

Eco-justice

The discussion of justice in the distribution of health care and in economic life has provided us with brief glimpses of how love operates through justice in seeking the common good. When our understanding of love-based justice is expanded to include Christian responsibility for the environment, we move beyond customary understandings that apply love and justice solely to human affairs. This requires some special theological reflection.

The groundwork for this transition was laid in chapter 2 when we observed that the biblical hope for God's promised future is for the whole person and the whole world of God's creation. A harmonious creation fulfilled and filled with life is among those goods we anticipate as a witness to our gospel hope through responsible concern for the whole creation. Joseph Sittler, whose reflections on Col. 1:15-20 earlier helped us to that vision, can help at this juncture also. Sittler was famous for making the theological connection between nature and grace. Since love and justice had usually been thought of only in terms of human relationships, Western traditions had also thought of God's grace solely in terms of God's relationship to humanity. Sittler challenged that tradition by drawing on the biblical vision of God's presence in all of nature and of God's redeeming activity as inclusive of the whole creation:

> There [in the Bible] nature comes from God, cannot be apart from God, and is capable of bearing the "glory" of God. Such a view of God and nature makes it completely clear why the redemption of God is celebrated in proleptic visions of a restored nature. For the realm of redemption cannot be conceived as having a lesser magnitude than the realm of creation.[29]

As God's love has extended God's grace to us in Christ, so that same self-giving love of God is graciously extended to creation, to the entire world that God loves. As we are to love one another as we have first been loved, so we are to love what God loves also in regard to nature. We are created in the divine image with a mandate to care for the creation as God does. However, the "dominion" of Gen. 1:26 does not mean that we have been given the imperial power to do as we please, but that we are to represent God's loving dominion of care.[30]

James Nash has made loving nature an integral expression of the Christian ethic of agape love. "If God is love, for instance, the process of creation itself is an act of love. All creatures, human and otherkind, and their habitats are not only gifts of love but also products of love and recipients of ongoing love."[31]

If God's love for nature and God's promise for its future implicate us in love for the whole creation, what does that mean specifically in terms of justice for the creation? I think we are helped in answering this question if we recognize in explicit terms how the good of the human community and the good of all else are tightly and inextricably woven together. The beauty of a document called "The Earth Charter" is that it does just that. Approved by its international commission in 2000,[32] the document was developed by people from all over the world. It started out as an initiative to develop a manifesto for environmental activism but was soon expanded as people began to recognize the need to link environmental integrity concerns with social and economic justice, sustainability, peace and nonviolence. These linkages are reflected in the titles of the main sections of the charter. In this context, love seeking justice is well described as "eco-justice," justice for the entire ecosystem (where "ecosystem" designates an organically integrated vision or communal vision of humanity and all creation).[33] It is a vision the Bible itself provides in Isaiah's glorious proleptic portrait of a harmonious creation at the arrival of God's promised future (Isa. 11:6-9).

The norms for eco-justice set forth by the Presbyterian Church (USA)'s Eco-Justice Task Force are consistent with the sort of comprehensive ecological perspective on reality we see in "The Earth Charter." These four norms continue to be representative of much of the discourse on eco-justice, both inside and outside the Christian community:[34]

Sustainability

"As a norm of human behavior, sustainability requires that we relate to the realm of nature in ways that respect its integrity, so that natural systems continue to function properly, the earth's beauty and fruitfulness may be maintained and kept sufficient for human sustenance, and life may continue also for the non-human species."[35]

Participation

God's gifts of creation are for everyone. If some are left out of adequate access to nature's bounty, something is awry. Economic arrangements should enable participation. Caring for the integrity and sustainability of the earth is in the service of participation and is directly related to the concerns of economic justice I spoke of earlier.

Sufficiency

A companion to participation, sufficiency underscores our obligation to provide for the basic needs of all. That entails setting limits on our levels of consumption for the sake of the common good. So "sufficiency" means a self-imposed commitment to "enough" but not "too much." It points us in the direction of a sharing society as foundational to justice.

Solidarity

This norm has several aspects to it. First, it means solidarity with the creation as a whole, recognizing ourselves as part of it and caring for it. Secondly, it means solidarity with all those who share our commitment to the good of the earth. We are created for community with God, one another, and the earth. This is an implication of our previous discussion of the image of God and the communal dimensions of our creation theology. Finally, solidarity means standing together with those poor who are the most profoundly affected by the economic and ecological imbalances and injustices of our world. We are brought back to the Beatitudes and the various aspects of solidarity we discovered there.

Overall, these norms and their explanations fall into the realm of middle axioms that take the general principle of egalitarian justice and the material principle of each according to need into the realm of ecology in its broadest sense. We can see the self-giving, other-regarding character of love and its drive toward the communal values of God's promised future infusing this account of eco-justice with energy and direction.

At the same time, we can also sense that the agape love standing behind the Christian commitment to justice will force some discerning choices. Love's commitment to "equal regard" refers to our neighbors and the equal dignity they possess and deserve by virtue of their creation in the divine image, even if they are our enemies. How, then, are we to regard other creatures who do not share that status? When conflicts occur between human needs and the needs of other species and natural systems, how do we resolve them?

In the next chapter we will be looking at some axioms for the resolution of conflict that would certainly come into play with regard to the more challenging decisions of eco-justice. For now, simply posing the questions involved not only warns against oversimplification but drives us back ever again to the trust we have in God's promises and the guidance of the Holy Spirit as we face vexing choices. This thought, then, leads us to some concluding observations.

Conflict, Compromise, and Consensus

The discussions of justice in the delivery of health care, economic justice, and eco-justice in general present us with topics that seem vast and impersonal. Most often, these are issues that seem quite remote from our daily life and thinking.

Yet these very issues of justice are often met in highly personal decision-making situations over which individuals must agonize. The following brief case serves to illustrate that point.

This is the case—reported by Beauchamp and Childress—of Mark Dalton, a histology technician employed in a large chemical plant who was diagnosed with chronic renal disease. Given his condition and the danger chemical vapors posed to his health, remaining in his present position seemed too risky. He was offered another job within the company. However, there were two other employees—one a woman—interested in this job and who had more seniority and training.

Beauchamp and Childress point out that all three could appeal to different material principles of justice to support their claim to the job. Dalton could appeal to need based on his health. The others could appeal to merit and contribution based on their seniority and superior training. Equal opportunity considerations might also be a point in favor of the woman employee.[36] In a situation such as the Dalton case, abstract principles suddenly become real and concrete; matters of justice, rather than being global and seemingly remote, become personal for those who must decide.

Whether operating on small-scale personal levels, as in this case, or on large-scale social and political levels, we are faced with a dialogue of decision that forces us to struggle not only with the choice of which material principle of justice is most appropriate to a given area of human activity but also with constantly conflicting claims arising from the pursuit of justice. In the face of those choices, compromises appear inevitable, and consensus, even among like-minded Christians, seems virtually impossible. This is especially true when it comes to choosing the exact policy initiative required or the exact course of action most morally responsible. It also needs to be recognized that what is possible at different times and in different places will change. Working for justice in the economic sector or in other areas of human endeavor will require a pattern of constant adjustment and readjustment, balancing of legitimate interests, and a mixture of short- and long-range solutions.

Nevertheless, despite the fact that it will be virtually impossible to achieve total consensus among Christian people on a specific course of action related to many issues, there can be consensus on several points. First of all, Christians can and ought to agree that the ethic of love in which they are formed and by which they are informed is in some real way relevant to the concerns of justice in society. Second, the Christian community can be expected to bring its moral principles into dialogue with issues of justice—in society and the world—as part of its calling to witness to the hope that is within it and as a reflection of the mercy with which God has called it into being. While not all

Christians may agree with these two points, all we have said thus far about the biblical witness for the life of the Christian community points in the direction of this minimal commitment for the people of promise.

Questions for Discussion

1. Some contend that our society has placed more stress on the rights of individuals pursuing their aims and too little stress on the good of the whole community. Do attitudes, behavior, and policies regarding health care, economic justice, and eco-justice provide evidence for this contention?

2. Think back to part 2 and our discussion of the virtues of love's character. How does our formation in the character of agape and its virtues equip us to respond to the enormous challenges we face in matters such as economic justice and eco-justice?

3. Look at the brief case of Mark Dalton. If you were a leader in that company, how would you sort out the conflicting claims of the three employees?

SANCTITY OF LIFE

You shall not murder.

—Exodus 20:13

In the previous two chapters, a good bit of interpretation and discussion were required to spell out the relationship of the commandments involved to the general rules I formulated. As we take up the commandment against killing, it seems far easier to draw a direct connection between this commandment and love's general rule of responsibility to respect the sanctity of life. That is indeed the case. Yet the commandment and the general rule are both so sweeping in their implications that they direct us to a wide range of issues, including murder, capital punishment, war, abortion, euthanasia, suicide, and assisted dying.[1] The scope of concerns involved becomes even broader when we consider that the obligation not only prohibits the taking of life but also commits us to enhancing the quality of life, preserving it, and protecting it. Therefore, I would suggest that a fuller formulation of the general rule is required to pick up the positive dimensions of our obligation under this commandment to respect the sanctity of life. Such a formulation might go something like this: "Love does not take life or do harm to the health of persons but preserves, protects, and promotes life and health, physically, psychologically, and emotionally."[2]

When the positive implications of the rule are paired with the negative prohibition, the application of this general rule to various areas of decision making involves us with many conflicts. As we explore some of the implications of love's obligation to respect the sanctity of life, we will look at some illustrations representing the form of the decision-making dialogue I have described as conflict resolution.

Before we get down to that business, one further note of introduction to this general rule is needed. For the biblical tradition from which the commandment against killing emanates, there is no sense of sanctity of life based on qualities inherent in life itself. Life is holy, and we are commanded to care for it in love because life is holy to God, and in creation and redemption God has cared for it in love.[3] This observation helps us make the connection between this general rule of love and those values of life and wholeness that are part of that ultimate good promised in the fulfillment of the reign of God. These values toward which love strives in anticipation of the fullness of that promise are, then, directly correlated with this general rule to respect the sanctity of life.

Resolution of Conflict

In chapter 8, I gave a brief description of conflict resolution and illustrated this with the conflict faced by the woman with multiple sclerosis who became pregnant and had to decide between the life of her unborn child, on the one hand, and her own health and the well-being of her family, on the other hand. In deciding how to resolve a conflict such as this and a myriad of others we could imagine, we can find some help toward a morally responsible choice by employing what I have called *adjudicating axioms*. To adjudicate means simply to hear, judge, and decide an issue. These axioms help us do this in the process of conflict resolution by providing us with some guidance on how to weigh conflicting rules and claims. They are not themselves moral imperatives. We are not obliged to follow one or the other of them. Furthermore, to use an adjudicating axiom as the basis of making a decision does not guarantee that the decision is justified or clearly the best decision. However, these axioms do help us organize our thinking as we struggle with the dilemmas of conflict, and they help us see our way toward what might be a responsible decision. Here I describe briefly four such axioms, which I have drawn from ethicist George F. Thomas and have worked with consistently in my own thinking.[4] We will see them further illustrated in the situations that follow.

Distinguishing between Interest and Need

Sometimes competing claims on my commitments are unequal because one represents an interest and the other a need. Where this distinction is relevant, interest gives way to need. For example, abortion for the sake of career plans may be rejected because the career plans are finally an interest whereas the preservation of life is a need. In our consumer culture some things we think of as "needs" may well be more like "interests" upon further examination. Our commitment of resources to such interests may well create a conflict with our obligations to genuine needs such as environmental resource conservation or the concerns of charity. The distinction between interest and need in these examples reveals what are truly obligations of love and what are not. That will not always be the case, however. Some healthy interests that enhance life are compatible with love's concern for the neighbor or family member but may be compromised in a situation of scarcity by pressing needs.

Limitation or Modification

When we have conflicting obligations to two or more parties, we may decide we can responsibly resolve the conflict by partially meeting the needs of all through limiting or modifying our response to their claims on us. This is simply the art of compromise. Recalling our discussion of justice and the delivery of health care in our previous chapter, it is easy to see that our society's current response to the conflict between high cost and the need for better health care has been one of modification or compromise. In addition to the objections of many special interests, our society's strong commitment to individual rights and freedom of choice has made the rationing of health care many fear entailed in a universal health-care program a major roadblock to establishing such a program. At the same time, most in our society do recognize that the most vulnerable may need help. Therefore, we have met these competing claims with a modified response. Rather than enacting a comprehensive national health insurance program, we have limited coverage to Medicare, Medicaid, and children in poverty and modified our approach to better public health by focusing on preventive health programs.

The Gradation of Higher and Lower Needs

One may decide to favor one obligation over another on the grounds that one need is of greater magnitude than the other. So, for example, persons in government have frequently withheld or obscured the truth because they believed it was in the interest of national security. Preserving security in this case is deemed a higher need than telling the truth. Business leaders are often confronted with this kind of assessment when the needs of all their stakeholders—shareholders, customers, employees, communities of location, the natural environment, affiliates, suppliers—cannot be met optimally. How does one decide which needs are the higher or lower? Which needs deserve first priority? Here is still another question: Do those closest to us, our family members, deserve priority of need over those further removed? Persons in helping professions and public service frequently face this question as they strive daily to allot their time, energy, and emotional commitments in the most responsible ways possible.

Inclusiveness

Sometimes we may resolve conflicting obligations by choosing to fulfill the one that appears to benefit the most people. The pitfall here is to easily justify the neglect of the one for the sake of the many. Nonetheless, this can be a credible and responsible way of resolving a conflict. Public policy decisions often operate on this premise, but it is also a common approach to decision making in families and smaller communities.

Once again, adjudicating axioms do not provide us with a rationale that justifies our decisions in the sense of eliminating the ambiguity of conflict resolution or demonstrating definitively the rightness of our choice. They do not protect us against the self-deception of using them to justify our own selfish motives. We are not delivered from the ambiguous and sometimes tragic nature of many of the moral dilemmas that confront us in a fallen world. We are empowered by the gospel to choose with confidence and assured by the gospel of God's mercy toward us. Our confidence does not reside in the excellence of our decision-making process but in the promise of God's faithfulness and mercy. Dietrich Bonhoeffer's words speak to this reality:

> The will of God may lie very deeply hidden among many competing possibilities. It is also not a system of rules that are fixed from the outset, but always new and different in each life circumstance. This is why it is necessary to discern again and again what the will of God is. Heart, intellect, observation, and experience must work together in this discernment. This discernment of the will of God is such a serious matter precisely because it is no longer our own knowledge of good and evil that is at issue here, but the living will of God; because knowing the will of God is not at our human disposal, but dependent entirely on God's grace.[5]

Decision at the End of Life

In chapter 6, I introduced the concept of passive euthanasia. There is a high degree of moral consensus among medical professionals and ethicists that passive euthanasia, when indicated, is a morally responsible course of action. As you recall, passive euthanasia is the practice of withdrawing and withholding further life-sustaining treatment for the irreversibly dying in order to make them as comfortable as possible and let death come naturally with the highest possible quality or dignity of life at its end. When a person is irreversibly dying, such a decision takes into account the probability that providing life-sustaining treatment when there is no hope of recovery is really a process of prolonging dying rather than prolonging life. The conflict faced by those involved in such cases is one of competing obligations under the requirement to respect the sanctity of life: the obligation to relieve suffering and the obligation to prolong life. Passive euthanasia in the face of this conflict is a form of applying the adjudicating axiom of limitation or modification; it is a form of compromise. To favor the obligation for prolonging life would mean to exert every possible effort to keep the person alive regardless of his or her condition. To favor the obligation to relieve suffering in its most radical mode would mean active euthanasia or mercy killing. Passive euthanasia is a compromise between these two extremes; it allows death to come without intervention or without deliberately hastening it, and it provides as much relief from suffering as is possible under the circumstances.

In many cases, there are other features that make this decision more problematic than it appears in the brief description I have just given. I alluded briefly to some of these features in chapter 6. For example, the traditional approach to passive euthanasia dictates that, while we withhold life-sustaining treatment to the dying, we still provide "ordinary" care. However, defining ordinary care versus extraordinary care is in some cases notoriously difficult. I mentioned one example of this in citing the possibility of a dying cancer patient, in great pain, contracting pneumonia. Is there an obligation to treat that person's pneumonia with antibiotics, or should this condition be allowed to run its course so that death might come more quickly and peacefully? In cases such as this, it may not be possible to analyze the conflict resolution as an issue of modification or limitation. In deciding whether or not to treat the pneumonia, for example, we may now need to see the choice in terms of which is the higher need, relieving suffering or prolonging life. If the patient is unable to participate in the decision, the family and the physician must make the agonizing choice.

Equally vexing are those cases where the patient has lapsed into what is called "persistent vegetative state" (PVS), mentioned in chapter 6. To reiterate, PVS is a condition in which all of the brain except the brain stem has died. Since the brain stem is still alive, breathing and circulation continue and the patient is not legally dead because there is still brain activity. Through intravenous feeding and hydration, such patients may live for long periods of time. Here the choice to let death come passively requires a decision to remove food and water, allowing the body to die of starvation and dehydration. Such a decision involves not only the axiom of determining the greater need, but also may involve the axiom of inclusiveness, since the cost of keeping such patients alive, both emotionally and financially, is an extreme drain on families and health-care institutions. Would not the well-being of the many be better served if tube feeding and hydration were withdrawn and the patient allowed to die? The answer to that question depends on how one interprets the facts.

There is considerable disagreement in such matters of interpretation. The recent case of Terry Schiavo (mentioned in chapter 6) illustrates this disagreement vividly. Those who opposed removal of her feeding tube did so out of religious conviction about the sanctity of life. They argued that the removal of the tube was an act of direct killing. Others who favored removal said that death was not intended by that action but simply accepted as inherent in her state of affairs. Those favoring the removal of the tube regarded it as an extraordinary measure in this circumstance while those opposed argued that providing food and water is as ordinary a form of care as one can imagine. Also disputed is the question of whether or not there was truly any consciousness in this and other PVS cases. Even the postmortem findings of Terry's massive brain damage did not resolve that particular dispute. In the final analysis, those opposing removal of her feeding tube did so out of the absolute conviction that we should never take life, and, they reasoned, the removal of the tube was a matter of taking life. In this case, the axiom of higher need or value would trump considerations of inclusiveness mentioned earlier.

Case Study One

There are other kinds of dilemmas that do not fit the pattern of the situations just described and challenge our moral sensitivities in different ways. Allow me to present a true case that helps to illustrate:

Mr. W., age eighty-one, had a cardiac pacemaker implanted seven years ago. Though physically capable of handling his own needs, his mental capabilities have failed to the point where nursing-home care has been necessary for the past three years. His pacemaker battery needs replacement; without this minor surgical procedure, he would be likely to die of cardiac arrest within two months.

Mr. W.'s mental status is such that he has no sense of time or place, and he is declared incompetent to sign his own operative consent. To everyone's surprise his competent, loving wife of many years refuses to give permission for the battery change. She says, "We are turning him into a vegetable. I cannot take it any longer. Let him die in peace." Mr. W.'s children concur in their mother's feelings and decision.

The attending doctor, who is also the family physician of many years, is upset at the prospect of accepting this verdict. The hospital attorney tells him he could probably get a court order to override Mrs. W.'s decision. Instead, he calls on the family pastor to talk with Mrs. W. and with him about this dilemma.

If you were that pastor, how would you help the family and the physician understand the situation and arrive at a decision? There are of course a variety of pastoral care and counseling issues in this situation. We cannot speculate on the kind of technique and approach the pastor might employ. However, we can do some ethical analysis that might be helpful to the parties involved.

The problem faced by Mrs. W. and the family seems to be one of concern for the quality of Mr. W.'s life versus concern for the preservation of his life. From their vantage point, preserving that life in its present deteriorated state seems a poor way to respect the sanctity of their husband and father's life. From the standpoint of the physician, the priorities seem to be reversed. Mr. W. is not dying and can be easily kept alive through a minor surgical procedure. However diminished his quality of life, it seems a dangerous precedent to arbitrarily withhold life-support measures from persons who are not dying simply because others have decided that their life is not worth living. For the physician the higher need is to prolong life. For the family the higher need is to end what they consider to be a poor quality of life. The problem is even more complicated because there is no reason to believe that Mr. W. is suffering and there is no way of knowing what his desires would be.

There is, of course, one other element we have yet to mention. That element is Mrs. W.'s feeling of desperation and her inability to continue to cope with her husband's deteriorated state. Perhaps the real issue is that Mrs. W. and her children are at the end of their rope and are looking for a way out of the suffering they are experiencing. Exploration of this possibility is a critical challenge to the pastoral caregiver.

If we assume for the sake of argument that this is in fact the real issue, then the ethical decision takes on a different cast. Now it may be possible to look at this conflict as a conflict between interest and need. The desires of the family to be rid of their own suffering might responsibly be considered more of an interest than a need, whereas the claim on continuing the life of Mr. W. and all those in similar circumstances may readily be considered a need that should take priority. If we were to resolve the conflict in this manner, we would need to remember that making a decision we believe is responsible does not exhaust the obligations of those involved. Mrs. W. and her family need support and help in coping with Mr. W.'s deteriorated health situation. If she is persuaded that it is right to give consent or if the court is brought in to overrule her refusal, a ministry to her and her family that can help them deal with their own suffering is an obligation of love entailed by this situation.

Case Study Two

One final case will help us explore a bit further some of the conflicts involved in decision making at the end of life. In a bioethics course I taught for nursing students some years ago, an anesthesiologist visiting the class provided this real-life case in which he was involved:

> A young man, twenty-five years old, was dying of inoperable cancer of the rectum. His days were numbered, but no one could predict exactly how long he would live. In the meantime, he was in intense pain and experienced very little relief from normal pain medications.
>
> The anesthesiologist was called in and asked by the family physician attending this young man whether or not he could give a spinal anesthetic that would give the young man some relief from his pain. The anesthesiologist indicated that he could indeed do that and it would provide pain relief. However, the process had a high risk of rupturing the bowel. The result would be that death would follow quickly.
>
> The young man, his wife, and the family physician conferred on this prospect and concluded that, since he was dying anyway and his pain was intolerable, it was worth the risk to do the procedure. The anesthesiologist consented to give the spinal anesthetic. The bowel ruptured, and death came quickly thereafter.

In reflecting on this experience with the class, the doctor raised the question of whether or not, knowing the high risk of death, he had been involved in a form of active euthanasia? Of course, the doctor might have justified his decision to administer the anesthetic on the basis of the rule of double effect. In chapter 8, I discussed this rule, which allows that some normally unjustifiable consequences may occasionally be justified when they are the result of a double effect or when they are secondary and unintended consequences. By this reasoning the death that occurred could be morally justified as a secondary unintended consequence of the primary intention, which was to relieve the patient's suffering. However, the fact that the anesthesiologist is questioning his actions suggests that he is not inclined to resolve the matter in that fashion. Indeed, dialogical ethics would regard it as more honest in this situation to live with the ambiguity of what was a difficult and even tragic choice. Obviously, all concerned in this decision reached the conclusion that the greater need, in view of the young man's imminent death, was the relief of suffering even to the point of taking the risk involved.

Decisions to End Life

The general rule to respect the sanctity of life requires that the burden of proof be on any decision to take life or hasten death. However, in the situations people often face, the manifold demands of this rule lead us to the reality of conflict and help us see that preserving bodily life is not the only way and not always the most responsible way to respect the sanctity of life once we understand that life is more than simple bodily existence.

As my last statement suggests, decisions about when to continue life support for the dying are related in part to an understanding that the "life" whose sanctity we are pledged to uphold is not defined simply in terms of physical existence. Human life is multidimensional and characterized by personhood and an inherent relationship to God and other persons, as we observed in our previous discussion of the image of God. Consequently, when illness has destroyed much of what we are and dying is in process, extreme efforts to keep a body alive can be a violation of the sanctity of life rather than respect for it. Christians living in the hope of the resurrection understand better than most that clinging to bodily life at all costs can be a form of idolatry. In this vein, ethicist Harmon Smith has recast a saying of Jesus to make the point: "A person does not live by life alone."[6] However, as fitting and useful as these observations may be, the business of deciding when life is less than fully life can result in ethical mischief as well. We have already met the temptation to draw such lines in the case of Mr. W., and in the case of Donald C., few would contest the fact that the quality of Mr. W.'s life was greatly diminished and the burden on the family was greatly increased. Few would also deny that the quality of Donald C.'s life was one of almost unbearable physical and emotional agony. However, many would regard the refusal of minor surgery to Mr. W. or the assistance to Donald C. in gaining release from his treatment and being allowed to die as active euthanasia in the one case and assisted suicide in the other case. If looked at in that light, most would regard both of these actions as morally unacceptable.

Yet a growing number in ethics and medicine argue that when the quality of life has dramatically deteriorated, active euthanasia or assisted suicide should be permitted when it is the autonomous choice of the patient.[7] In these instances of extreme loss in the quality of life, advocates of assisted dying would argue that the distinction between active and passive euthanasia is not morally significant, since the end in both cases is the same. This is particularly true, advocates of this position contend, in light of the blurred line that often exists between passive and active euthanasia in real life as illustrated in the debate of the Terry Schiavo case and the experience that the anesthesiologist related to my class.

They point to the fact that there are a growing number of cases produced by modern medicine in which the agony of the final days is simply unbearable. To this is added the complaint that pain management is woefully inadequate in today's medicine. Finally, they point out that assisted suicide has been practiced legally in the Netherlands for years without noticeable harm to the country's ethos. The same case has also been made in relation to Oregon's death with dignity law, which also provides for assisted suicide for the dying.°⁸

Daniel Callahan, by contrast, maintains that the distinction between active euthanasia in assisted dying and passive euthanasia is still morally important. He contends that the renewed interest in active euthanasia is due to a fear of medicine's ability to keep us alive under the worst of circumstances, a fear that need not be realized with good comfort care at the end of life.⁹ Former U.S. surgeon general C. Everett Koop fears that the development of active euthanasia based on arbitrary decisions of when life has lost its value will almost inevitably work against the underclass, the handicapped, and those marginal to society. He, like Callahan, wants to emphasize an ethic of passive response to terminal illness and compassionate care for the dying.¹⁰

There is much more to be said to fill in all the details of the debate over assisted dying. However, in terms of ethical decision making, we have yet another clash of obligations and claims. Those advocating assisted dying for those dying in agony argue that such relief from suffering upholds the sanctity of life at its end and honors the rule of respect for autonomy that has already been invoked in connection with other patient's rights to informed consent and to the choice of refusing treatment. This argument appeals to what it considers to be the higher value.

Those who oppose and would outlaw assisted dying in any circumstances believe such a prohibition is the best way to respect the sanctity of life when combined with adequate measures of pain management and comfort care. Here the resolution of the conflict between the relief of suffering and the preservation of life by passive euthanasia that includes pain management and comfort care is essentially an application of the axiom of modification or compromise. Some opponents would argue further that autonomy is limited by the good of the larger community and should therefore be limited in the case of

---

°At this writing the Oregon law is under attack in the U.S. Supreme Court by the federal government, which contends that the law violates federal law against controlled substances because of the chemicals used to bring about death.

choosing assisted suicide because legalizing the process would jeopardize the valuation of life in our society and open up the possibility for abuses. Here the axiom of inclusivity is being invoked.

Decision at the Beginning of Life

In both ancient and modern times, efforts have been made to establish the onset of human life; it has been hoped that such a determination will enable Christians and others to resolve the ethical debate over abortion. Theologians like Augustine and Aquinas made distinctions between the fetus in its early stages before it had received a soul and its full human status once ensoulment occurred. The time of ensoulment was clearly not conception, but exactly when this occurred might be a matter of debate. In any case, the sin incurred in aborting an unensouled fetus differed from the homicide clearly involved once the fetus had received a soul. As a result, some moral theologians, following these thinkers, argued that therapeutic abortion may be justified as a lesser sin if the fetus had as yet no soul.[11]

Many arguments for the beginning of life that we hear of today almost seem to be modern scientific versions of older beliefs:

> Some argue that the fetus is a person from the moment of conception on the ground that the fetus is a human being and all human beings are persons. This stipulation begs the question and is not particularly convincing. Others argue that there is no person before the development of a functioning brain. Even if one agrees with that, it does not follow that there is a person present after the development of a functioning brain; other considerations ranging from viability to self-awareness might be necessary. In short there is no neat biological answer to the moral status of the fetus.[12]

At the end of chapter 8, I mentioned that the abortion debate in the Christian community is an example of an issue in which there is disagreement both over the facts and over what the Bible directs. Determining the moral status of the fetus—key to the ethics of abortion—is complicated by combining our lack of a "neat biological answer to the moral status of the fetus" with debate about biblical guidance. Ethicist Gilbert Meilander admits that the Bible does not resolve the question of when life begins.[13] This recognition opens the door to a variety of proposals among Christians for when life begins, ranging from conception to viability, the point of development at which the fetus can survive outside the mother with reasonable medical help.

For Meilander, individual human life begins approximately fourteen days after the fertilized ovum successfully implants in the uterine wall. Prior to this time it is still possible that the developing blastocyst can divide into two or more individuals of the same genotype. This is called "twinning."[14] At conception, all the genetic material is present for the development of a fully individuated human being (or human *beings* should "twinning" occur), and at implantation its survival and further development become possible. If abortion is permitted at all in this view, it cannot proceed on the basis that we are doing anything less than taking a human life. Though this nascent life is yet to be a person among persons, its *potential* assures that it will be and is therefore deserving of the same regard as all persons.

In 1973 the Supreme Court essentially determined in the *Roe v. Wade* decision that philosophical or theological opinions about the beginning of life and the consequent permissibility of abortion were beyond the ability of the courts to adjudicate. Therefore, abortion was judged to be a private decision under the constitutional right to privacy until the time of viability during the last ten weeks of pregnancy, the time when the fetus might be expected to live outside of the uterus with reasonable medical attention. The battle to restore some legal sanctions against abortion has continued unabated, however. Arguments on both sides have become more sophisticated, and public opinion has shifted more than once.

Since our primary purpose is to elaborate a model of Christian decision making in the context of faith and formation, we cannot undertake the job of reviewing and evaluating various positions in the abortion debate. Nonetheless, I still need to say something about my own basic position if anything that follows is to make sense.

It seems to me that there is, in the minds of people, a kind of commonsense distinction between fetal life in its earliest stages and life as we experience it at the time of viability or birth. This distinction is likely to remain embodied in our laws for the foreseeable future despite hopes that a new mix of philosophies on the Supreme Court will lead to overturning *Roe v. Wade.* However, I do not regard this commonsense approach or any of the more detailed biological and philosophical arguments for the beginning of life as definitive in establishing whether or not abortion is wrong in a given case.

Throughout this book, I have stressed that the Christian community approaches ethics as a people of promise. We live in the promise of God's gracious presence with us in all circumstances of life. We live also in the promise of God's future for us in that final reign revealed by the victory of Jesus Christ over sin and death. Living in the promise means that the life of love is a possibility. With this mind-set, I suggest that we can approach the question of abortion in terms of promise and possibility rather than prohibition and permission. The ethics of love will look to fetal life and its claim on our obligation to respect the sanctity of life not in terms of some definition of its stage of development but in terms of the common future that all life has in the promise of God's final dominion. In this perspective we are committed to the triumph of life over death that the resurrection has revealed as the essence of God's future. Because that future is "not yet," there will be tragic choices for abortion that may need to be made. However, we will not seek to permit or prohibit abortions on the basis of speculations concerning the beginning of human life. Rather, we will be committed to life as the promise of God and exercise our freedom and responsibility in the confidence of that gospel promise. To borrow a phrase from Paul Ramsey, "We are all fellow fetuses"; we are united with all human life at every stage by the common future we share; we are all "not yet." God has shown in Christ the desire to consummate our creation. We are thus brought back to the observation made at the beginning of this chapter that, for the Bible, life is holy not because of something inherent in life itself but because it is holy to God. From this vantage point, ethically speaking, the burden of proof is on the choice to abort.

Having said this, I am ready to present yet another type of abortion decision involving the kind of conflict in which the tragic choice to abort may be the most responsible choice available and the choice not to abort may have tragic consequences. I have in mind choices created by our new knowledge in the field of genetics.

In our time, the increasing capacity to predict genetic abnormalities has brought with it new burdens of decision. These decisions include whether or not to risk pregnancy, whether or not to undergo testing as prospective parents, and whether or not to abort when prenatal diagnosis signals the risk or certainty of a genetic defect. Such decisions will increase in frequency because our knowledge of genetics is increasing rapidly. The National Institutes of Health (NIH), along with a private commercial research company working on its own initiative, has concluded a project called The Human Genome Initiative. This research effort has completed mapping and identifying every one of the genes on human chromosomes. Such information will immeasurably expand our understanding of a wide variety of health problems, our ability to predict them, and our ability to treat them.[15] As knowledge increases, public awareness will increase as well and use of diagnostic techniques for features of genetic inheritance will certainly expand with it. For this reason, the ethical discussion of these matters becomes more urgent than ever before. Recognizing this, the original NIH project budgeted 90 million dollars to explore the ethical aspects of the genome initiative.

With specific reference to genetic abortion, there are currently available a number of prenatal genetic tests that raise this volatile issue. Best known of these is perhaps the practice of amniocentesis. In this procedure, a needle is inserted through the abdomen of the expectant mother to draw off a portion of the amniotic fluid that surrounds the developing fetus in the uterus. Cells suspended in the fluid, which have been sloughed off by the fetus, are then cultured and grown in the laboratory so that they can be analyzed for genetic makeup. Amniocentesis cannot be done until fourteen to sixteen weeks into the pregnancy. In addition, several weeks are required after the fluid has been withdrawn to culture and analyze the cells before a diagnosis can be made. By this time, the pregnancy is into the middle of the second trimester.

More recently, a procedure called chorionic villus sampling (CVS) has been developed as an alternative. The chorion, a membrane surrounding the embryo, develops a series of fingerlike projections called villi, which form the placenta. In most cases, a thin flexible tube can be inserted into the vagina, through the cervix, and into the uterus to suction off some of the villi. The procedure can be done at nine to eleven weeks of pregnancy, and because fetal cells are plentiful in the villi, a lengthy culturing process is not needed; genetic analysis is possible immediately, and results can be available within a few days. The obvious advantage of CVS is that it can be done and provide results early in the pregnancy when abortion is less risky and perhaps more palatable.

Both amniocentesis and CVS also carry a small risk of miscarriage (for amniocentesis and probably slightly higher for CVS); the procedures may not be recommended if the risk of the suspected abnormality is statistically less than the risk of the test itself. In addition to these techniques, ultrasound, blood sampling from the umbilical cord and alpha-fetoprotein screening are also used to detect fetal abnormalities. By the mid-1990s, prenatal diagnosis was available for hundreds of disorders.[16]

The genetic defects detectable by this kind of prenatal testing vary greatly in their severity. One of the most notorious of the severe conditions is Tay-Sachs disease. Tay-Sachs is the product of recessive genetic traits (both parents must carry the trait) found among Jews of Eastern European origin. A baby with Tay-Sachs will appear normal at birth, but within four to eight months symptoms will begin to occur and become progressively worse. Ultimately, the child will be overtaken by blindness, deafness, seizures, paralysis, and total mental retardation. Death will occur by three to five years of age. There is no treatment on the horizon. A similarly deadly disorder is Edward's Syndrome or Trisomy 18. In this condition there is an extra eighteenth chromosome, which produces profound physical and mental retardation and death during infancy.

Parents who face prospects such as Tay-Sachs or Trisomy 18 during pregnancy face a conflict between the prevention of suffering and the preservation of life. Given the quality of life their unborn child inevitably faces, they need to ask which, in this situation, is the higher value. Is the higher value in respect to the sanctity of life served by preventing suffering through abortion or by carrying the child to term and preserving its life for as long as possible? For many ethicists (I count myself among them), cases like these are instances where the burden of proof has been satisfied and abortion may be regarded as a responsible choice. While a certain amount of ambiguity may remain and an element of tragedy is unquestionably present, the harshness of the life awaiting the child after birth represents a strong argument against continuing the pregnancy. At least one ethicist has suggested that abortion in cases like these may even be consistent with the obligation of the parental care implicit in pregnancy, an obligation that would normally constrain us from choosing abortion.[17]

More recently, another type of prenatal diagnosis has become available in conjunction with *in vitro* fertilization. This practice is called preimplantation diagnosis. In *in vitro* fertilization a number of eggs are fertilized before choosing one or more to implant in the mother's uterus. When they develop into four to eight cell embryos, they can be examined for certain genetic or chromosomal disorders so that only those that test healthy will be implanted. Because it is a process linked to *in vitro* fertilization, it is not readily available and not all clinics doing *in vitro* fertilization have the capacity to do this diagnosis.[18] In addition to the problem of the availability of this procedure, there is also ethical dispute about *in vitro* fertilization itself. Persons who oppose abortion without qualification usually oppose *in vitro* as well because they claim that the developing embryos are human life, even though not yet implanted. The fact, then, that some will end up being discarded is considered taking life as sure as abortion is. Life in this view begins at conception. For this reason the same objections are raised when science proposes to do embryonic stem-cell research in quest of cures for various conditions and diseases.

However, we need to say more about the various choices parents may face when prenatal diagnosis is done. As we try to discern the higher value in our attempts to resolve conflicts that arise from such testing, we find that a variety of other detectable conditions are not as easily evaluated as Tay-Sachs or Trisomy 18. What does one do if one of the following conditions is diagnosed?

Down Syndrome

This condition is marked by the physical characteristics of slanting eyes, curving folds of skin at the eyes, and shorter than average stature. It involves varying degrees of mental retardation and is sometimes accompanied by heart disease and other complications in the development of the digestive system. Life expectancy may be nearly normal. Persons with Down Syndrome are often happy and loving in nature. The condition is the result of a chromosomal abnormality.

Cystic Fibrosis

This condition is characterized by unusually thick mucous buildup, which blocks the lungs, resulting in coughing, difficulty in breathing, infections, and distended lungs. Further complications are poor digestion, thin body build, poor tolerance for exercise, abnormally short stature, and excessive loss of salt through perspiration. Treatment can be given through physical therapy to improve breathing. Synthetic digestive enzymes and salt tablets as well as antibiotics can help with the other complications. Life expectancy is shorter than normal, frequently not beyond age twenty. Cystic fibrosis is caused by a recessive genetic trait possessed by both parents.

Spina Bifida

A defect in the bone structure of the spinal column frequently results in a large cyst containing parts of the spinal cord observable at birth. This condition, caused by a variety of genetic and environmental factors, can be treated by corrective surgery. However, those treated sometimes will be paralyzed from the waist down, and other times the condition is inoperable and will result in death shortly after birth. Thus, there is uncertainty involved in diagnosing how severe the case may really be. Those who respond well to treatment can have a happy and meaningful life despite the disabilities involved.

In these instances, arguing that preventing suffering through abortion is the higher value is far more difficult to sustain. Meaningful life, despite its serious difficulties, is possible over a fairly long period of time in most cases of the sort mentioned above. However, some may be prepared to argue that it is not simply a matter of preventing suffering on the part of the unborn child but also a matter of relieving the burdens on the family and relieving society of additional burdens for special education and the cost of medical resources. To argue in this fashion would be to argue from the axiom of inclusiveness, an attempt to insure the good for the greatest number of people. This is problematic, however, because we can easily argue that inclusiveness should be overridden when it compromises our basic obligation to protect life. Moreover, in the three conditions we have just mentioned, the case for abortion is further complicated by the fact that there is a measure of predictive uncertainty. Even if we could mount a compelling argument to abort for the prevention of suffering, we would have to admit that we are uncertain as to how severe the condition may be in any given case. This makes the burden of proof for abortion even heavier than at first glance.[19]

Without pretending to resolve all the issues involved even in this narrow range of cases under the heading of genetic abortion, it seems to me that several important observations follow. First of all, whether it is a case of deciding to abort or a case of carrying the pregnancy to term, there is an inescapable measure of tragedy and ambiguity in our decision. Once again, we come up against the reality of life in a fallen world and we fall back upon the grace of God—not for easy forgiveness, but for the courage to act in the confidence of our faith and for the assurance that God is with us to sustain us in that decision and in our life with the consequences that result. We are not left with an iron-clad rational justification of our actions once the dialogue has been completed with decision. We have only the promise.

In the end, we are brought back to our earlier discussion of Christian character formed in love as the expression of faith. Stanley Hauerwas has argued that Christians have often failed in the public debate on abortion because they have tried to sustain their opposition to abortion in terms of rational arguments instead of getting in touch with the roots of their views in the faith and character of the Christian community.[20] From the standpoint of our own discussion, we can follow Hauerwas's lead by referring back to our previous consideration of the Christian virtue of solidarity in suffering. The readiness to accept a child we know will be born with a genetic defect such as Down Syndrome or cystic fibrosis or spina bifida is finally not a matter simply of rational argumentation, as we have observed, but a matter of readiness to live in love with those who suffer, to embrace the promise and the possibility of Jesus' beatitude: "Blessed are those who mourn."

Finally, we are also led back to our overall emphasis on ethics as an expression of the community of promise. There is more to ethics than simply determining what is right in a given instance: to abort or not to abort. The ethics of love also demand that persons faced with those decisions receive the support of the community or communities in which they live. Advocacy for the sanctity of life in the case of unborn children with genetic defects requires that the Christian community take the lead in providing support for the parents, ready acceptance of the child in the life of the community, and support in society for adoption services, special education, necessary health-care resources, and whatever else is needed to complete love's obligation to each and every life. This is so, for each and every life stands under the promise of God.

Questions for Discussion

1. Review the section on *adjudicating axioms*. What are some examples from your own experience or observation that illustrate the application of each of these axioms?

2. Look at the case of Mr. W. How would you interpret the situation and what would you decide? In your decision making would one particular adjudicating axiom prove most helpful? Which one and why?

3. In what respects, if at all, is the decision facing the parents of a Trisomy 18 fetus and that facing parents of a Down Syndrome fetus morally different? What factors other than the relative severity of the two conditions play a part in this decision?

12

TRUTH-TELLING AND PROMISE-KEEPING

You shall not bear false witness against your neighbor.

—Exodus 20:16

You shall not commit adultery.

—Exodus 20:14

Perhaps one of the most commonly held beliefs about moral obligations is the conviction that we ought to tell the truth. Certainly honesty is one of the most highly prized virtues. Yet, for all of that, truth-telling and honesty are not simple, straightforward matters. Sissela Bok begins her impressive and durable book, *Lying*, with the following set of questions:

> Is it not naïve to set forth on a general exploration of lying and truth-telling? Some will argue that the task is impossible. Life is too complex they will say, and societies too diverse. How can one compare the bargaining in an Eastern bazaar, the white lies of everyday life, the lie for national defense, and that to spare a dying child? Is it not arrogant and myopic to conceive of doing so? . . . How can one, in fact, do full justice to the words used in court: "The truth, the whole truth, and nothing but the truth"?[1]

Bok concedes that in the complexities of life the whole truth is out of reach. "But this fact has very little to do with our choices about whether to lie or speak honestly, about what to say and what to hold back. These choices can be set forth, compared, evaluated. And when they are, even rudimentary distinctions can give guidance."[2] Thus Bok sets the stage for her argument that the difficulties in mapping our obligations to tell the truth in a variety of circumstances should not deter us from examining those obligations and charting a course for a morally responsible approach to telling the truth in a wide variety of personal and social interactions.

In this regard it is helpful to observe her distinction that the moral problem of telling the truth or lying is not the same as the issue of seeking the truth as a philosophical question about the meaning of life or the nature of reality. Obviously, those kinds of truth questions are important to our lives together, but the ethical issue of truth-telling as she deals with it and as we shall deal with it revolves around the statements that we make to each other in representing or misrepresenting the facts as we know them. In these transactions between people, even our grasp of the facts is not the nub of the issue, ethically speaking. The moral question is joined when we ask whether or not what we say to another intends to mislead that person.[3] From that point of departure she goes on to examine the various forms and contexts of lying, the excuses that are given for doing so, the arguments mounted for why false statements might not be considered as real lies, and the situations in which lying might be justified in the name of a higher moral obligation.° Throughout this investigation she pointedly asks us to look at the rationalizations of the liar from the point of view of the one lied to, the dupe. In effect, she is asking us to examine the matter from the standpoint of the Golden Rule, "Do unto others as you would have them do unto you." Even the use of the term *dupe* or the thought of being labeled a dupe says something about the impact on the personal dignity of those who are the victims of untrue statements. In a manner that echoes our concerns for truthfulness in chapters 5 and 7, Bok points out that lies hurt people in various ways and undermine the trust necessary for sound and rewarding personal, social, and political relationships.[4] In this regard I recently offered the following thoughts:

> For some time after it became clear that Iraq did not have weapons of mass destruction, polls showed that a majority of Americans still believed they did. Why? One reason is, I believe, that no one wants to feel as though they have been duped. To be duped is to be made foolish, robbed of your dignity, and made accomplice to something built on falsehood. When one is duped, one stops trusting.[5]

This perspective of the victim leads us to an understanding of the dynamics of truth-telling and lying that stress that concern for the well-being of our neighbor, and the quality of the relationships in which we live is the focus of the commandment against bearing false witness. In that regard I want to try

---

°A recent search I did on the Internet of the word *lying* turned up an almost endless supply of references expressing concern for children's lying, corporate lying, government lying, marketing lying, and media lying. Also available were scientific studies on the psychological indicators of lying and even some sites on how to lie effectively.

to emphasize the positive thrust of truth-telling in a manner consistent with the governing commandment of love for the neighbor as well as examining the negative prohibition against lying.

Love for the Neighbor Tells the Truth

As Luther observed and as is obvious from the text itself, the primary reference for this commandment is the arena of the courtroom. In that setting, truth serves the ends of justice and false testimony jeopardizes the reputation, property, and freedom of the neighbor. There is, of course, a law against perjury with severe penalties that attempts to enforce this requirement of truthful testimony in court proceedings. Undoubtedly, however, volumes could be written about the way in which contemporary courtroom procedures and legal maneuvers enable people to conceal or manipulate the truth without running afoul of perjury laws. It has become commonplace to observe that those guilty of crimes who can afford good legal defense fare better in the courtroom than those who lack the resources to purchase the services of the most skillful trial lawyers. In the courtroom, issues of truthfulness and justice are interwoven.

However, I know of no commentator on this commandment who would not say that its implications go beyond the immediate reference to courtroom proceedings. The truthfulness demanded of us in the courtroom is demanded also in all our relationships, especially if those relationships are to be governed by love's regard for the neighbor. Luther is particularly concerned about the damage we do to the neighbor by the sin of slander. Public falsehoods and evil judgments about our neighbors immeasurably damage their reputations and effectively deny them the respect and community that they need and deserve. Instead, it is our obligation to speak well of our neighbors whenever we have opportunity and thereby support and enhance their reputations and places in the community. Moreover, as we hear reports of our neighbors or observe our neighbors' statements and behaviors, we are similarly obligated to put the best construction on what we see and hear.[6] In this way, Luther means for us to understand that love demands an orientation to the good of the neighbor rather than a malicious desire to see evil wherever possible and to build ourselves up by enjoying the failure of others, whether real or imagined.

Lewis Smedes helps us to further our discussion of how our general rule obligation of love to tell the truth serves the needs of our neighbors. He offers three reasons from a biblical perspective as to why we should tell the truth for the sake of our neighbors. First of all, to be truthful is to be trustworthy. This is the counsel of James 5:12, where we are enjoined to say what we mean and mean what we say. Such trustworthiness is characteristic of God and the promises of God. Such truthfulness builds that trust in our neighbors who, then, know that they can rely on us. Second, Smedes says, community cannot survive without trust. He cites Eph. 4:25: "So then, putting away falsehood, let all of us speak the truth to our neighbors, for we are members of one another." Finally, our neighbors need to be able to trust us in order to be free. Freedom requires truthfulness in order to make genuine choices. If we misrepresent the facts—Smedes uses the example of lying about the condition of a car we want to sell—we deny our neighbors the truth needed to make good choices important to their well-being. In this fashion we treat our neighbors as though they were merely a means to our own ends rather than persons deserving of equal regard.[7]

It requires but a moment's reflection, in recalling our previous discussion of *agape,* to understand that self-serving falsehoods, which threaten our neighbors' well-being and break down the trust essential to community, are antithetical to the ethic of love. At the same time, truthfulness regards the needs of neighbors first, contributes to their well-being, and builds the trust that is the cornerstone of the community *agape* seeks to realize.

Truth-telling: Interpretation, Limits, and Conflict

As a general rule of love, truth-telling is always our obligation. However, in real-life situations fulfillment of this obligation may require some intuitive forms of direct interpretation. Helmut Thielicke discusses an encounter with a child's question that provides us with a good example of this interpretive demand. The scene Thielicke sets is that of a very young child asking his mother where babies come from. He allows for the possibility that the mother might respond by trotting out the old legend of the stork delivering babies. While the mother would be correct in assuming that the child could not grasp the biological facts and would not be helped by hearing them, Thielicke suggests that the stork legend is, nonetheless, a self-serving evasion that unnecessarily deceives the child in order to arrive at an easy solution to a difficult question.

How can one tell the truth to this child when a scientific version of that truth would not be helpful or meaningful? This is the interpretive challenge. Thielicke answers by relating how one mother he knew of responded to this question from her small son. The account is too lengthy to reproduce here, and some may question whether the mother's attempt was as successful as Thielicke thinks it was. However, the gist of her answer was that children come from the creative hand of God to people who are in love, and the mother lovingly carries this gift of God under her heart until the little child has grown sufficiently and God takes it from under the mother's heart and lays it in the cradle. Thielicke's approval of this attempt to tell the truth is based on his conviction that the mother's explanation of pregnancy and birth is accessible to the child, not deceitful, and includes important values about God, love, and parenthood.[8] Regardless of our judgment about the adequacy of the mother's response, the point is clear: following the general rule to tell the truth will at times require sensitive direct interpretation in dialogue with the situation we face.

If some situations require sensitive interpretation, are there not other situations that seem to require that we limit the degree of truthfulness we want to convey? Certainly there are instances where telling the truth can be cruel. When we insist on disclosing to another something that is hurtful, even though it is true, simply in the name of telling the truth for its own sake, we are certainly not telling the truth in love. An examination of our judgment and sensitivity to the neighbor is in order, if not an examination of our motives and the degree of care we really have for the other person. We often think of so-called white lies as being occasioned by this kind of sensitivity for the feelings of the other. Certainly, in everyday society, we do operate by custom with the mutual expectation that politeness and diplomacy will lead us to sharing less than the whole truth about the impressions we have or the opinions we hold.

Thielicke provides us with another example of the courteous white lie that is at the same time an amusing anecdote. He tells of a sexton at whose church theological students frequently preached. "He always had three stock answers when they asked with anxious curiosity how they had done. If they had done well, he would reply, 'The Lord has been gracious'; if moderately well, 'The text was difficult'; and if badly, 'The hymns were well chosen.'"[9] However, while we may applaud the tact of the sexton, we should also recognize that lies we excuse as white lies because we tell them to protect the feelings of others or for some expediency we feel will produce the greater good are often more dangerous than we might think. Furthermore, whether we are engaged in interpreting how to tell the truth or engaged in determining whether a lie is a white lie, we are always in danger of self-deceptive rationalizations for escaping the hard and sometimes painful work of telling the truth.

The hazards of rationalization and self-justification are no less real in circumstances where telling the truth seems to be in conflict with other obligations of love. Is a physician justified in withholding the truth from a patient about his or her true condition because the physician believes that such knowledge would be so demoralizing as to interfere with the patient's will to live? Is the truth really a problem for the patient to deal with, or is it more a problem for the physician to deal with? Family members may face the same questions in relating to loved ones who are gravely ill. Is it justified for governments to lie for the sake of national security? There may be cases where it arguably is, but it may also be argued that such justifications lead to a pattern of deceiving the public in order to protect the standing of the government or of one political party and manipulate public opinion to support its own ends.

During the vice presidential and presidential debates leading up to the 2002 election, a new feature was added to the media coverage. Reporters were given the special assignment to identify how many times each candidate misrepresented the truth. Apparently the networks added the feature in the full expectation that they would have something to report. However, perhaps nothing about that campaign was more distressing that the storm brewed by the Swift Boat Veterans for Truth who accused John Kerry of lying about his war record and the medals he won under allegedly false pretenses as a "swift boat" captain in Vietnam. Claims and counterclaims flew back and forth. The fact that credibility on either side of the controversy was so obviously tainted by political partisanship fed the already cynical belief of the public that lying and politics simply go together. Reasonable, nonpartisan presentations of the evidence of what really happened seemed to have little impact.[10]

Is Honesty Really the Best Policy?

I suppose most of us grew up hearing a parent or teacher repeat the old saying "Honesty is the best policy." The presumption in this saying seems to be that if we tell the truth we will not only have done the right thing, but things will also work out better in the end. This statement is frequently made after the truth has been told and things have worked out for the best. However, in the reality of resolving the conflict between telling the truth and other competing obligations, it is not always self-evident that things will work out for the best. In some conflict situations, the decision to tell the truth may have painful consequences. I have in mind the kind of situation that has become a critical issue in the ethics of the business world. This is the issue of the whistle-blower, the employee of a corporation who discovers that his or her company is engaged in some kind of unethical practice and, in conscience, feels compelled to tell the truth about it, perhaps first to upper-level management but maybe even to outside agencies of government or the press.[11] To illustrate the problem, we can look at the following case, which, though fictitious, is very true to life and has many analogues throughout business, industry, and other walks of life.

Howard is a fifty-year-old engineer who has an excellent job working for a large corporation that manufactures aircraft parts. He is a husband and father with three children, one of whom has just begun college, with the other two close behind. In the course of Howard's work, he discovers that his corporation has been manufacturing a defective part that has thus far escaped detection but that could in the long run pose serious safety hazards once the parts have been in use for some time. Howard goes to his immediate supervisor with his discovery, but to his dismay the supervisor, instead of sharing his concern, tries to persuade him that he is mistaken in his judgment and warns him to take the matter no further. But Howard is sure of his facts. Howard discusses it with some of his colleagues, but to his surprise he finds very little support from them for pursuing his concerns. They realize, as Howard himself does, that a recall of the parts and the possible loss of valuable contracts would be a terrible financial blow to the corporation and could threaten the job security of those who work there. Nonetheless, Howard feels conscience-bound to keep after this problem. Therefore, despite the warnings of his supervisor and his peers, he presents his evidence to the highest level of management. His appeals for corrective action fall on deaf ears. Like his supervisor, they try to persuade Howard that his perception of the liabilities involved in this presumed defect is erroneous and exaggerated. Finally, they warn him that if he were to take the matter outside the company, he could expect to lose his job and find it virtually impossible to get another position in the industry. Other corporations would be advised of his problematic behavior. For several months thereafter Howard struggles with his conscience, trying to decide whether or not he should make his information public and trying to decide if he can still trust his own judgment. His wife stands behind him and promises her support for doing what he feels he must do. However, he senses her growing anxiety over what would happen to the family if Howard were to lose his job and be unable to find another one that would provide the needed income. Howard recognizes this danger as well and realizes that starting a new career at age fifty would be extremely difficult if not impossible. In the meantime, he also notices that his fellow employees and supervisor have become increasingly less friendly, and he is being given fewer and fewer responsibilities.

Howard is a typical whistle-blower who is having an all-too-typical experience as a consequence of his honesty. As one author has observed, "From a distance, the general public often regards the whistle blower as a sort of culture hero; examples are Frank Serpico, who uncovered widespread bribery in the New York City Police Department, and Karen Silkwood, who alleged that the Kerr McGee Plant was producing unsafe plutonium products that leaked radiation."[12] However, this same author goes on to point out that in ordinary daily life, whistle-blowers have very little real support from their peers or from society in general for their efforts at being morally responsible. "Few people have heard of Joseph Whitson, Jr., an Air Force chemist, who refused to falsify drug tests so that certain commanders could 'get at' certain people. He told his story at a drug trial, and within a few months, his job was 'abolished.' He is now unemployed and paying off $100,000 in legal fees."[13] More recently, the senior civilian contracting officer for the Army Corps of Engineers, Ms. Bunnatine H. Greenhouse, was suddenly demoted for "poor performance" after she publicly criticized the Corps for circumventing her authority and awarding a noncompetitive contract for work in Iraq to a subsidiary of Halliburton, the company once run by Vice President Cheney.[14]

Members of the "whistle-blower's hall of fame" like Serpico, Silkwood, and Roger Boisjoly, who issued repeated warnings about the O-rings on the ill-fated space shuttle *Challenger*, share with their lesser-known colleagues in truth-telling the common burden of material, emotional, and social suffering. Some research has found that whistle-blowers frequently suffer depression and anxiety under stress, sometimes coupled with allergies, divorce, and suicidal tendencies.[15]

Fostering Truthfulness

For Howard and others like him, the conflict is a serious one. While we may be quick to say that Howard's obligation to tell the truth is stronger than other considerations, and especially so because the safety of unknown people is also involved, Howard himself must balance this against the needs of his family in the face of painful and predictable consequences. A decision to do what is right could be potentially disastrous to the well-being of his household. While few of us may face such drastic choices, to live the ethic of love means that we will often be confronted with choices and obligations that we would just as soon avoid but that we cannot ignore.

The plight of the whistle-blower in business raises questions regarding how we create a climate in which truth-telling is encouraged and even rewarded. This concern is germane since we are stressing the positive qualities of relationships of trust that are associated with this rule of love. If, as we have said, truthful communication is essential to the trust that builds community and mutual well-being in community with each other, then the relationships and communities in which we live must provide fertile ground for that truth. When disclosures of truth are met only with judgment, punishment, and disapproval, for example, in a family, and with little in the way of grace or understanding, we can hardly expect truthfulness to flourish. I am not suggesting that we should not suffer the just consequences of our misdeeds simply because we have been truthful about them. However, I am suggesting that building an atmosphere conducive to truthfulness in personal sharing is everybody's job in whatever the community of interaction may be. If there is within the family, community, or work setting a disposition to value truth, to be willing to hear it graciously and with a constructive response, to be understanding, forgiving, and ready to receive what is disclosed in the best possible light, then we have the kind of context of mutual acceptance that is an encouragement to truthfulness.

In terms of our concern for the whistle-blower, corporations have a responsibility to provide an atmosphere that encourages truthfulness and that can, in turn, eliminate some of the terrible conflicts endured by whistle-blowers of good conscience. Corporations may, of course, take steps to accommodate the whistle-blower and deal with his or her concerns constructively in order to avoid legal action on the part of the whistle-blower or legal and financial consequences for not dealing with the whistle-blower's particular disclosures. However, companies concerned about a high level of ethical responsibility in their operation may wish to seek a higher ground by developing an ethos and procedures congenial to employee truthfulness.

If a company itself is committed to truthfulness, concerned employees will be assured that they will be treated with fairness and that their concerns will be dealt with responsibly and promptly. As one writer in business ethics has put it, "There needs to be a clear process of receiving complaints, conducting impartial investigations, to finding standards of judgment, providing a fair hearing procedure, and reaching the most objective and responsible decision possible."[16] Various procedures for accomplishing this goal have been discussed in the literature of business ethics. However, once again, the key is in the disposition to truthfulness prevailing within the corporate community itself. Where there is an atmosphere of acceptance and mutual respect, effective procedures can be readily developed and truthfulness encouraged.

Bok explains how lying makes an impact on the liar. It damages one's own sense of personal integrity and adversely alters the relationship one has with those to whom one has lied.[17] For many, if not most, this is a heavy burden to bear for one's failure to tell the truth. To be sure, when we lie we bring this burden on ourselves. But when we make it hard for people to tell the truth, it seems to me that we are responsible in part for their own internal conflict and loss of integrity. The degree to which we can determine that responsibility in personal interactions, family life, or in the life of organizations may be difficult, but I am convinced this is an important part of our consideration of truth-telling.

Motives toward Truth

If those who would lie must examine their motives, and if individuals, communities, or corporations must examine the manner in which they succeed or fail to provide an atmosphere for truthfulness, there are times when those who would tell the truth must examine their motives for doing so as well. The truth can be used deliberately to harm or to advance one's own ambitions. Some whistle-blowers may not be driven by pangs of conscience but may be driven by revenge or a perceived opportunity for advancement at the expense of another. Some may even see the possibility of a successful and rewarding lawsuit against the company. In short, the fact that what one tells is the truth does not in itself guarantee that what one has done is morally noble or ethically responsible.

In keeping with our emphasis on the roots of the Christian ethic in the faith life of the community, it seems to me that several observations are in order. Congregations are just as likely to be places where deception, duplicity, and slander thrive as anywhere else. To foster a community in which people are able to speak and seek the truth in love and in an atmosphere that is gracious, forgiving, accepting, and supportive is obviously a goal for the congregation consistent with our vision of the people of God as a people of anticipation. To explore ways in which the congregation can get at this goal through the resources of its faith life brings us to our previous discussion of formation. There, as we explored the virtue of poverty of spirit, we noted that a profound sense of reliance on the grace of God, which is at the heart of this virtue and its spirituality, frees us from self-deception and the temptation to compromise the truth in an effort to justify ourselves or gain our own security. While the rule of love to tell the truth is concerned with whether or not the things we say are in fact true, it is the disposition of the individual and the community that finally ensures that there is a commitment to truthfulness even under the most ambiguous and confusing circumstances. In the context of this attention to our formation as a community and as individuals we can begin to develop ministries to our members that are sensitive to the problems they face in this area of moral concern. In our society, it is certainly urgent that our congregations develop a keener sense of the daily challenges to truth-telling that persons in the business world and other occupations must face. The notion that business and professional activities are of necessity conducted by different standards from those we embrace in our personal ethics is another version of the dichotomy between personal ethics and social concern that frustrates our need to let the full scope of God's promises speak to all aspects of life.[18]

Promise-Keeping and the People of Promise

It is fitting that we should reserve for last a discussion of the general rule of love that we should keep our promises. It will provide us with an opportunity to look back on what we have tried to do in this book even as we explore one final implication of love.

The commandment that is our point of reference is the prohibition against adultery. To be sure, the commandment focuses on marital infidelity and calls upon us to actively pursue faithfulness to the marriage covenant. However, at the same time, it suggests a broader consideration of promise-keeping. In the play by Thornton Wilder, *The Skin of Our Teeth*, the playwright explores the human condition through the highly symbolic drama of the Antrobus family. At a crucial moment in the play, Mrs. Antrobus confronts her husband with his betrayal and unfaithfulness. Her words speak not only to that dramatic moment in their marriage but also to a fundamental truth concerning the very foundations of our relationships:

> *Mrs. Antrobus:* I didn't marry you because you were perfect. I didn't even marry you because I loved you. I married you because you gave me a promise. That promise made up for your faults. And the promise I gave you made up for mine. Two imperfect people got married and it was the promise that made the marriage.
> *Mr. Antrobus:* Maggie, . . . I was only nineteen.
> *Mrs. Antrobus:* And when our children were growing up, it wasn't a house that protected them; and it wasn't our love that protected them— it was that promise.[19]

On a more popular level, radio personality Garrison Keillor, in one of his reports from Lake Wobegon, has also made the connection between fidelity in marriage and fidelity in general. The story he tells is in the form of a letter from a boyhood friend. A man, now happily married with a family, found himself becoming more and more attracted to a woman with whom he worked at the local college. He had reason to think that her feelings for him were mutual. They were about to travel together to a professional conference and the opportunity to act upon those feelings would doubtless present itself. As he waited in front of his house for her to come and pick him up, he admitted to himself that he had adultery on his mind. Then he began to reflect on the community around him, how it was a decent place with decent people who worked hard and cared about each other. What would happen, he thought, if everyone behaved in their various activities of life in the same manner he was now contemplating? Maybe people would suddenly stop paying their bills or stop taking part in the civic activities so important to the quality of life in the community. Maybe the butcher would leave the sausage in the meat case a day or two longer than it should be. Maybe people would stop caring about each other and their life together in many big and little ways that were, together, so very important. It was then that he decided to do nothing with his colleague except go to the conference with her.[20]

The great theologian Karl Barth made a point in discussing the doctrine of the image of God that fits well here. In reflecting on the phrase in Gen. 1:27—"male and female God created them"—Barth sees a reference to the marriage bond. For him the unity of male and female in the marriage bond is a paradigm or model for the fundamental relationship we have to all other human beings as a part of our creation in the image of God. In our cohumanity with others, there is a bond of implicit promise or fidelity that is analogous to the covenant of marriage.[21] While it is doubtful that the Genesis passage really says all that Barth wants it to say, it seems clear to me that his theological instincts are correct in seeing that our creation in the image of God not only bespeaks a bond of fidelity to God but also that we are created for community and unity with each other.[22]

Joseph Allen makes promising a central theme in his understanding of Christian ethics by choosing the biblical idea of *covenant* as a model for understanding the Christian life and ethic. The covenant relationship God initiates with all of humanity and promises to fulfill in the ultimate future is the framework for understanding the fundamental relationships in which we exist with other people, along with the moral obligations those relationships entail. To live in a manner appropriate to the covenant relationship God has designed for humankind is to live in a relationship in which we entrust ourselves to one another and accept the responsibilities over time that such a relationship of mutual trust requires.[23] In terms of our present discussion, what Allen seems to be saying is that to live in the covenant relationship God has ordained for us all is to keep our promises to each other in loving care for each other.

In Allen's scheme of things, the covenant of marriage and the faithfulness to promise involved there is one example of a number of special covenants in which we live. Special covenants provide particular instances of the general and all-encompassing covenant. The marriage covenant and other special covenants each have their own peculiar demands of faithfulness or promise-keeping, but all are related to the fundamental relationships of mutual trust in which God has placed us as a human family.[24]

Allen goes on to speak of faithfulness as characteristic of promise-keeping in the special covenant of marriage. Faithfulness is described as fidelity, constancy, loyalty, steadfastness, and dependability; these characteristics are contrasted with infidelity, inconstancy, disloyalty, and fickleness. Such faithfulness, he indicates, requires also fairness, sexual exclusiveness, and a commitment to the permanence of the covenant relationship. The process of fulfilling these obligations of love in marriage requires the kind of creative and insightful pro-active effort characteristic of agape love's commitment to the needs and well-being of the other person in the intimacy of a lifelong relationship that is truly "for better or for worse."[25] A great deal more could be said to elaborate on this portrait of marriage both in terms of Allen's comments and from a myriad of other sources. However, the point I want to stress, with Allen, is the manner in which promise-keeping in marriage is a particularly important paradigm for promise-keeping in general and the manner in which this is fundamental to the constitution of human life in its wholeness and authenticity.

It follows that if we enter marriage with this profound understanding, we encounter marriage as anything but a commonplace contractual arrangement; marriage is not like a business contract or a contract for professional services, subject to negotiation of terms with the understanding that such a contract can then be abrogated when the terms are no longer being met to the satisfaction of each party. Civil law permits this model to thrive through the ease of gaining a divorce or dissolution and by recognizing prenuptial agreements. The irony of this system, which permits people to move in and out of marriage practically at will, is that it belies the real situation. Despite the ease of ending marriage, divorce remains, along with the death of a spouse, at the very top of the list of the most stressful experiences of life. Moreover, an increasing number of studies detail the profound and debilitating effects of divorce on the children of broken families.

Ethically speaking, the state of marriage and divorce in our society is certainly a complicated matter. We could analyze the enormous sociological changes that have characterized the last few decades and created new and different pressures on marriage. We could cite conflict resolution decisions in a myriad of cases and question whether the tragic choice of disillusion or divorce is the most responsible choice. But the most important thing to say is that when it is a choice, it is a *tragic* choice! While it may be a necessary and responsible choice in some instances, it is nonetheless a failure in one particular and highly significant instance of promise-keeping.

The congregation gathered in faith, as the fount of ethics for the Christian community, needs to provide a ministry to people for strengthening marriage, for guarding its integrity in congregational and daily life as well as providing a ministry for those whose marriages have failed.

Such a ministry is a function of Christian ethics and congregational life because it supports and instructs us in the obligations of love so that we may find help in meeting them on a daily basis as well as being prepared for moments of greatest challenge. Whether we are talking about promise-keeping in marriage or any other issue of ethical concern, exploring it together in the community of faith builds resolve and prepares us all, individually and as a group, for the challenges we may meet at any time.

I still remember the pastor who came to my office asking for advice as to whether he should discuss issues of euthanasia in his congregation. He reflected on the way in which members of his congregation had approached him distraught over how to decide about treatment for a dying loved one. He wished he had a set of the "right questions" to ask them since they were looking to him for absolute answers he felt unable to give. Maybe a set of the right questions would be helpful to have in mind because pastors will always have to face these circumstances. But the upshot of our conversation was the point I just made in the last paragraph. Talking about issues of euthanasia in the congregation is a way of providing moral leadership in preparing people for the crises they may face and laying the foundations of love's future decisions. Such conversations in the community may help everyone to better understand what the right questions are when the time comes.

From the standpoint of Christian education, Maria Harris has written that the congregation's educational program is not defined by those who teach, the classes offered, and the lessons used: "The church does not *have* an educational program; it *is* an educational program."[26] Rather than seeking just the right educational program for a particular parish, Harris insists,

> a fuller and more extensive curriculum is already present in the church's life: in teaching, worship, community, proclamation, and outreach. Printed resources that serve this wider curriculum are in the treasury of the church, especially the comprehensive curricular materials designed over the last century in the United States. These, however, are not *the* curriculum. *The* curriculum is both more basic and more profound. It is *the entire course of the church's life*, found in the fundamental forms of that life.[27]

From the standpoint of Christian ethics, I have been trying throughout to make a point similar to Harris's. At the end of chapter 1, I reflected on experiences in which I saw people in congregations attempting to avoid discussion of hard ethical questions. But to avoid these conversations is to overlook that fact that the ethical witness of the Christian community is integral to our life in the gospel of Jesus Christ and proclamation of that gospel; it is not an aside. To overlook this fact is, then, to fall short in mutual preparation for the fullness of our vocation.

Our reflections on promise-keeping serve to remind us that God has specifically fashioned us as a people of promise. Our mandate, our vocation, is to keep faith with our neighbor and our world in love, as God has kept faith with us and, by our witness of love, to anticipate the fullness of God's promised future. We are a people with promises to keep.

One final memory helps to bring our thoughts to a conclusion. I recall being an awkward thirteen-year-old boy, newly enrolled in junior high school, encountering my first gym class. Our gym teacher was a gruff man whose teaching methodology was fear. He would line us all up on the gym floor for basketball drills and, after we had gone at it for a while, would blow his whistle and scream at us for how poorly we were doing. One of his favorite phrases was, "Look at all that deadwood out there." Except for a talented few, most of us were consigned to the deadwood pile as hopelessly bumbling and inept would-be athletes.

Years later, I thought of my gym teacher at the time of the volcanic eruption of Mount St. Helens. A television commercial for a leading lumber company gave us a panoramic view of all the trees that were wiped out by the volcano. There they were, scattered like so many toothpicks all over the mountainside, as far as the eye could see. What a deadwood pile *that* was! The commercial went on to say how the lumber company moved in to retrieve the fallen trees and turn them into useful products. Notwithstanding the self-serving purposes of the lumber company commercial, it struck me that the lumber company functioned more as God does than did my gym teacher. In some sense we are all deadwood and apparently not good for much. But God graciously retrieves us and fashions us anew into a thing of beauty that is a service to humankind: a church, a people of promise, a people of anticipation:

> *Once you were not a people, but now you are God's people;*
> *once you had not received mercy, but now you have received mercy.*

> —1 Peter 2:10

Questions for Discussion

1. How many relationships and arrangements in human society can you mention that depend on people telling the truth? What happens when they lie instead? Try to give specific examples.

2. Put yourself in the place of Howard, our fictional whistle-blower. What would you do and how would you reach that decision? Can you think of other situations in which telling the truth seems to be in conflict with other obligations?

3. What are some of the forces that work against keeping our marriage covenant promises? Do people actually take these promises—"for better or for worse," etc.—seriously nowadays, or are they really only conditional upon whether we stay happy together? What can Christian communities do to strengthen marriages?

APPENDIX 1

A Theology for Outreach

Trinity Episcopal Church and St. Paul's Lutheran Church are old established congregations situated close to each other in an urban environment. It is a midsize city with some big-city problems. Both parishes have seen membership dwindle in recent years as older members have died and others have moved outside the city. Still, both congregations retain a core of committed members who are convinced they have an important ministry to offer in their city neighborhood. They want to stay where they are.

Phyllis Carlson, the pastor at St. Paul's, and Steve Graham, the priest at Trinity, have become good colleagues, sharing experiences and ideas and getting their congregations together at various times for worship and service projects. Both Phyllis and Steve have come to the conclusion that their ministry in the community would be better served if Trinity and St. Paul's would merge and become a joint Lutheran-Episcopal congregation. They find that the shared activities they have fostered have created openness to that idea among their members.

In separate congregational meetings, the two congregations agree to consider a plan for such a joint venture. They ask their pastor and priest to work together to develop a statement of common faith that could provide the spiritual foundation for their merger and a vision for mission and ministry in which they could unite.

Both Steve and Phyllis share a vision for mission in the neighborhood that includes community outreach. While the details and possibilities are not yet clear, such outreach might include over time: (1) programs for the youth who are constantly tempted with drugs and gang activities; (2) help in parenting for teen mothers; (3) emergency hunger aid; (4) job counseling; (5) low cost housing for persons in need; (6) counseling services; (7) addressing the problems of the homeless; (8) being a catalyst for community in a racially and ethnically diverse neighborhood.

Phyllis remembers how Luther worked with local government to set up a community chest for the poor and victims of misfortune in the city of Leisnig and surrounding villages. Their own efforts might also involve cooperation with local leaders, she thought. Moreover, Luther grounded his advocacy for community welfare in the church's worship in word and sacrament.[1] She also noted that her national church office now has a person in place responsible for promoting faith-based community organizing and helping congregations get started in this kind of outreach.

Steve had heard about the Episcopal Church of the Messiah in Detroit whose circumstances were similar to his own parish: an old-line congregation with dwindling membership in a changing urban setting. Over the years Messiah renewed its congregational life and successfully incorporated a variety of neighborhood outreach ministries. This long list of services included a food pantry, various youth ministry initiatives, covenant communities to bring ethnically diverse people together in the community, a housing corporation to provide low-cost housing, and more. The leadership at Messiah believed that activities like creating affordable housing are a genuine form of evangelism.[2]

Both Phyllis and Steve also want their community outreach vision to be a clear expression of their basic statement of faith in the triune God and in the gospel of Jesus, the Christ. They share a conviction that the ministry and mission of the church are rooted in word and sacrament. They don't want to appear to be more like a social agency than a church. They are also aware of how the social activism of liberal Protestant churches during the '60s and '70s backfired. They are sensitive to the fact that many of today's growing churches have a more conservative posture regarding social concerns. Nonetheless, they are sure that they can craft a statement of faith that will provide the theological grounding for their comprehensive vision of community outreach in mission and ministry.

Put your self in the role of the two ministers.

1. In what ways can the material in this book be helpful to these pastors in developing a statement of faith that integrates the various possibilities of outreach ministry with the proclamation of the gospel in word and sacrament? What might this statement of faith look like?

2. What theological resources in this book might be used to address specific outreach initiatives?

3. Congregations have not always been committed to community outreach and social concerns. What aspects of the faith and biblical resources would you want to stress in an effort to educate the congregation to its new mission vision?

APPENDIX 2

The Stem-Cell Bill

George Coleman is a veteran member of the state senate in what many consider a rather conservative-leaning state. Though he would consider himself a political moderate, he has managed to earn the trust of his mixed constituency of liberal, conservative, and independent voters. With a reelection campaign looming in the near future, George has a feeling that this trust may be put to the test when he is forced to take a stand on a highly volatile bill coming before the senate. The bill in question would ban state funding for embryonic stem-cell research.

Stem cells are indeterminate cells not genetically programmed to develop into a specific tissue or organ of the body. They have the capacity to develop into a variety of tissues and organs, given the appropriate stimulus. While stem cells occur in adults, their potential for a wide variety of therapeutic applications seems limited when compared to embryonic stem cells. Embryonic stem cells are what scientists call "pluripotent," able to develop in a wide variety of ways for a wide variety of therapeutic applications. Embryonic stem cells can be harvested from blastocysts created in the process of *in vitro* fertilization. When *in vitro* fertilization is done, more eggs are fertilized in the laboratory than are implanted in the uterus. Those blastocysts not chosen for implantation are most often discarded. These are the ones that can be chosen to have their stem cells extracted, a process which then kills the blastocyst.

George has been listening carefully to the voices of people who hold a variety of views on stem-cell research.

People with Parkinson's disease, families with loved ones in the grip of Alzheimer's disease, and others beset with end-stage kidney disease, certain forms of cancer, liver failure, or paralysis see the promise of embryonic stem-cell research as a virtual godsend. Their stories are moving. Even if it is too late for them or their loved ones, their experience with these fatal and debilitating diseases evokes a compassionate advocacy for this work to go forward. How can one say no to them?

One also hears from the scientists who have these diseases in their cross-hairs. They are eager to forge ahead, whether out of an authentic vocational drive to combat disease and death or the thrill of the hunt and the glory of the prize—or both. Their ambition raises George's suspicions, but their arguments on behalf of the advancement of medicine are persuasive nonetheless.

The people behind the bill to ban stem-cell research have their own ideas about what constitutes a passionate commitment to the sanctity of life. While stem-cell research may promise some healing consequences, it does so at the price of intentionally destroying human life. Persons holding this view regard the early-stage embryos used to obtain stem cells as human life. Many would say that human life begins at conception and has a moral claim on us from that moment on.

Of course, George is aware that the debate over when life begins has a long history. The fact that there has never been a consensus on the answer to this question is at the bottom of the endless debate over abortion. The intractable nature of this ongoing religious and philosophical dispute prompted the Supreme Court in *Roe v. Wade* to make the decision to abort prior to the "viability" of the fetus outside the womb a matter of private decision. Consequently, there has been no legal constraint regarding the discarding of blastocysts in the process of *in vitro* fertilization, whatever the ethical qualms some may feel. However, the idea that we might deliberately conceive and grow human life in the laboratory for the sole purpose of extracting stem cells for research purposes adds a new ethical dimension in the minds of many. Some may reason that the fact that many fertilized eggs never implant in the natural course of things provides a ground for excusing the loss of some in the process of *in vitro* fertilization. Still, to deliberately sacrifice them to research raises questions.

Concerns over the deliberate creation and destruction of human life are heightened by the fact that many stem-cell researchers want to employ "therapeutic cloning" as a source of stem cells. Therapeutic cloning removes the nucleus from a donor egg and replaces it with the DNA from another person. An electric impulse reprograms the nuclear DNA, and the egg divides as if a sperm had fertilized it. The blastocyst that develops in five days is then split apart to harvest the stem cells in its cavity. Researchers see the development of this method as particularly promising because the stem cells used in treating the person whose DNA was inserted in the donor egg would not be subject to rejection by the immune system. The cells would have his or her own DNA.

Opponents of stem-cell research find the prospect of therapeutic cloning to be particularly insidious. Now we are clearly creating human life for no other purpose than to destroy it for research or therapy. Moreover, we are doing it by the morally questionable process of cloning. While no one in the stem-cell debate is suggesting we make babies by cloning, there are those who see no distinction between therapeutic cloning and reproductive cloning. If life begins at conception, cloning is cloning. If we allow therapeutic cloning, we place ourselves on a slippery slope toward reproductive cloning.

Some states have passed legislation to support stem-cell research, and a license for therapeutic cloning has been issued in the United Kingdom. At the same time, the federal government has severely limited this research thus far although a numbers of legislators in Washington have attempted bills from a variety of viewpoints. The political landscape is mottled.

George is also aware of the fact that a good bit of the opposition to stem-cell research and support for the bill that faces him is coming from religious conservatives among his constituents. George himself is a Christian, a lifelong member of a so-called mainline Protestant denomination. He is uncomfortable with what he considers the moral absolutism among Catholics and conservative evangelicals. His belief in the separation of church and state makes him leery of having such a rigid position imposed on the entire populace. At the same time, his own faith often serves as a guide in his thinking about political decisions. There is no doubting the influence of our faith traditions on our laws and public policies, even if the influence is indirect. For George, the struggle is over how best to honor the sanctity of life. Both the commitment to heal and the commitment to preserve life appeal to his Christian conscience. From his standpoint, Christians should recognize that there are times when we can't be absolutely sure what course of action to pursue. We need to pray and search and then decide, trusting in God's mercy.

While George struggles with how best to respect the sanctity of life, he also is concerned with the questions of justice involved in this debate. With over 43 million people without health insurance, how do we set priorities in the allocation of public funds spent in medicine? For that matter, support of public health measures and human services to the needy and persons with disabilities are immediate life-saving measures too. Must we follow every lead no matter what the cost? However, in reality, will a vote for or against this bill actually have any impact on these other areas of concern?

George has been in conversation with other senators who are similarly conflicted by this bill. They are working hard to try and find a compromise.

1. How would you state the ethical issue for George?

2. In one respect, the decision George faces on this bill is a matter of resolving conflict. Do we pursue the therapeutic possibilities to relieve horrible diseases and conditions, or do we forgo this avenue of research in respect for all forms of nascent human life? What is the best way to follow love's general rule of respect for the sanctity of human life? Are the adjudicating axioms in chapter 11 of any help in sorting out this conflict? Would their application to this deliberation likely lead to a compromise bill of some sort? If so, what might it look like?

3. How much weight would you place on the justice dimension of this matter? Why?

4. Does this situation qualify as one of those ethical issues in which there is no agreement among Christians on either what the Bible says about the matter or what the true facts are? Why or why not?

5. If George loses in the next election as a result of his vote on this bill or his involvement in a possible compromise measure, the state will lose a fine legislator of good character who has served well. Does this consideration have any ethical standing in his decision?

APPENDIX 3

The Just War Debate

Introduction

Just war thinking in Christian tradition goes back at least as far as the fourth-century writings of Ambrose of Milan and has been prominently associated with such towering theological figures as Augustine, Thomas Aquinas, and Martin Luther. By the end of the Middle Ages, the criteria for determining a just war were well established. Despite the fact that they have undergone much refinement in the discussions and debates of modern warfare, these criteria remain with us in contemporary discussions of just war. Though one can find variations in the listing of just war criteria, the following are representative of the tradition.

First, we have criteria for whether or not deciding to go to war is a just decision (jus ad bellum):

- **War must be declared by a legitimate authority.** *This means there should be a public declaration. It precludes sneak attacks and represents a legal exercise of authority on the part of government.*
- **War must be fought only for a just cause.** *This may include defense against unprovoked aggression, defense of one's allies, deterrence of a threat to peace, humanitarian assistance to those under oppression, etc.*
- **War must be fought with the right intention.** *This means that the decision to wage war should be driven by the desire for peace and the common good and not conducted, for example, out of vengeance, the will to power, or material and territorial gain.*
- **War must be a last resort.** *All means to avoid war should be exhausted, at which point war becomes one's tragic duty if it is truly a just cause.*
- **The values gained by the war effort should be proportionately greater than evils of the war itself.** *This precludes wars that are futile.*

Second there are two primary criteria for how a war must be waged if it is to be considered just (jus in bello):

- **War must be waged in respect for the lives of noncombatants.**
- **The means used must be proportionate to the ends.** *This criterion precludes "overkill," using more force and doing more damage than is required to achieve the just goals of the war.*

I have taken the position that just war criteria are not a means to "justify" war but rather a means by which we determine whether or not the tragic choice of going to war is the most responsible course of action possible, the lesser of evils but clearly an evil.[1] *Given this perspective, criteria for determining whether or not to go to war* (jus ad bellum) *function as a form of adjudicating axioms, axioms for the resolution of conflict (see chapter 11). Criteria for how just war is waged* (jus in bello) *function as middle axioms related to general rules of justice and the sanctity of life.*

The Christian's call to peacemaking, the promise of God's future reign as one of peace in which the reconciling work of Christ is fully realized, and the rule of love to respect the sanctity of life in anticipation of its ultimate triumph over death in God's future all combine to commit Christians to peace over war. The burden of proof is on those who would argue the necessary evil of war. In this regard my understanding of just war thinking shares a conviction with pacifism that war is always evil. At the same time, it allows for a realistic perspective on a world that we have seen is not yet the reign of God, a world in which sin still abounds among individuals and within the social, political, and economic structures of human devising.

Julie Pearson was struggling. She had a paper due in a week's time for her Religion and Politics course at State University. That paper assignment was causing her some real personal turmoil. It was not that she wasn't good at writing papers; it was *this* paper that was the problem.

The professor had just taken the class through the history of just war thinking in Christianity and the pacifist alternative espoused especially by the so-called "peace churches." That part of the course was fine. Learning about a tradition and grasping its main concepts and their historical development was par for the course in college education. Things got a bit more difficult when it came time to make present applications, particularly to the war going on in Iraq. Then came the paper. Each student was to write a personal evaluation of whether or not the U.S. war in Iraq (waged beginning in 2003) could be considered a "just war" by the criteria of the Christian just war tradition.

Many of Julie's best friends at college were opposed to the war. She suspected her professor, whom she admired for the clarity of his thought, was also, even though he tried hard not to tip his hand. The antiwar movement was very much alive on campus, although the absence of the draft in the present conflict made a big difference in the level of student activism compared to the Vietnam era. As these perspectives critical of the war exerted their influence on her thinking, she was also keenly aware of the fact that her family strongly supported the U.S. presence in Iraq. Her favorite uncle was serving there now. At her home church, they regularly prayed for him and for others in the military in Iraq and Afghanistan. How to sort all this out!

Readings for the paper didn't clarify matters for her.

First, she read a strong argument from a well-known and highly respected theologian for the judgment that the war in Iraq is indeed a just war. The argument sought to demonstrate that, regardless of the existence or not of weapons of mass destruction (the threat of such weapons in the hands of an aggressive tyrant being the initial premise for war) there is enough evidence of human rights violations under Saddam Hussein to constitute a just cause. His track record of breaking promises was sufficient reason for thinking that stopping him by this war was truly the last resort. The argument went on to assert that our intentions are right: to establish democratic rule and move out. Finally, various efforts to protect civilian populations demonstrated conformity to *jus in bello*.[2]

Julie then quickly discovered that there were other views just as strongly argued. In a widely read book, another religious leader had this to say as part of his contention that the Iraq War is not a just war:

> Neither international law nor Christian just war doctrine allow preemptive military action by one state against another. The U.N. Charter and international law only allow for individual states to go to war in situations of self-defense or after an armed attack. And in both international law and just war doctrine, there are scrupulous conditions even for self-defense. For the United States to unilaterally initiate military action was a dangerous precedent; it severely undermined the system of international security established since World War II.[3]

As arguments on one side or the other multiplied in Julie's readings, she became aware of other claims. Those arguing for the war often said that our way of life was at stake in the face of extremists who hate what America stands for. Others pointed out that we are losing lives and running up a colossal deficit that will burden our children and grandchildren and that is already cutting into our ability to provide needed social programs and foreign aid. Some claimed that patriotism required support of troops and the war. Others claimed that one can be patriotic in criticizing the war and still support the troops.

Perhaps most confusing of all to Julie was her discovery of the argument that just war doctrine is not useful because it has never been credibly employed to say "no" to going to war. While the principles of just war teaching have a noble ring to them, the reality of human sin tempts people to use these principles to rationalize a war that is really being driven by self-serving impulses or bad intentions.[4] This fact was displayed in public suspicion, whether founded or not, about the honesty of the administration pursuing the war in Iraq. Maybe, Julie thought, pacifism is the only alternative after all.

As Julie finally sat down to write, she was still unsure how she would come out. If it was anything less than full support of the war, could she share that with her family when she came home for break and they asked about her courses?

---

1. Put your self in Julie's place. Knowing what you do about just war teaching, what would you write?

2. Even if you think the U.S. war in Iraq was a just cause, do you think it was a last resort? A group of Christian ethicists have sought to formulate and advance principles for just peacemaking. These are not designed to supplant just war doctrine but to press the case for the kind of peacemaking initiatives that make war less likely. Peacemaking practices see the connection between justice, nonviolent action, negotiation, and the capacity for peace.[5] On the eve of the war, former president Jimmy Carter urged that continued inspection for the indefinite future would contain Saddam Hussein and be a nonviolent alternative. Was that a realistic possibility?

3. Is it possible to criticize a war and still support the troops? Are Christians able to disagree on this and still be together in communion?

4. If just war criteria functioning as "adjudicating axioms" can be used to rationalize self-serving decisions, are they still useful? What marks of Christian character discussed in part 2 of this book might need to be in place to insure their usefulness?

5. Remembering our discussion of truth-telling in chapter 12, how should Julie handle the discussion with her family about her paper should she end up as a critic of the war?

6. Are there other questions prompted by this discussion?

APPENDIX 4

Sexual Ethics and Parental Responsibility

Jill is a bright and attractive seventeen-year-old about to start her senior year in high school. Along with others in her class, she is preparing to select a college. She wants to go to a college away from home but not too far. She wants to be independent but not too distant from the security that home represents. It is also the case that she and her parents get along great. She even gets along well with her younger brother. Jill wants to be close enough to be able to see them frequently.

Jill has enjoyed popularity in school and has dated a number of different boys. None of these relationships has been much more than friendly until recently. She now has what seems to be developing into a serious relationship with a boy in her class.

An aspect of the good relationship enjoyed between Jill and her parents, Neil and Laura, has been their ability to talk openly and honestly about all kinds of things. Neil and Laura talked with Jill about sex and sexual conduct from early on, adding more information and counsel as Jill grew more mature. As Christian parents they shared their beliefs. They spoke of how our sexuality is part of God's good creation. They emphasized that sex belongs within the intimacy of a marriage marked by love, faithfulness, kindness, and fairness. Sexual intercourse in that sort of ideal context becomes something very wonderful and if it leads to having children, something more wonderful still.

When sex is only casual or a matter of individuals satisfying their own desires—something that happens within some marriages—it is disappointing and even at times degrading. Christians have a vocation, they said, to lift up the ideal of sex in a loving and just marriage. This is a particularly important witness in our sex-saturated culture in which promiscuity seems widespread and acceptable to many.

Jill told her parents that many of the same points were made in the presentation on sexual ethics by the youth pastor at their church's youth group retreat.

In the discussion among the kids, however, there was much more questioning. While everyone agreed that sex in marriage was the ideal and no one would say that being promiscuous was okay, some wondered whether it might not be all that bad to have sex with someone if you really love each other and practice "safe sex." One girl talked of what she had heard from her older sister about what goes on at her college campus. Kids who didn't have sex during the high school years suddenly felt they were adult enough to now do as they pleased. It no longer seemed a big deal. Someone else spoke of how he knew of couples in college who were really in love and wanted to get married but could not afford to do it until after they graduated and went to work. Should they really have to wait years before having sexual intercourse when they are really married in spirit?

One of the youth said they all ought to follow the example of the Christian teenagers who took a public pledge to abstain from sex until marriage. She thought this was a good witness. Others were more skeptical, however. Some pointed out that most of those who took the pledge ultimately broke it, and a lot who didn't still did other stuff sexually. One of the group added that he had read in a magazine how young people who pledge to abstain often get into trouble when they break the pledge. They don't take precautions because that would mean they *intended* to have sex all along, so they end up with a pregnancy on their hands.

"All in all," Jill told her parents after relating this youth group experience, "I still believe what you have taught me is right. But I was surprised at how many of the other kids were so uncertain or at least had real questions about the right thing to do in some cases. They are Christians too. Some of them are the kindest and most generous friends I have ever had."

Later, Neil and Laura talked about what Jill had shared from her youth group discussion. They trust Jill and do not think that she is the kind of person that will be promiscuous and casual about sex. They trust Jill's sincerity in her expressed intention to wait until marriage before having sexual intercourse. They also know that as a good relationship develops with another, it isn't easy to refrain from a natural desire to make love with that person. They remember their own struggles when they were young and not yet married. Jill is getting serious with this boy now, and college away from the influences of home is looming too. Jill is their unique daughter and no mere statistic, but Neil and Laura are also aware of studies reporting that over two-thirds of high school youth are sexually active by the time they graduate. The percentages get even higher after graduation. Jill has already told of how some of her best church friends are ambivalent about traditional sexual ethics.

Neil and Laura know that their strong relationship with Jill means that she will take what they say seriously. But what if what they say turns out to be unrealistic and they fail to give her some important practical advice about sex? Laura wonders aloud whether or not they should still lift up the ideal of marriage but also counsel Jill to be prepared should that ideal be impossible for her to attain. Maybe, she allows, we should counsel her to at least refrain from casual sex and make sure that, if she can't wait till marriage, it should be with a loving and responsible person. It should be something they both want, not something coerced. Of course, if Neil and Laura were to go this far, they would also have to encourage Jill to take birth-control precautions.

Neil agrees that this approach is simply common sense; if you can't manage the ideal of keeping sex for marriage, your sexual activity should be loving and responsible However, he also questions whether such an approach really abandons the ideal: sex belongs in marriage, but in a loving and responsible relationship it's okay too? Since they have stressed the ideal of sex in marriage as a matter of Christian ethics and Christian witness, must they say that any deviation from that norm is wrong? A sin? If so, then how can they tell Jill anything other than their conviction that she should try her best and pray for help to remain a virgin until her wedding night?

1. Some might argue that marriage is a civil matter to be honored for the stability of the family in society, but sex is a matter of morality, and the moral norm for sex is its occurence in a loving, faithful, and just relationship. Is there anything said in chapter 12 about promise-keeping that could contradict that argument? If not, what do you think of it and why? If you disagree that the primary test for ethical sex is a loving and just relationship, would you say that such sexual conduct is a sin or simply less than the ideal?

2. We have spoken in this book of the witness of the Christian ethic. Is the ideal of sex only in marriage an important part of that witness? Is it simply a thing of the past and Christians should revise sexual ethics to reflect the changing times? Can you cite evidence that this has already happened in some parts of the Christian church, officially or unofficially?

3. If Laura and Neil do counsel Jill on what to seek in a relationship if she can't wait until marriage, are they being dishonest since they themselves are committed to that ideal? Even if you think it is dishonest, is it a responsible compromise in the interest of their daughter's well-being?

For Further Reading

Modern Foundational Works

Althaus, Paul. *The Ethics of Martin Luther.* Translated with foreword by Robert C. Schultz. Philadelphia: Fortress Press, 1972.

Barth, Karl. *Ethics.* Dietrich Braun, editor. Translated by Goeffrey Bromily. New York: Seabury, 1981.

Bonhoeffer, Dietrich. *Ethics.* Dietrich Bonhoeffer Works, Vol. 6. Edited by Clifford J. Green. Translated by Reinhard Krauss, Charles C. West, and Douglas W. Stott. Minneapolis: Fortress Press, 2005.

Elert, Werner. *The Christian Ethos.* Translated by Carl J. Schindler. Philadelphia: Fortress Press, 1957.

Fletcher, Joseph. *Situation Ethics: The New Morality.* Philadelphia: Westminster, 1966.

Gustafson, James. *Christ and the Moral Life.* New York: Harper and Row, 1968.

———. *Church as Moral Decision-Maker.* Philadelphia: Pilgrim Press, 1970.

———. *Ethics from a Theocentric Perspective.* Chicago: University of Chicago Press, 1981.

Niebuhr, H. Richard. *The Responsible Self: An Essay in Christian Moral Philosophy.* New York: Harper and Row, 1978.

Niebuhr, Reinhold. *An Interpretation of Christian Ethics.* New York: Seabury, 1973.

———. *Moral Man and Immoral Society: A Study in Ethics and Politics.* Louisville: Westminster/John Knox, 2001.

Nygren, Anders. *Agape and Eros.* Translated by Philip S. Watson. Chicago: University of Chicago Press, 1982.

Outka, Gene H. *Agape: An Ethical Analysis.* New Haven: Yale University Press, 1972.

Ramsey, Paul. *Basic Christian Ethics.* Louisville: Westminster/John Knox Press, 1993.

Sittler, Joseph A. *The Structure of Christian Ethics.* Louisville: Westminster/John Knox Press, 1998.

Thielicke, Helmut. *Theological Ethics.* 3 volumes. Edited by William Lazareth. Grand Rapids: Eerdmans, 1979.

Yoder, John Howard. *The Politics of Jesus.* Grand Rapids: Eerdmans, 1994.

Recent: Foundational and Topical

Allen, Joseph L. *Love and Conflict: A Covenantal Model of Christian Ethics.* Nashville: Abingdon, 1984.

Benne, Robert. *Ordinary Saints: An Introduction to the Christian Life*. Minneapolis: Fortress Press, 2003.

Beuchamp, Tom L., and James F. Childress. *Principles of Biomedical Ethics*. 5th edition. New York: Oxford University Press, 2001.

Birch, Bruce, and Larry L. Rasmussen. *Bible and Ethics in the Christian Life*. Minneapolis: Augsburg, 1989.

Cahill, Lisa Sowle. *Sex, Gender and Christian Ethics*. New York: Cambridge University Press, 1996.

————. *Theological Bioethics: Participation, Justice and Change*. Washington, D.C.: Georgetown University Press, 2005.

Cannon, Katie. *Black Womanist Ethics*. Atlanta: Scholars Press, 1988.

Curran, Charles E. *The Catholic Moral Tradition Today: A Synthesis*. Washington, D.C.: Georgetown University Press, 1999.

Finn, Daniel. *Just Trading: On the Ethics and Economics of International Trade*. The Churches' Center for Public Policy. Nashville: Abingdon, 1996.

Gudorf, Christine. *Body, Sex, and Pleasure: Reconstructing Christian Sexual Ethics*. Cleveland: Pilgrim Press, 1995.

Hauerwas, Stanley. *Character and the Christian Life: A Study in Theological Ethics*. San Antonio: Trinity University Press, 1985.

————. *The Peaceable Kingdom: A Primer in Christian Ethics*. Notre Dame: University of Notre Dame Press, 1983.

Jersild, Paul T., Dale A. Johnson, Patricia Beattie Jung, and Shannon Jung, editors. *Moral Issues and Christian Response*. 6th edition. New York: Harcourt Brace, 1998.

Küng, Hans. *Global Responsibility: In Search of a New World Ethic*. New York: Crossroad, 1991.

Lebacqz, Karen. *Six Theories of Justice: Perspectives from Philosophical and Theological Ethics*. Minneapolis: Augsburg, 1986.

Lovin, Robin W. *Christian Ethics: An Essential Guide*. Nashville: Abingdon, 2000.

Maguire, Daniel C. *A Moral Creed for All Christians*. Minneapolis: Fortress Press, 2005.

Meilaender, Gilbert. *Bioethics: A Primer for Christians*. Grand Rapids: Eerdmans, 1996.

Nash, James A. *Loving Nature: Ecological Integrity and Christian Responsibility*. Nashville: Abingdon, 1991.

Nelson, James B. *Embodiment: An Approach to Sexuality and Christian Theology*. Minneapolis: Augsburg, 1978.

Paris, Peter. *Virtues and Values: The African and African American Experience*. Minneapolis: Fortress Press, 2005.

Townes, Emilie. *In a Blaze of Glory: Womanist Spirituality as Social Witness*. Nashville: Abingdon, 1995.

Verhey, Allen. *Remembering Jesus: Christian Community, Scripture, and the Moral Life*. Grand Rapids: Eerdmans, 2002.

Wogaman, J. Philip. *Christian Ethics; A Historical Introduction*. Louisville: Westminster/John Knox, 1993.

Notes

Chapter One

1. Jane Parker Huber, "Let Justice Flow Like Streams," *With One Voice* (Minneapolis: Augsburg Fortress, 1995).

2. Stanley Hauerwas, *Performing the Faith: Bonhoeffer and the Practice of Nonviolence* (Grand Rapids: Brazos Press, 2004), 77.

3. Stanley Hauerwas has argued that we cannot understand each other's ethical reasoning or decisions until we fully appreciate how our thinking and dispositions have been shaped by the "story" we have lived. Everyone's outlook, he maintains, has been formed by the story or stories characteristic of their community. Thus, "Pro- and anti-abortion advocates do not communicate on the notion 'abortion,' since each group holds a different story about the purpose of the notion. At least so far as 'abortion' is concerned, they live in conceptually different worlds. This fact does not prohibit discussion. But if it takes place, it cannot begin with the simple question of whether abortion is right or wrong. It is rather more like an argument between a member of the PLO and an Israeli about whether an attack on a village is unjustified terrorism. They both know the same 'facts' but the issue turns on the story each holds, and within which those 'facts' are known." "From System to Story," in *Truthfulness and Tragedy* (Notre Dame: University of Notre Dame Press, 1977), 22. See also, *The Peaceable Kingdom: A Primer in Christian Ethics* (Notre Dame: University of Notre Dame Press, 1983), in which Hauerwas's understanding of the narrative character of Christian convictions is clearly foundational to his account of Christian ethics.

4. A helpful collection of articles on issues of death and dying, including the matter of assisted dying, is in part 6 of *Contemporary Readings in Biomedical Ethics,* ed. Walter Glannon (New York: Harcourt College Publishers, 2002).

5. Douglas John Hall, *Bound and Free: A Theologian's Journey* (Minneapolis: Fortress Press, 2005), 9–14.

6. For one of the best-known discussions of the failure of the Enlightenment project, see Alasdair MacIntyre, *After Virtue* (Notre Dame: University of Notre Dame Press, 1981).

7. For a discussion of postmodernism, see Stanley Grenz, *A Primer on Postmodernism* (Grand Rapids: Eerdmans, 1996), and Paul Lakeland, *Postmodernity: Christian Identity in a Fragmented Age* (Minneapolis: Fortress Press, 1997).

8. Allen Verhey, *Remembering Jesus: Christian Community, Scripture, and the Moral Life* (Grand Rapids: Eerdmans, 2002), 6.

9. Theodor Seuss Geisel, *The Sneetches and Other Stories* (New York: Random House, 1961).

10. On the basis of his study of congregations, James F. Hopewell made the following observation that supports my concern and is relevant to our previous point about the loss of moral authority in the contemporary world: "As I conducted world view interviews I was surprised how infrequently, in even conservative Protestant congregations, the name of Christ was mentioned in response to questions about crises such as death, family instability, or world catastrophes. Although the name of Christ is regularly used by church members in the intensive, self-identifying acts of worship and evangelism, it seems now to be infrequently employed to fathom situations that challenge personal or corporate identity. The formidable pedagogy developed by the church to inculcate the person of Christ into the total world view and ethos of Christian life has today largely failed, the house of authority, to use Edward Farley's image, having collapsed. Structures within which the congregational household has for millennia made its home have lost an earlier power both to explain the world in Christian terms and to form behavior by norms readily acknowledged as those of Christ. The authority of Scripture, dogma, organization, and theological reasoning that once constituted the church, the *ekklesia,* has waned to the point of inconsequentiality for most Christians trying to make sense of their existence." From *Congregation* (Philadelphia: Fortress Press, 1987), 165. More recently, Allen Verhey has spoken of his discussions with individuals about their hard moral choices. He finds them willing to talk about those choices in private conversation but not in their congregations. They don't trust the congregation to be a place where difficult decisions about sensitive matters can be aired. Sadly, he observes, patterns of judgmentalism or avoidance justify that lack of trust. *Remembering Jesus,* 7–8.

11. The *Report and Recommendations from the Task Force for Evangelical Lutheran Church in America Studies on Sexuality* was released to the public on January 13, 2005.

Chapter Two

1. Martin Luther, "The Freedom of a Christian (1520)," trans. W. A. Lambert; rev. Harold J. Grimm, *Luther's Works,* American ed. (Philadelphia: Fortress Press; St. Louis: Concordia, 1955–86), 31:367–68.

2. Helmut Thielicke, *Theological Ethics,* ed. William H. Lazareth (Philadelphia: Fortress Press, 1966), 1:51–52.

3. See Ronald M. Hals, *Grace and Faith in the Old Testament* (Minneapolis: Augsburg, 1980), 62–64.

4. Dietrich Bonhoeffer, *Discipleship,* Dietrich Bonhoeffer Works, vol. 4, ed. Geffrey B. Kelly and John D. Godsey, trans. Barbara Green and Reinhard Krauss (Minneapolis: Fortress Press, 1996), esp. 43–44, 50–55.

5. See James M. Childs Jr., *Ethics in Business: Faith at Work* (Minneapolis: Fortress Press, 1995), 14–18.

6. Dietrich Bonhoeffer, *Ethics*, Dietrich Bonhoeffer Works, vol. 6, ed. Clifford J. Green, trans. Reinhard Krauss, Charles C. West, and Douglas W. Stott (Minneapolis: Fortress Press, 2005), 382–83.

7. Jan Milic Lochman, *Signposts to Freedom*, trans. David Lewis (Minneapolis: Augsburg, 1982), 18–20.

8. "Holy Communion, Setting 1," *Lutheran Book of Worship* (Minneapolis: Augsburg, 1978), 69.

9. John Bright, *The Kingdom of God* (New York: Abingdon, 1953), 92.

10. "The Assumption of Moses," 10:1, in R. H. Charles, ed., *The Apocrypha and Pseudepigrapha of the Old Testament* (Oxford: Clarendon, 1913), 2:421.

11. See N. T. Wright, *The Challenge of Jesus: Rediscovering Who Jesus Was and Is* (Downers Grove, Ill.: InterVarsity, 1999), esp. 53, 89, 131–37. Wolfhart Pannenberg, *Jesus—God and Man*, trans. Lewis L. Wilkins and Duane A. Priebe (Philadelphia: Westminster, 1968), 66–88.

12. Elisabeth Schüssler Fiorenza, *In Memory of Her* (London: SCM Press, 1983), 123.

13. Ibid.

14. Joseph Sittler, "Called to Unity," *Evocations of Grace: The Writings of Joseph Sittler on Ecology, Theology, and Ethics*, ed., Steven Bouma-Prediger and Peter Bakken (Grand Rapids: Eerdmans, 2000), 39–40.

15. Jürgen Moltmann, *The Coming of God: Christian Eschatology*, trans. Margaret Kohl (Minneapolis: Fortress Press, 1996), 270–79.

16. Glen H. Stassen and David P. Gushee have argued that Isaiah is the best place to look for the background of Jesus' teaching on the kingdom of God. Their investigation of seventeen passages in Isaiah that speak of God's deliverance of his people leads them to conclude that there are seven marks of God's reign discernible in the prophet that form the background of Jesus' teaching and his work: (1) deliverance or salvation; (2) righteousness/justice; (3) peace; (4) joy; (5) God's presence as Spirit or Light; (6) healing (includes the restoration of outcasts to community; (7) return from exile. *Kingdom Ethics: Following Jesus in Contemporary Context* (Downers Grove, Ill.: InterVarsity, 2003), 25–28. While their list differs in some particulars from the one I have proposed, it is really a compatible finding once you unpack the potential meanings of their "marks" and my list of "values."

Chapter Three

1. Stephen King, *The Stand* (New York: NAL Penguin, 1980), 53–54.

2. Jürgen Moltmann, "Progress and Abyss: Remembrances of the Future of the Modern World," in *The Future of Hope: Christian Tradition amid Modernity and Postmodernity*, ed. Miroslav Volf and William Katerberg (Grand Rapids: Eerdmans, 2004), 16.

3. Studs Terkel, *Hope Dies Last: Keeping Faith in Troubled Times* (New York: New Press, 2003), xv.

4. T. R. Taylor, "I'm But a Stranger Here," *The Lutheran Hymnal* (St. Louis: Concordia, 1941), #660.

5. Paul Gerhardt, "A Pilgrim and a Stranger," *The Lutheran Hymnal* (St. Louis: Concordia, 1941), #586.

6. Although Martin Luther provided considerable encouragement and guidance for conscientious Christian involvement in the concerns of society and the world, he also had a rather disparaging attitude about the characteristics of our sinful world and the possibility of progress. In his well-known doctrine of the "two kingdoms," Luther explained that God rules in two different ways. God's right-hand dominion is exercised through the gospel in the hearts of believers. The left-hand rule comes through the authorities of society and government by which God provides order to punish the wicked and protect the good in order to preserve the world from itself. Christians are called to obey God's left-hand rule by upholding the authorities and working for justice and peace, but this is not an arena of great hope and expectation. Something of Luther's attitude is reflected in the following. If evil were not restrained by the authority of government, Luther says, "men would devour one another, seeing that the whole world is evil and that among thousands there is scarcely a true Christian. . . . The world would be reduced to chaos. For this reason God has ordained two governments: the spiritual, by which the Holy Spirit produces Christians and righteous people under Christ; and the temporal, which restrains the un-Christian and wicked so that—no thanks to them—they are obliged to keep still and maintain the outward peace." Martin Luther, "Temporal Authority: To What Extent It Should Be Obeyed," trans. J. J. Schindel, rev. Walther I. Brandt, *Luther's Works*, American ed. (Philadelphia: Fortress; St. Louis: Concordia, 1955–86), 45:91.

7. Wolfhart Pannenberg, *Theology and the Kingdom of God* (Philadelphia: Westminster, 1969), 111–12.

8. Dietrich Bonhoeffer, *Ethics*, Dietrich Bonhoeffer Works, vol. 6, ed. Clifford J. Green, trans. Reinhard Krauss, Charles C. West, and Douglas W. Stott (Minneapolis: Fortress Press, 2005), 150–70.

9. Walter Rauschenbusch, *Theology for the Social Gospel* (Nashville: Abingdon, 1987), 54, 143.

10. Pannenberg, *Theology and the Kingdom of God*, 82.

11. H. Richard Niebuhr, *The Kingdom of God in America* (New York: Willett, Clark & Co.: 1937), 45–87.

12. Langdon Gilkey, *Blue Twilight: Nature, Creationism, and American Religion* (Minneapolis: Fortress Press, 2001), 45–46.

13. *Religion &Ethics News Weekly*, "Justice Sunday" (April 29, 2005) http://www.pbs.org/wnet/religionandethics/week835/cover.html.

14. In response to "Justice Sunday" evangelical president and CEO of Central Dallas ministries, Larry James, said, "We have some demagoguery going on here. Let's face it. This is a constitutional matter and we live under a democracy—a constitutional democracy. We're not a theocracy." (Ibid.) Jim Wallis, founder of the periodical *Sojourners,* and himself a conservative evangelical with a passion for justice, has

labeled Christian right leaders Jerry Falwell and Pat Robertson as theocrats who hold much in common with fundamentalists in Judaism and Islam who want their religious agenda enforced by the state. See *God's Politics: A New Vision for Faith and Politics in America* (San Francisco: HarperSanFrancisco, 2005), 67–68.

15. Douglas John Hall, *The Cross in Our Context: Jesus and the Suffering World* (Minneapolis: Fortress Press, 2003), 20.

16. Dietrich Bonhoeffer, *Discipleship*, Dietrich Bonhoeffer Works, vol. 4, ed. Geffrey B. Kelly and John D. Godsey, trans. Barbara Green and Reinhard Krauss (Minneapolis: Fortress Press, 1996), 173.

17. James M. Childs Jr., "Ethics and the Promise of God: Moral Authority and the Church's Witness," *The Promise of Lutheran Ethics*, ed. Karen L. Bloomquist and John R. Stumme (Minneapolis: Fortress Press, 1998), 112–14.

18. Douglas John Hall, *The Cross in Our Context*, 195.

19. Any number of biblical scholars have made this observation. Perhaps the eminent New Testament theologian Rudolf Bultmann is as appropriate as any to cite on this matter: "That the earliest church regarded itself as the Congregation of the end of days, is attested both by Paul and the synoptic tradition." *Theology of the New Testament,* trans. Kendrick Grobel (New York: Charles Scribner's Sons, 1951), 1:37.

20. The story is related by Ulrich Bach in *Partners in Life: The Handicapped and the Church*, ed. Geiko Mueller-Fahrenholz, Faith and Order Paper No. 89 (Geneva: World Council of Churches, 1979), 115.

Chapter Four

1. Victor Paul Furnish, *Theology and Ethics in Paul* (Nashville: Abingdon, 1968), 218.

2. See the discussion of *nous* and *phroneite,* the Greek words for "mind" and "have this mind" in these two passages, in Walter Bauer and Frederick William Danker, eds., *A Greek-English Lexicon of the New Testament and Other Early Christian Literature,* 3rd ed. (Chicago: University of Chicago Press, 2000).

3. See "Character" in *The Westminster Dictionary of Christian Ethics,* ed. James F. Childress and John Macquarrie (Philadelphia: Westminster, 1986).

4. In the New Testament we see that we are being transformed according to the "image of God" revealed in Christ. In Christ, through baptism, we put off the old nature and put on the new nature. In so doing, our lives follow the example of the Christ in whose image we finally will be perfected at the resurrection. James M. Childs Jr., *Christian Anthropology and Ethics* (Philadelphia: Fortress Press, 1978), esp. 117ff.

5. In this discussion of *agape,* I am especially indebted to two excellent books: Gene Outka, *Agape* (New Haven: Yale University Press, 1972); and Victor Paul Furnish, *The Love Command in the New Testament* (Nashville and New York: Abingdon, 1972). Outka provides a threefold analysis of *agape* as involving equal regard, self-sacrifice, and mutuality. I have freely adopted this scheme, reflecting his basic insights and providing my own development of the thoughts.

6. When we trace the doctrine of the image of God through the Old and New

Testaments, it is clear that dignity and identity as persons are not inherent in us, our accomplishments, or our contributions; they are rather conferred upon us as a gift from God in creating us in the divine image and in promising the fulfillment of that image through Jesus Christ. See Childs, *Christian Anthropology and Ethics*, esp. chap. 6.

7. Quoted in Daniel Day Williams, *The Spirit and Forms of Love* (New York: Harper and Row, 1968), 193.

8. Dorothee Soelle, *Beyond Mere Obedience*, trans. Lawrence Denef (New York: Pilgrim Press, 1982), 30–35.

9. Lisa Sowle Cahill, "Feminism and Christian Ethics," in *Freeing Theology: The Essentials of Theology in Feminist Perspective*, ed. Catherine Mowry LaCugna (New York: HarperSanFrancisco, 1993), 217. Cahill is reflecting here on Valerie Saiving's influential essay, "The Human Situation: A Feminine View," *Journal of Religion* 40 (1960), 71–83.

10. See James M. Childs Jr., *Greed: Economics and Ethics in Conflict* (Minneapolis: Fortress Press, 2000).

11. Childs, *Christian Anthropology and Ethics*, 89–96.

12. Dietrich Bonhoeffer, *Ethics*, Dietrich Bonhoeffer Works, vol. 6, ed. Clifford J. Green, trans. Reinhard Krauss, Charles C. West, and Douglas W. Stott (Minneapolis: Fortress Press, 2005), 335–36.

13. E. M. Good, "Peace in the Old Testament," and C. L. Mitton, "Peace in the New Testament," in *The Interpreter's Dictionary of the Bible* (Nashville: Abingdon, 1962).

14. Stanley Hauerwas, *A Community of Character* (Notre Dame: University of Notre Dame Press, 1981).

15. Louis B. Weeks, *Making Ethical Decisions* (Philadelphia: Westminster, 1987), 32–33.

16. Bruce C. Birch and Larry L. Rasmussen, *Bible and Ethics in the Christian Life* (Minneapolis: Augsburg, 1976), 104–11.

17. Allen Verhey, *Remembering Jesus*, 22.

18. Pinchas Lapide, *The Sermon on the Mount*, trans. Arlene Swidler (Maryknoll, N.Y.: Orbis, 1986), 31–33. Bonhoeffer addresses the question of the relationship between the will (being) and the act (doing) in conjunction with Jesus' saying about the good tree bearing good fruits (Matt. 7:17). He concludes that the saying's "meaning is not that first the person is good and then the work, but that *only the two together*, only both united as one, are to be understood as good or bad" (*Ethics*, 51).

19. The connection between the Sermon on the Mount and Jesus' inauguration of the reign of God has been reiterated recently by N.T. Wright, *The Challenge of Jesus*, 46–47.

20. Robert A. Guelich, *The Sermon on the Mount* (Waco, Tex.: Word, 1982), 67. Stassen and Gushee have also followed Guelich's lead in this regard. They see the Beatitudes as gracious gifts for participation in the blessedness and deliverance of the reign of God. See *Kingdom Ethics*, 33ff.

21. Stassen and Gushee have provided helpful charts comparing virtues listed in the Epistles with those of the Beatitudes and their location. See *Kingdom Ethics*, 48, 50.

Chapter Five

1. Robert Guelich, *The Sermon on the Mount* (Waco, Tex: Word, 1982), 67.

2. Ibid., 72.

3. Michael H. Crosby, *House of Disciples* (Maryknoll, N.Y.: Orbis, 1988), 154, makes the point that nowhere in Matthew does the writer canonize poverty.

4. Jamse H. Evans Jr., *We Have Been Believers: An African-American Systematic Theology* (Minneapolis: Fortress Press, 1992), 69–70.

5. Gustavo Gutiérrez, *A Theology of Liberation*, trans. and ed. Caridad Inda and John Eagleson (Maryknoll, N.Y.: Orbis, 1973), 297.

6. Henri Nouwen, "Bearing Fruit in the Spirit," in *Sojourners* 14, no. 7 (July 1985), 30.

7. Jürgen Moltmann, *The Trinity and the Kingdom: The Doctrine of God* (Minneapolis: Fortress Press, 1993), 198–99. See also Leonardo Boff, "Trinity," *Systematic Theology: Perspectives from Liberation Theology*, ed. Jon Sobrino and Ignacio Ellacuria (Maryknoll, N.Y.: Orbis, 1996), 75–90.

8. Theologian Ted Peters proposes that we think of the marks of the church (one, holy, catholic, and apostolic) as "dispositions of moral resolve that should characterize the various members of the Body of Christ." *God—The World's Future: Systematic Theology for a New Era*, 2nd ed. (Minneapolis: Fortress Press, 2000), 304. This fits nicely in the present discussion in which I am linking the moral disposition or virtue of poverty of spirit with the call of the church to live into its so-called "marks."

9. Joseph Allen, *Love and Conflict* (Nashville: Abingdon, 1984), 169.

10. James H. Cone, "The White Church and Black Power," in *Black Theology*, ed. Gayraud S. Wilmore and James H. Cone (Maryknoll, N.Y.: Orbis, 1979), 126–28.

11. James H. Cone, *God of the Oppressed* (New York: Seabury, 1975), 15.

12. "The global legacy of racism persists like an inheritance that heirs cannot or will not dispose of, either because they believe it still provides wealth or because it is all they know. This legacy has even infected feminism to the extent that white feminists have often sustained fundamentally racist attitudes and practices in assumptions that white women's experiences adequately represent all women." Laurel C. Schneider, "God Beyond Racism and Sexism," *Constructive Theology: A Contemporary Approach to Classical Themes*, ed. Serene Jones and Paul Lakeland (Minneapolis: Fortress Press, 2005), 69.

13. Joy Ann McDougall, in her article, "Women's Work," *Christian Century* (July 26, 2005), 20–25, provides a helpful brief introduction to this developing work among contemporary feminist theologians.

14. Wolfhart Pannenberg, *What Is Man?* trans. Duane A. Priebe (Philadelphia: Fortress Press, 1970), 28–40.

15. Robert M. Veatch, *The Foundations of Justice* (New York: Oxford University Press, 1986), 119–29.

16. Ibid., 125.

17. For a fuller discussion of affirmative action, see my chapter "Beyond Affirmative Action," in *Ethics in Business: Faith at Work* (Minneapolis: Fortress Press, 1995),

88–101. I argue that there are both moral and practical reasons for businesses to value diversity and not simply regard seeking it as a matter of compliance with an undesirable law.

18. Crosby, *House of Disciples*, 155: "Thus we discover two significant factors related to being 'poor in spirit.' First, by their knowledge of God, the 'poor in spirit' recognize their own need for God. Recognizing their dependence on God, they become abandoned; they trust in God's loving care to meet their needs. Second, by their awareness of the Spirit of the Lord given over to them (see 27:50), they recognize their responsibility to image God by working to reorder creation. They abandon themselves to cooperate with God in renewing God's household on the earth. The passive dimension of abandonment or being 'poor in spirit' involves the admission of one's need before God; the active dimension recognizes God's need to use humans to continue the divine creative activity of bringing about the original order envisioned by God."

19. Martin Luther, "Heidelberg Disputation (1518)," trans. Harold J. Grimm, *Luther's Works*, American ed. (Philadelphia: Fortress; St. Louis: Concordia, 1955–86), 31:40.

20. Josef Pieper, *The Four Cardinal Virtues* (Notre Dame: University of Notre Dame Press, 1975), 15, 20–21.

21. Dietrich Bonhoeffer, *Discipleship,* Dietrich Bonhoeffer Works, vol. 4, ed. Geffrey B. Kelly and John D. Godsey, trans. Barbara Green and Reinhard Krauss (Minneapolis: Fortress Press, 1996), 131.

Chapter Six

1. Jerzy Kosinski, *The Painted Bird* (New York: Bantam, 1972).

2. Stanley Hauerwas, *Suffering Presence* (Notre Dame: University of Notre Dame Press, 1986), 81.

3. Martin Luther, "The Sermon on the Mount," trans. Jaroslav Pelikan, *Luther's Works,* American ed. (Philadelphia: Fortress; St. Louis: Concordia, 1955–86), 21:17–18.

4. Douglas John Hall, *The Cross in Our Context: Jesus and the Suffering World* (Minneapolis: Fortress Press, 2003), 21.

5. Robert Guelich, *The Sermon on the Mount* (Waco, Tex.: Word, 1982), 100–101.

6. William Barclay, *The Plain Man Looks at the Beatitudes* (London: William Collins Sons, 1963), 28–29.

7. Luther, "Sermon on the Mount," 19.

8. Kosuke Koyama, *No Handle on the Cross* (Maryknoll, N.Y.: Orbis, 1977), 1–7.

9. James B. Nelson and Jo Anne Smith Rohricht, *Human Medicine* (Minneapolis: Augsburg, 1984), 151.

10. Paul Ramsey, *The Patient as Person* (New Haven: Yale University Press, 1970), 114.

11. Nelson and Rohricht, *Human Medicine,* 172–73.

12. The American Cancer Society Web site (www.cancer.org) offers a helpful description of hospice care with links to other resources.

13. Ronald Bayer, "The Duty to Prevent, the Duty to Care: Social Challenges of the AIDS Epidemic," in *AIDS Issues*, ed. David G. Hallman (New York: Pilgrim, 1989), 64.

14. See the discussion in Diane Baker, et al. eds., *Sexuality in America: Understanding Our Sexual Values and Behavior* (New York: Continuum, 1999), 244–45.

15. Sonja Weinreich and Christoph Benn, *AIDS—Meeting the Challenge: Data, Facts, Background* (Geneva: WCC Publications, 2003), 46.

16. Donald E. Messer, *Breaking the Conspiracy of Silence: Christian Churches and the Global AIDS Crisis* (Minneapolis: Fortress Press, 2004), 27–29.

17. Ibid., 43–45. Patricia Beattie Jung and Ralph F. Smith have provided a helpful analysis and discussion of various positions taken by churches on the morality of homosexuality and homosexual conduct in their book *Heterosexism: An Ethical Challenge* (New York: SUNY Press, 1993), 22–33.

18. James B. Nelson, "Responding to, Learning from AIDS," *Christianity and Crisis* (May 19, 1986), 176.

19. Beryl Ingram-Ward, "Space for Hospitality and Hope," *The Church with AIDS: Renewal in the Midst of Crisis*, ed. Letty M. Russell (Louisville: Westminster/John Knox, 1990), 76.

20. George A. Buttrick, *The Beatitudes* (Nashville: Abingdon, 1968), 24.

21. John R. Belcher, "Helping the Homeless: What about the Spirit of God?" *Pastoral Psychology*, 51, 3 (January 2003), 184.

22. Rebecca Anne Allahyari, *Visions of Charity: Volunteer Workers and Moral Community* (Berkeley: University of California Press, 2000).

23. Ibid., 138

24. Ibid., 142.

25. Ibid., 74–104.

26. Belcher, "Helping the Homeless," 184.

27. *Patripassionism* was not only condemned in defense of the essential impassibility of the divine but also because Sabellius, who was associated with the teaching, based it on a modalistic monarchian view of the Trinity, which maintained that God is one simple being manifested in three different modes.

28. Daniel Day Williams, *The Spirit and Forms of Love* (New York: Harper and Row, 1968), 159ff.; and Jürgen Moltmann, *The Experiment Hope*, ed. and trans. M. Douglas Meeks (Philadelphia: Fortress Press, 1975), 75–76.

29. Jürgen Moltmann, *The Trinity and the Kingdom*, trans. Margaret Kohl (Minneapolis: Fortress Press, 1993), 23.

30. Ted Peters, *God—The World's Future: Systematic Theology for a New Era*, 2nd ed. (Minneapolis: Fortress Press, 2000), 207.

31. Hall, *The Cross in Our Context*, 85.

Chapter Seven

1. Robert L. Coutts, *Love and Intimacy* (San Ramon, Calif.: Consensus, 1973), 172–73.

2. Ibid., 174. See also the chapter "Forgiveness and the Restoration of Intimacy" in Howard Markman, Scott Stanley, and Susan L. Blumberg, *Fighting for Your Marriage* (San Francisco: Jossey-Bass, 1994), 211–30.

3. Michael H. Crosby, *House of Disciples* (Maryknoll, N.Y.: Orbis, 1988), 163.

4. William Barclay, *The Plain Man Looks at the Beatitudes* (London: William Collins' Sons, 1963), 57–64.

5. Ibid., 62.

6. Robert Guelich, *The Sermon on the Mount* (Waco, Tex.: Word, 1982), 104.

7. Coutts, *Love and Intimacy*, 173–74.

8. Michael Obstatz, *From Stalemate to Soulmate: A Guide to Mature, Committed, Loving Relationships* (Minneapolis: Augsburg, 1997), 97.

9. Guelich, *Sermon on the Mount*, 104–5.

10. See Crosby's discussion in *House of Disciples*, 163.

11. Sharon Ringe, *Jesus, Liberation and the Biblical Jubilee* (Philadelphia: Fortress Press, 1985), 16–32. See also John Howard Yoder, *The Politics of Jesus* (Grand Rapids: Eerdmans, 1972), 64–77.

12. Karen Lebacqz, *Justice in an Unjust World* (Minneapolis: Augsburg, 1987), 122–35.

13. Ringe, *Jesus, Liberation, and the Biblical Jubilee*, 17–22.

14. For background to these comments, see ibid., 29–30, and passim.

15. On this point Ringe and Lebacqz agree.

16. For a discussion of the outcomes and related concerns of the Jubilee 2000 campaign see Jim Wallis, *God's Politics: A New Vision for Faith and Politics in America* (San Francisco: HarperSanFrancisco, 2005), 272–87.

17. Wolfhart Pannenberg, *Theology and the Kingdom of God* (Philadelphia: Westminster, 1969), 126.

18. Lebacqz states: "The jubilee is a vision of new beginnings, but it is a cyclical vision implying the need for a new jubilee. The story goes on. And as the human community writes its story, new injustices will happen. Justice is a constant process of correction, not a once-and-for-all program." *Justice in an Unjust World*, 153.

19. Guelich, *Sermon on the Mount*, 107.

20. Crosby, *House of Disciples*, 166.

21. Martin Luther, "The Sermon on the Mount," trans. Jaroslav Pelikan, *Luther's Works*, American ed. (Philadelphia: Fortress; St. Louis: Concordia, 1955–86), 21:39–44.

22. Ibid., 41.

23. Martin Luther, "The Smalcald Articles (1537)," in *The Book of Concord: The Confessions of the Evangelical Lutheran Church*, ed. Robert Kolb and Timothy J. Wengert (Minneapolis: Fortress Press, 2000), 298, 5.

24. Alan Geyer, *The Idea of Disarmament* (Elgin, Ill.: Brethren, 1982), 194.

25. Luther, "Sermon on the Mount," 44.

26. James Cone, *God of the Oppressed* (New York: Seabury, 1975), 226.

27. Ibid., 228–34.

28. Ibid., 242.

29. Søren Kierkegaard, *Purity of the Heart Is To Will One Thing*, trans. Douglas V. Steere (New York: Harper and Brothers, 1948), 175.

30. Ibid., 218.

31. Dietrich Bonhoeffer, *Ethics*. Dietrich Bonhoeffer Works, vol. 6, ed. Clifford J. Green, trans. Reinhard Krauss, Charles C. West, and Douglas W. Stott (Minneapolis: Fortress Press, 2005), 346. See n. 32 on that page for commentary on the context of Bonhoeffer's remarks.

32. Paul Tillich, *The Courage to Be* (New Haven: Yale University Press, 1952), 163.

33. Robin W. Lovin, *Christian Ethics: An Essential Guide* (Nashville: Abingdon, 2000), 72.

34. Daniel C. Maguire, *A Moral Creed for All Christians* (Minneapolis: Fortress Press, 2005), 105.

Chapter Eight

1. Martin Luther, "Letter to Philip Melanchthon, August 1, 1521," in *Luther's Works*, American ed. (Philadelphia: Fortress; St. Louis: Concordia, 1955–86), 21: 39–44.

2. Martin Luther, "Sermons on the First Epistle of St. Peter," trans. Martin H. Bertram, in *Luther's Works*, vol. 30, esp. pp. 27, 68, 70.

3. Quoted from Mary B. Mahowald, "Is There Life after *Roe v. Wade?*" *Hastings Center Report* (July/August 1989): 25.

4. I first introduced the method of dialogical ethics in my book, *Christian Anthropology and Ethics* (Philadelphia: Fortress Press, 1978). Since that work I engaged in testing and revising that proposal particularly in the area of formulating general rules. That subsequent work, then, came to expression in the first edition of *Faith, Formation, and Decision* (Philadelphia: Fortress Press, 1992). I have continued to work with this model in my teaching, consulting, and other publications and have been satisfied that it is a sustainable approach.

5. Two durable studies stand behind my understanding of *agape* as the foundational principle of the Christian ethic: Victor Paul Furnish's *The Love Command in the New Testament* (Nashville: Abingdon, 1972) and Gene Outka's *Agape: An Ethical Analysis* (New Haven: Yale University Press, 1972).

6. Herbert Waddams, *A New Introduction to Moral Theology* (New York: Seabury, 1964), 43–62. Charles E. Curran, *The Catholic Moral Tradition Today: A Synthesis* (Washington, D.C.: Georgetown University Press, 1999), 35ff. and *passim*. Curran's book includes a discussion of the natural law characteristics of Pope John Paul II's 1993 encyclical, *Veritatis splendor*.

7. For a critique of natural law theory, see Joseph Fletcher, *Moral Responsibility* (Philadelphia: Westminster, 1967), 58ff.; Helmut Thielicke, *Theological Ethics*, ed. William H. Lazareth (Philadelphia: Fortress Press, 1966), vol. 1, 383ff., 420ff.; "Natural Law," in *The Westminster Dictionary of Christian Ethics*, ed. James F. Childress and John Macquarrie (Philadelphia: Westminster, 1986), 412–14.

8. Curran, *The Catholic Moral Tradition Today*, 37–47.

9. Richard A. McCormick, "Human Significance and Christian Significance," in *Norm and Context in Christian Ethics*, ed. Gene H. Outka and Paul Ramsey (New York: Charles Scribner's Sons, 1968), 241.

10. George F. Thomas, *Christian Ethics and Moral Philosophy* (New York: Charles Scribner's Sons, 1955), 256.

11. Reinhold Niebuhr, *The Nature and Destiny of Man* (New York: Charles Scribner's Sons, 1964), 2:246–56.

12. Joseph Fletcher, *Situation Ethics* (Philadelphia: Westminster, 1966), esp. chap. 4.

13. Thielicke, *Theological Ethics*, 1:351, George Forell, *Ethics of Decision* (Philadelphia: Fortress Press, 1955), 104. Jan Milic Lochman is worth quoting here: "The Ten Commandments retain their undiminished validity and authority as a clear declaration of the public will of God, at least for Christians and Jews, despite all the cultural changes. But this validity is not the validity of an abstract law; the commandments are valid in the living context in which they were set and given to us by God himself. In other words, as rooted in the history of the liberation of God's people and with the object of 'increasing' life in freedom and love. Within this life-giving context we must seek the concrete meaning of the Ten Commandments for the actual situation of our churches and congregations. This meaning is not something we already have or will ever have 'at our fingertips,' firmly in our possession. God's commandment is never valid as a dead and deadening 'letter' but only as an imperative venture of freedom and love, the precise content of which must always be sought and practiced in the given circumstances in which we find ourselves." *Signposts to Freedom,* trans. David Lewis (Minneapolis: Augsburg, 1982), 85–86.

14. For a discussion of casuistry in the Catholic Moral Theology tradition see Curran, *The Catholic Moral Tradition Today*, 164–65. For a recent discussion of casuistry in the Jewish tradition, see Dena S. Davis, "Abortion in Jewish Thought: A Study in Casuistry," *Journal of the American Academy of Religion* 60, no. 2 (Summer 1992): 313–24.

15. See H. Richard Niebuhr, *The Responsible Self* (New York: Harper and Row, 1963), 61–65.

16. Lewis B. Smedes, *Mere Morality* (Grand Rapids: Eerdmans, 1983), 62–63.

17. *Caring for Creation: Vision, Hope, and Justice,* A Social Statement of the Evangelical Lutheran Church in America adopted by the Churchwide Assembly on August 28, 1993, 7.

18. Ibid.

19. Alan Verhey, *Remembering Jesus*, 15–16. Verhey offers extensive references on this point from the literature of Christian ethics including the well-known volume by James Gustafson, *The Church as Moral Decision Maker* (Philadelphia: Pilgrim, 1970).

20. Mark Allan Powell, "Binding and Loosing: Asserting the Moral Authority of Scripture in Light of a Matthean Paradigm," *Ex Auditu* 19 (2003): 81–96.

21. See Dietrich Bonhoeffer, *Discipleship*, Dietrich Bonhoeffer Works, vol. 4, ed. Geffrey B. Kelly and John D. Godsey, trans. Barbara Green and Reinhard Krauss (Minneapolis: Fortress Press, 1996), 49–53.

Chapter Nine

1. See a discussion of these challenges and their importance for the modern perspective, see Jan Milic Lochman, *Signposts to Freedom*, trans. David Lewis (Minneapolis: Augsburg, 1982), 13–18. Although this analysis is over twenty years old, it remains a statement of valid concern.

2. Paul Lehman, *The Decalogue and a Human Future: The Meaning of the Commandments for Making and Keeping Human Life Human* (Grand Rapids: Eerdmans, 1995), 31.

3. Walter Harrelson, *The Ten Commandments and Human Rights* (Philadelphia: Fortress Press, 1980), 191.

4. Ibid., 192–93.

5. This is such a pervasive theme in Hauerwas's work that one hardly knows where to begin in choosing a citation. His book *After Christendom? How the Church Is to Behave If Freedom, Justice, and a Christian Nation Are Bad Ideas* (Nashville: Abingdon, 1991) is a good example of this perspective.

6. See Michael J. Perry, *Love and Power* (New York: Oxford University Press, 1991). Perry believes that religion should have a voice in the shape of political life, a voice among many voices in a pluralistic society, and a voice that retains the integrity of its faith in the public dialogue. I have written briefly on this matter, "Religion and Politics: Tradition and the Post-Modern Agenda," *Capital University Law Review* 20 (1991): 154–57.

7. For Martin Luther's most complete discussion of the First Commandment, see "The Large Catechism (1529)," in *The Book of Concord: The Confessions of the Evangelical Lutheran Church*, ed.,Robert Kolb and Timothy J. Wengert (Minneapolis: Fortress Press, 2000), 386–92.

8. Harrelson, *Ten Commandments*, 186.

9. Ibid., 189.

10. *The Decalogue and the Human Future*, 31.

11. Terence E. Fretheim, "Law in the Service of Life: A Dynamic Understanding of Law in Deuteronomy," *God So Near: Essays in Honor of Patrick D. Miller*, ed. Brent Strawn and Nancy Bowen (Winona Lake, Ind.: Eisenbrauns, 2002), 184–86.

12. James M. Childs Jr., *Christian Anthropology and Ethics* (Philadelphia: Fortress Press, 1978).

13. The discussion of the "image of God" in the New Testament is quite complicated. However, a few things can be simply stated to help make our point. When Christ is called the "image of God" in the New Testament, it is a reference to his *divinity*. First Corinthians 15:44–49 tells us that in the resurrection we will bear the *image* of the "heavenly man" (Jesus, the Christ). Thus, as we are perfected in the resurrection according to Christ's image, we are perfected in the *image of God*.

14. Henrik Ibsen, *A Doll's House* (New York: Charles Scribner's Sons, 1911), Act 3, pp. 179, 183.

15. See James F. Childress, *Priorities in Biomedical Ethics* (Philadelphia: Westminster, 1981), 21–22. Childress gets the concept of "sick role" from sociologist Talcott Parsons.

16. Ibid.

17. Ibsen, *A Doll's House,* Act 1, p. 85.

18. Robert M. Veatch, "Models for Ethical Medicine in a Revolutionary Age," *Hastings Center Report* (June 1972): 5–7.

19. Ibid., 6.

20. Ibid., 9.

21. William F. May, *The Physician's Covenant: Images of the Healer in Medical Ethics* (Philadelphia: Westminster, 1983), 116–44.

22. Howard Brody, "Physician-Patient Relationship," *Medical Ethics,* 2nd ed., ed. Robert M. Veatch (Sunbury, Mass.: Jones and Bartlett, 1997), 74–101.

23. Robert B. White, "A Demand to Die," *Hastings Center Report* (June 1975): 9–10.

24. Ibid.

25. Philosopher Bruce L. Miller has delineated different senses of autonomy, one of which is "authentic autonomy." That is, actions are truly autonomous when they are authentic expressions of a person's character and personality. When actions are at variance with what we expect from a given individual, we may question whether they are truly autonomous actions rather than actions distorted by some alien influence. See "Autonomy and the Refusal of Lifesaving Treatment," *Hastings Center Report* (August 1981), 24.

26. See James F. Childress, "Autonomy," in *The Westminster Dictionary of Christian Ethics,* ed. James F. Childress and John Macquarrie (Philadelphia: Westminster, 1986), 53.

Chapter Ten

1. N. T. Wright, *What Paul Really Said* (Grand Rapids: Eerdmans, 1997), 110–11.

2. Jan Milic Lochman, *Signposts to Freedom,* trans. David Lewis (Minneapolis: Augsburg, 1982), 76–77.

3. Ibid., 78–85.

4. Walter Harrelson, *The Ten Commandments and Human Rights* (Philadelphia: Fortress Press, 1980), 136–38.

5. Ibid., 142.

6. Robert Gnuse, *You Shall Not Steal* (Maryknoll, N.Y.: Orbis, 1985), 31.

7. Ibid., 112.

8. Paul Lehman, *The Decalogue and a Human Future: The Meaning of the Commandments for Making and Keeping Life Human* (Grand Rapids: Erdmans, 1995), 80–81.

9. Lochman, *Signposts to Freedom,* 78.

10. See Daniel Callahan, *Setting Limits: Medical Goals in an Aging Society* (New

York: Simon and Schuster, 1987), and *False Hopes: Why America's Quest for Perfect Health Is a Recipe for Failure* (New York: Simon and Schuster, 1998). I have made use of these books by Callahan in the discussion of this issue in James M. Childs Jr., *Greed: Economics and Ethics in Conflict* (Minneapolis: Fortress Press, 2000), 47–61.

11. Gerard F. Anderson and Jean-Pierre Poullier, "Health Spending, Access, and Outcomes: Trends in Industrialized Countries," *Health Affairs* (May/June 1999): 178–92.

12. Tom L. Beauchamp and James F. Childress, *Principles of Biomedical Ethics* (New York: Oxford University Press, 1979), 171–72. See also the 5th edition of *Principles* (New York: Oxford, 2001), 227–28.

13. Ibid., 172 (5th ed., 228).

14. Ibid., 173 (5th ed., 229).

15. Gene Outka, "Social Justice and Equal Access to Health Care," *Journal of Religious Ethics* 2 (Spring 1974): 11–32.

16. Ibid., 15.

17. Ibid., 21–23.

18. Reinhold Niebuhr, *Moral Man and Immoral Society* (New York: Charles Scribner's Sons, 1960), xi.

19. Childs, *Greed*, 4.

20. M. Douglas Meeks, *God the Economist* (Minneapolis: Fortress Press, 1989), 123. Karen Lebacqz makes a similar comment on the conflict between freedom and equality in contemporary theories of justice; see *Six Theories of Justice* (Minneapolis: Augsburg, 1986), 65.

21. Childs, *Greed*, esp. chaps. 2 and 6.

22. Daniel C. Maguire, *A Moral Creed for All Christians* (Minneapolis: Fortress Press, 2005), 50.

23. *Economic Justice for All: Catholic Social Teaching and the U.S. Economy* (Washington, D.C.: National Conference of Catholic Bishops, 1986).

24. See the various discussions of the pastoral letter on the economy in Charles P. Lutz, ed., *God, Goods, and the Common Good* (Minneapolis: Augsburg, 1987).

25. *Economic Justice for All*, para. 68.

26. Ibid., paras. 69–76. The bishops employ the traditional Catholic distinctions of *commutative, distributive,* and *social* justice. Commutative justice refers to fairness in agreements and exchanges. Distributive justice refers to the allocation of income, wealth, and power in society vis-à-vis those whose basic material needs are unmet. Social justice refers to everyone's obligation to actively and productively participate in society and society's obligation to enable that participation by all. I have omitted these designations from the discussion for the sake of simplicity.

27. Ibid., paras. 77–93d.

28. Ibid., para. 94.

29. Joseph Sittler, "Essays on Nature and Grace," *Evocations of Grace: The Writings of Joseph Sittler on Ecology, Theology, and Ethics,* ed., Steven Bouma-Prediger and Peter Bakken (Grand Rapids: Eerdmans, 2000), 104.

30. Among many discussions of how the interpretation of Genesis 1:26 has shaped attitudes toward the environment and how contemporary understandings have corrected past assumptions about human dominion, see H. Paul Santmire, *Nature Reborn: The Ecological and Cosmic Promise of Christian Theology* (Minneapolis: Fortress Press, 2000), especially chap. 3.

31. James A. Nash, *Loving Nature: Ecological Integrity and Christian Responsibility* (Nashville: Abingdon, 1991), 140–41. Nash provides a comprehensive theological analysis of how the main themes of our faith are intertwined with the concerns of ecology.

32. The charter can be found at www.earthcharter.org.

33. For an expansive theological treatment of this communal vision, see Larry L. Rasmussen's highly acclaimed book, *Earth Community, Earth Ethics* (Maryknoll, N.Y.: Orbis, 1996).

34. *Keeping and Healing the Creation* (Louisville: Committee on Social Witness Policy, Presbyterian Church [USA], 1989). The discussion of norms I cite is in chap. 5, 61–81. The same norms also appear in the Social Statement of the Evangelical Lutheran Church in America, *Caring for Creation: Vision, Hope, and Justice* (1993), the product of a task force on which I was privileged to serve.

35. Ibid., 63.

36. Beauchamp and Childress, *Principles of Biomedical Ethics*, 229.

Chapter Eleven

1. Walter Harrelson, *The Ten Commandments and Human Rights* (Philadelphia: Fortress Press, 1980), 109, citing Karl Barth.

2. James M. Childs Jr., *Decisions at the Beginning and End of Life* (Columbus: SELECT, 1984), 50.

3. Harrelson, *Ten Commandments*, 119.

4. George F. Thomas, *Christian Ethics and Moral Philosophy* (New York: Charles Scribner's Sons, 1955), 441–44. Thomas used the term *middle axioms* to describe these four principles. Historically, I think this is a misappropriation of terms, so I have renamed them *adjudicating axioms*.

5. Dietrich Bonhoeffer, *Ethics*, Dietrich Bonhoeffer Works, vol. 6, ed. Clifford J. Green, trans. Reinhard Krauss, Charles C. West, and Douglas W. Stott (Minneapolis: Fortress Press, 2005), 321.

6. Harmon L. Smith, *Ethics and the New Medicine* (Nashville: Abingdon, 1970), 125.

7. See the comments of Edmund D. Pellegrino in *The Journal of the American Medical Association* (May 19, 1989), 2843–44. In "The Theologic Ethics of Euthanasia" Kenneth L. Vaux says, "Today a vivid set of cases involving patients who are not dying but are suffering from the final stages of Lou Gehrig's disease, cystic fibrosis, cerebral palsy, or other irreversible and fatal afflictions have been set before us in newspapers, courts and television dramas. Some of these patients eventually ask their physicians to disconnect life-supports and ease them into death with barbiturates and muscle relaxants. In my view such cases are compelling and justify active euthanasia" (*Hastings Center Report* [January/February 1989], 21).

8. See, Margaret Pabst Batten, *The Death Debate: Ethical Issues in Suicide* (Upper Saddle River, NJ: Prentice-Hall, 1996), Tom L. Beauchamp, ed., *Intending Death: The Ethics of Assisted Suicide* (Upper Saddle River, NJ: Prentice-Hall, 1996), and Ronald Hamel and Edwin R. DuBose, eds., *Must We Suffer Our Way to Death? Cultural and Theological Perspectives on Death by Choice* (Dallas: Southern Methodist University Press, 1996). My own article in that volume is entitled, "Anna, Ambiguity and the Promise: A Lutheran Theologian Reflects on Assisted Death," 198–225.

9. Daniel Callahan, "Can We Return Death to Disease?" *Hastings Center Report* (January/February 1989), 4–6.

10. C. Everett Koop, "The Challenge of Definition," *Hastings Center Report* (January/February 1989), 2–3.

11. John T. Noonan, "An Almost Absolute Value in History," in *The Morality of Abortion*, ed. J. T. Noonan (Cambridge: Harvard University Press, 1970), 1–27.

12. Thomas M. Garrett, Harold W. Baillie, Rosellen M. Garrett, *Health Care Ethics: Principles and Problems* (Englewood Cliffs, NJ: Prentice-Hall, 1989), 142.

13. Gilbert Meilander, *Bioethics: A Primer for Christians* (Grand Rapids: Eerdmans, 1996), 29.

14. Ibid., 30–31.

15. For information on all aspects of the Human Genome Project see http://www.ornl.gov/sci/techresources/Human_Genome/home.shtml.

16. Hessel Bourma III, et al., *Christian Faith, Health, and Medical Practice* (Grand Rapids: Eerdmans, 1989), 246–47. Michael T. Menmiti, "Prenatal Diagnosis—Advances Bring New Challenges," *The New England Journal of Medicine* (March 9, 1989): 661–63. LeRoy Walters, "Reproductive Technologies and Genetics," *Medical Ethics*, 2nd ed., ed. Robert M. Veatch (Sudbury, Mass.: Jones and Bartlett, 1997), 221.

17. Edmund N. Santurri, "Prenatal Diagnosis: Some Moral Considerations," in *Questions about the Beginning of Life*, ed. Edward D. Schneider (Minneapolis: Augsburg, 1985), 133. So also, Bourma, et al., *Christian Faith, Health, and Medical Practice*, 249.

18. Walters, "Reproductive Technologies and Genetics," 221.

19. Santurri, "Prenatal Diagnosis," 135.

20. Stanley Hauerwas, *A Community of Character* (Notre Dame: University of Notre Dame Press, 1981), 212–23.

Chapter Twelve

1. Sissela Bok, *Lying* (New York: Vintage, 1999), 3–4.

2. Ibid., 4.

3. Ibid., 6.

4. Ibid., 21–24, 30.

5. James M. Childs Jr., "Hope and Truth: Why Theology Matters," *Trinity Seminary Review* 26, no. 2 (Summer/Fall 2005), 81.

6. Martin Luther, "The Large Catechism (1529)," in *The Book of Concord: The Confessions of the Evangelical Lutheran Church*, ed., Robert Kolb and Timothy J. Wengert (Minneapolis: Fortress Press, 2000), 420ff.

7. Lewis B. Smedes, *Mere Morality* (Grand Rapids: Eerdmans, 1983), 222–23.

8. Helmut Thielicke, *Theological Ethics,* ed. William H. Lazareth (Philadelphia: Fortress Press, 1966), 1:521–26.

9. Ibid., 549.

10. Robert McAfee Brown, *Saying Yes and Saying No* (Philadelphia: Westminster, 1986), 85–91. Brown suggests five ways governments can compromise the truth to their own advantage, such as stressing the small faults of the opponent without acknowledging your own large ones, floating undocumented statements that prove to be false, and engaging in extravagant rhetoric that distorts reality.

11. For a comprehensive discussion of whistle-blowing see Alan F. Westin, *Whistle-blowing! Loyalty and Dissent in the Corporation* (New York: Harper and Row, 1989).

12. Paul Hencke, ed., *What You Should Know about Business Ethics* (New York: National Institute of Business Management, 1987), 69.

13. Ibid.

14. See the Web site for the National Whistleblowers Center, http://www .whistleblowers.org, for this story and others.

15. James M. Childs Jr., *Ethics in Business: Faith at Work* (Minneapolis: Fortress Press, 1995), 131–32.

16. Hencke, *What You Should Know about Business Ethics,* 76.

17. Bok, *Lying,* 26.

18. On this point, see James Childs, *Ethics in Business: Faith at Work* (Minneapolis: Fortress Press, 1995), chap. 1.

19. Thornton Wilder, "The Skin of Our Teeth" in *Three Plays* (New York: Harper and Row, 1957), Act 2, pp. 200–201.

20. Garrison Keillor, "Letter from Jim," from *Spring News from Lake Wobegon,* audiocassette (St. Paul: Minnesota Public Radio, 1983).

21. Karl Barth, *Church Dogmatics 3.1: The Doctrine of Creation,* trans. G. T. Thompson (New York: Charles Scribner's Sons, 1936), 185ff., 195ff.

22. On this point, see Wolfhart Pannenberg's critique of Barth in *Systematic Theology,* trans. Geoffrey Bromiley (Grand Rapids: Eerdmans, 1994), 2:226.

23. Joseph Allen, *Love and Conflict* (Nashville: Abingdon, 1984), 32–39.

24. Ibid., 41–45.

25. Ibid., 231–46.

26. Maria Harris, *Fashion Me a People* (Louisville: John Knox, 1989), 47.

27. Ibid., 63.

Appendix One

1. Carter Lindberg, *Beyond Charity: Reformation Initiatives for the Poor* (Minneapolis: Fortress Press, 1993), 100–101, 123ff.

2. Nile Harper, *Urban Churches, Vital Signs: Beyond Charity to Justice* (Grand Rapids: Eerdmans, 1999), 138–56. See also, Dennis A. Jacobsen, *Doing Justice: Congregations and Community Organizing* (Minneapolis: Fortress Press, 2001).

Appendix Three

1. I believe this is the clear implication of the position I staked out some years ago in my chapter "Nuclear Policy and the Ethics of Anticipation" in *Peace and the Just War Tradition* (New York: Lutheran Council in the USA, 1986), 54–69.

2. Jean Bethke Elshtain, *Just War against Terror: The Burden of American Power in a Violent World* (New York: Basic, 2004), 182–92.

3. Jim Wallis, *God's Politics: A New Vision for Faith and Politics in America* (San Francisco: HarperSanFrancisco, 2005), 111.

4. See, John Howard Yoder, *When War Is Unjust: Being Honest in Just-War Thinking*, 2nd ed. (Maryknoll, NY: Orbis, 1996).

5. See the special section organized by Glen H. Stassen: "Just Peacemaking," *Journal of the Society of Christian Ethics* 23, no. 1 (Spring/Summer 2003), 169–267.

INDEX